Literacy

Literacy

An Introduction to the Ecology of Written Language

Second Edition

David Barton

Blackwell Publishing

BLACKWELL PUBLISHING
350 Main Street, Malden, MA 02148-5020, USA
9600 Garsington Road, Oxford OX4 2DQ, UK
550 Swanston Street, Carlton, Victoria 3053, Australia

First edition published 1994 by Blackwell Publishers Ltd
Second edition published 2007 by Blackwell Publishing Ltd

2   2009

Library of Congress Cataloging-in-Publication Data

Barton, David, 1949–
    Literacy : an introduction to the ecology of written language / David Barton. — 2nd ed.
        p. cm.
    Includes bibliographical references and index.
    ISBN 978-1-4051-1114-0 (hardback)
    ISBN 978-1-4051-1143-0 (pbk.)
1. Literacy.   2. Reading.   3. Composition (Language arts)   4. Linguistics.   I. Title.

    LC149.B28 2007
    302.2′244—dc22

                                                                        2006026292

A catalogue record for this title is available from the British Library.

Set in 11/13pt Dante
by Graphicraft Limited, Hong Kong
Printed and bound in Singapore
by Markono Print Media Pte Ltd

The publisher's policy is to use permanent paper from mills that operate a sustainable forestry policy, and which has been manufactured from pulp processed using acid-free and elementary chlorine-free practices. Furthermore, the publisher ensures that the text paper and cover board used have met acceptable environmental accreditation standards.

For further information on
Blackwell Publishing, visit our website:
www.blackwellpublishing.com

Contents

Preface

This book is intended as an introduction to literacy studies for students and for general readers. It is also aimed at specialists in one area of study who wish to understand the significance of literacy studies for their own work. The book explores competing definitions of literacy in contemporary society and examines the theories of language and learning which underpin new views of literacy. It also aims to provide a coherent view of literacy which can act as an antidote to the narrow technical views of reading and writing which are common in much public discussion, in the media and in political speeches.

This updated second edition brings together recent developments in a coherent manner, by showing how new research has contributed to our understanding of literacy. Since the publication of the first edition there have been many detailed studies of literacy practices in different settings. This new edition contains summaries of this research and provides extensive references to further research. There is also a section devoted to how literacy research is carried out.

There is now an international network of researchers contributing to the field of literacy studies and I am grateful to the many people I have talked to and corresponded with over the past decade, especially those who have organized seminars and conferences. The field has been taking great strides forward and this progress has been conducted in a collaborative and friendly way across many international boundaries. I owe particular thanks to the members of the Literacy Research Centre at Lancaster University, who have contributed to my thinking immensely, especially Yvon Appleby, Mary Hamilton, Rachel Hodge, Roz Ivanič, Karin Tusting, Uta Papen and Anita Wilson. Karin Tusting has helped in the development of this second edition in detailed ways, especially in contributing to the parts on workplace literacies and on new technologies; equally importantly she has suggested sections to shorten and has tried to keep me to a timetable for finishing this work. Of course I take full responsibility for the gaps when trying to keep up to date with this rapidly expanding field.

David Barton
Lancaster University
April 2006

Preface to the first edition

I mistakenly thought that writing an introductory text would be a simple and straightforward task; I assumed that *simple to read* meant *simple to write*. As I became more and more immersed in my project, I came to realize how wrong I had been and how difficult it is to be simple. I hope I have succeeded.

This book does several seemingly incompatible things at once. First, it is intended as an introduction to the growing field of Literacy Studies, accessible to the interested general reader as well as to the beginning student. It is also aimed at the specialist in one area of the field who wishes to have an up-to-date introduction to other related areas. Finally, I want to contribute to current discussions of literacy by articulating a coherent view of literacy, as an alternative to the narrowly technical views of reading and writing which are common in much public discussion, in the media and in political speeches, as well as in some areas of education and research.

There are several ways to read this book. It is possible to start at the beginning and read straight through to the end; alternatively, many of the chapters can be read independently: feel free to jump about and miss chapters out. To make the text easier to read I have put many of the references and extra examples into notes at the end, so a more detailed reading is also possible, with one finger in the endnotes.

I am conscious of my use of language. I do not use the supposedly generic personal pronouns *he* and *she*. As you can see, I am happy to use the word *I* in recognition of my self in writing. I use the word *we* but in several ways, so be aware of whether you are included when I use it, or whether I am drawing you along unwillingly with me. I try not to use *we* when I mean *I*! I am probably inconsistent in my use of tense, sometimes being in the past, sometimes the present and sometimes the future. My use of people's full names is erratic – I hope it is not gendered. While it is probably inevitable that thinking about literacy makes one reflective about one's own writing, I will avoid the temptation here to write pages about my own literacy practices, and about how I wrote this book; I will save that indulgence for another occasion.

I acknowledge the influence of many people. I am grateful to Charles Ferguson and Shirley Brice Heath for letting me realize many years ago that I did not have to measure spectrograms for ever and that literacy is a reasonable interest to pursue. Since that time, in the past decade I have talked to many people about literacy at meetings and conferences in Europe and North America. I owe a debt to all of them, especially Michael Cole, David Olson and Catherine Snow. Many colleagues who are also friends have contributed: including Brian Street, who has always been extremely generous in his support; Mukul Saxena and Mary Talbot, who commented on parts of the manuscript of this book; Kenneth Levine, who updated the table in chapter 2 for me; and especially David Bloome, Mary Hamilton, Roz Ivanič, Janet Maybin and Catherine Macrae who took the time to provide me with many detailed comments on the whole enterprise.

At Lancaster I have been grateful for support from colleagues in the Centre for Language in Social Life, and especially to staff and students who have participated in the activities of the Literacy Research Group over the years, including Rachel Rimmershaw, Sarah Padmore and Simon Pardoe. I am grateful to my colleagues in the Department of Linguistics for maintaining a sabbatical system which encourages people to take time off for writing and research, despite external pressures to constantly reduce this time. Above all, the endless discussions with and enthusiasm from Mary Hamilton and Roz Ivanič have contributed much to this book. Of course I take responsibility for all errors, omissions, confusions and lack of clarity which remain. Meanwhile, I have learned a great deal.

David Barton
Lancaster University
1994

1 An integrated approach to literacy

Introduction

Rapid technological and social change is affecting what we know and how we communicate. The nature of knowledge and the nature of communication are changing in fundamental ways, and literacy is central to this. Throughout the world, issues of literacy have moved to the top of the political agenda and in public debate everywhere there is perceived to be a crisis in education; literacy has become a contentious issue in schools and colleges, in the community and in political debate.

More than one hundred years after the introduction of compulsory schooling we do not have an educational system which turns out happy well-educated people. This can be demonstrated in many ways; with reference to reading and writing, it is generally agreed that around 10 per cent of adults in countries like Britain and the United States are not satisfied with their levels of literacy. After three decades of adult literacy provision in such countries, what was thought of as a minor social problem has not been solved; rather, basic education provision for adults now has to be seen as part of normal educational provision. Pressures are coming from governments and elsewhere for education to account for what it achieves and there are new demands from rapidly changing technologies. This is happening throughout industrialized countries. Meanwhile, in developing countries there is a realization that literacy rates are not increasing in the ways optimistically predicted before the year 2000 and there are debates on how to achieve 'education for all'.

Competing views of what education is for are being made more explicit. People may disagree about the nature of 'the crisis' but there is public unease about what is going on. The purpose of schools and education has often been taken for granted: more and more it is now being called into question. Questions about reading and writing turn up in a wide range of places: in discussions about falling standards in education; in calls for Plain English in documents; in debates about the economic cost of education, the requirements for a trained workforce, the effects of new technologies on our lives, the need for adult literacy provision.

All sorts of people talk about literacy and make assumptions about it, both within education and beyond it. The business manager bemoans the lack of literacy skills in the workforce. The politician wants to eradicate 'the scourge of illiteracy'. The radical educator attempts to empower and liberate people. The literary critic sorts the good writers from the bad writers. The teacher diagnoses reading difficulties and prescribes a programme to solve them. The pre-school teacher watches literacy emerge. These people all have powerful definitions of what literacy is. They have different theories of literacy, different ideas of 'the problem' and what should be done about it. Public discussion in the media is often at odds with what is going on in schools. Ideas about a 'literacy crisis' are constantly in the newspapers but public discussion of literacy issues is not very sophisticated; there is widespread ignorance about language, and the most simplistic approaches are latched on to.

Part of this current conflict revolves around what is meant by literacy and to some extent the disputes can be viewed as struggles between different definitions of literacy. The aim of this book is to try to understand the different ways in which people talk about reading and writing, and to draw together new views of literacy which have been developed in different areas. The question I am asking throughout is: what is literacy? In exploring this topic, I will cover many very different aspects of literacy. There are two starting points for the discussion: first, that of examining people's everyday reading and writing; and, secondly, the many areas of study which are contributing to new understandings of literacy.

Literacy in everyday life

The first starting point is people's everyday lives and how they make use of reading and writing. In going about their ordinary daily life, people today are constantly encountering literacy. This is true for most people in the world. Imagine a person waking up in the morning: they may well be woken up at seven o'clock in the morning by an alarm which turns on a radio automatically. The first voice they hear might well be someone reading the radio news to them, a written text which is being spoken. Going for breakfast, they pick up the newspaper from the door mat along with some mail. Breakfast, in England at least, might consist of drinking a cup of tea while listening to the radio, browsing through the newspaper and opening some letters. Other people might be present, adults and children, and they might participate in these activities. Already, at the beginning of the day, there have been several literacy events, each quite different from the other.

I have used this example elsewhere; I like it because it demonstrates that how people use literacy is tied up with the particular details of the situation and that literacy events are particular to a specific community at a specific point in history. The scene I describe may be very familiar to you or it may seem very distant. The precise details may not be right: there are many countries today where mail and newspapers are not delivered to the door in time for breakfast. I was thinking of Lancaster, England; in seemingly similar places such as Lancaster, Pennsylvania or Lancaster, Ontario things may be very different. It is only in some cultures that it is thought normal to start the day sitting at a table and simultaneously to listen to a radio, read a newspaper and drink a cup of tea, and where it may be acceptable and polite to ignore other people eating at the table, or to talk intermittently to them while reading. What is polite or acceptable in one situation may not be in another, and such behaviour might not be accepted at a different time of day or with different people present.

There are several other things about literacy which this example illustrates. The first point to be made is that literacy impinges on people in their daily lives, whether or not they regularly read books or do much writing. Literacy is embedded in these activities of ordinary life. It is not something which is done just at school or at work. It is carried out in a wide variety of settings. For the school child much of the literacy in the home may be quite unlike that encountered in the school classroom. Secondly, several people can be involved in reading or in writing, and they may participate in various ways, each treating the written word differently. There are many ways of reading in a particular situation with a particular text. The various texts are recognized as distinct and are read in different ways – there are many ways of taking meaning from the text. Listening to the news broadcasts, scanning the morning papers, sorting through the different letters in the mail may all involve different participants acting in different ways.

This example has been concerned with reading, but there may well be some writing involved. Around breakfast time there may be a hurried letter to be written to the teacher, or a school form to be filled in. There may be a note to be left for someone, or a bill which has to be paid urgently. People write reminder notes for themselves at the beginning of the day and write in diaries and on calendars. Some people get up early to write personal letters or log on to their email before the bustle of the day begins.

Using an everyday event as a starting point provides a distinct view of literacy. The most common views of literacy start out from the educational settings in which literacy is typically taught, that is, the school classroom. The dominant definitions in society, then, are school-based definitions of literacy. These views of what literacy is are often at odds with what people experience in their everyday lives. This can be in a very straightforward way where the kinds of reading and writing which people do in their everyday lives are different from those done in school. It can be in people's more general conceptions of literacy. Everyday literacy gives a richer view of literacy which demands a new definition of literacy, a new way of thinking about what is involved in reading and writing.

The main area for research on reading and writing up till now has been education. The main focus has been on individual learning. The main research paradigm has been psychological. Again this has been the most common approach. However, it is not just educators who are interested in literacy. If we look elsewhere, it is obvious that the more we dig at literacy, the richer it is. A wealth of recent ideas which are not encompassed by standard theories flood in from history, anthropology, sociology and a range of other disciplines. These ideas provide the second starting point for the exploration of literacy.

The study of literacy

There are many aspects of literacy to account for. Across a wide range of disciplines there has been an explosion of interest in literacy. Topics which were not mentioned a few years ago are now being researched and there is so much work going on that it is difficult to keep up with the books and articles which are being published. There are many strands of research taking the subject in different directions. It is necessary to bring these strands together, and much of this book will be devoted to doing this. To give an idea of what is ahead here is a brief list of some of the areas where there has been renewed interest in literacy and where we might look for ideas. The individual people working in these areas are moving in the same direction and I want to point to the unity of ideas in these seemingly diverse topics.

Across a range of disciplines the term **literacy** has become a code word for more complex views of what is involved in reading and writing. In each of the following subjects, people are making some contribution to the contemporary study of literacy:

- historical development
- the study of different cultures and subcultures
- oral cultures without literacy
- languages, scripts, bilingual literacy
- written and spoken language
- situated cognition
- social understanding of science and of new technologies
- processes of reading and writing
- pre-school literacy, emergent literacy
- learning in schools
- learning at home, in the community, at work
- adult learning, adult literacy, adults returning to study
- the politics of literacy, literacy and power

These are the topics I will be drawing upon throughout the book. I will provide references to work in these areas as they are encountered. In all these areas people are questioning what is meant by literacy. Although there are similarities, in some ways these different approaches with different philosophies underlying them are asking different questions and using different methodologies. There needs to be a way of talking about literacy which begins to bring together the many facets described so far. I will provide an overview of current approaches to literacy in these different areas at the same time as ensuring that they contribute to a common understanding of reading and writing. This is a complex interdisciplinary endeavour and I hope that the idea of an ecological approach, the subject of the next two chapters, will provide enough common threads to weave the topics together.

At different points in history disciplines go forward at different rates; in the past two decades the pace of change in the study of reading and writing has been rapid and the new field of literacy studies has come into existence. It is important to realize that there has been a significant paradigm shift going on in this area. It is exhibited in various ways, one of the most visible being the explosion of books, papers and conferences on the subject. The shift is in a particular direction. Many of the recent works I will refer to begin with summaries of changes in views and they are all shifts to some social perspective.

Another phenomenon is the plethora of reviews, reviews of reviews, special issues of journals and conferences devoted to the topic of literacy, each beginning with a discussion of what is meant by the word. There are even whole books devoted to defining literacy (such as Venezky et al., 1990). Writers, including myself, see the need to examine the metaphors and theories we are starting from. One way of going forward has been to regard the taken-for-granted ideas as **myths**, to list the myths associated with aspects of literacy and then to counter them.[1] While there has undeniably been a paradigm shift in the study of reading and writing, these changes are also part of more general trends in the social sciences of being more reflexive, focusing on the particular, and of being interdisciplinary. Like other shifts, this one is also leading to conflicting ways of talking about the topic and struggles over the meanings of words. A major goal of the book is to destroy common myths and widely accepted but wrong 'truths' about reading and writing, in order to build a different view. This will be evident in each of the topics covered.

Outline of the book

Chapter 2 is concerned with the need for a new way of thinking about reading and writing. It examines some of the metaphors which have been used when talking about literacy. Having outlined what is meant by a theory and the importance of metaphors in language, it explores some of the different ways of talking about literacy, including everyday usage, and how these metaphors are theories of literacy. Definitions of literacy from politicians, researchers and dictionaries are examined. The area of **literacy studies** is introduced and a final section discusses the metaphor of ecology and its potential application to the area of literacy.

Chapter 3 is an overview of what it means to think in terms of **the ecology of literacy**, arguing that literacy is best understood as a set of **practices** which people use in **literacy events**; that it is necessary to talk in terms of there being different **literacies**; that literacy practices are situated in broader social relations; that literacy is a symbolic system used both for communicating with others and for representing the world to ourselves; that attitudes and awareness are important aspects of literacy; that issues of power are important; and that current literacy events and practices are created out of the past.

Chapter 4 is about researching literacy practices. It describes methods for researching literacy practices and provides examples of research which has been carried out into everyday literacy practices. It then discusses several examples of multilingual literacy practices, then the ways in which all aspects of literacy are **gendered**, and finally examples of research into workplace literacy practices.

Chapter 5 explores contemporary ideas about language which are necessary for a sophisticated view of literacy. It provides a **constructivist** view of language, and it emphasizes the various **discourses** which different literacies are part of. Writing results in **texts**, which can be used, analysed and dissected, and they are connected to each other by **inter-textuality**. Several examples of texts are used as illustrations in the book. The idea of reading as **taking meaning from texts** is covered. Finally, the various senses in which language, and especially literacy, **mediates** our experience are described.

Chapter 6 covers views on differences between written and spoken language, and how they have developed from ideas of listing differences, through notions of **continua** from written to spoken, on to ideas of

configurations of language which utilize both written and spoken. Chapter 7 includes a brief description of different **writing systems** and some of the difficulties in making comparisons between them, and a discussion of writing in relation to other notations such as number, music, maps and visual layout. This is linked to the general discussion throughout on the limits of literacy.

Chapter 8 examines some crucial points in history and how they can provide insights into areas as diverse as: the learning of literacy, levels of literacy in society, literacy and technological change, and literacy and power relations. The first part, the **archaeology of literacy**, looks at the origin of writing, how it arose out of earlier systems, its relationship to social structure, and the wide range of functions existing from the beginning. Issues around the importance of early Greek literacy are covered, along with discussion of problems with the idea of writing **evolving**. A section on the **social history of literacy** looks at the importance of the development of printing in changing social practices, and the gradual development of a literate culture. The historical basis of contemporary literacy is covered through an examination of popular literacy and the introduction of compulsory schooling.

Chapters 9 and 10 turn to young children and the learning of literacy. As well as having ideas about language embedded in them, views of literacy also contain theories of learning. The roots of literacy are identified in learning to speak and in the practices associated with home literacy events. Views of learning which cover both written and spoken language are drawn upon. **Emergent** reading and writing are covered, along with the importance of children's developing awareness of language.

Chapter 11 explores two metaphors common in public discussion about reading and writing and in education: these are, first, ideas about literacy being a **skill** and, secondly, **literary** views of reading and writing. This includes discussion of how professional writers, mainly novelists, talk about the act of writing. What goes on in schools, the actual literacy practices, are the subject of chapter 12. School practices are described in brief, along with some of the ways in which schools as institutions sustain certain views of literacy. Some of the research on links between home and school is covered.

The next chapter, chapter 13, turns to adult literacy, covering literacy campaigns in developing countries as well as recent questions raised in industrialized countries. It includes a section on how ordinary people, especially those who identify problems with reading and writing, negotiate their day-to-day lives. The values and purposes underlying literacy campaigns are discussed. The ecological fact that languages are currently dying out at a phenomenal rate is pointed out, along with some discussion of the role of literacy in supporting **endangered languages**. In the final chapter some suggestions are made of how schools and adult literacy programmes can take account of these views of literacy, and some directions are suggested for developing an ecological view of literacy.

2   Talking about literacy

Metaphors for literacy

Like a germ that learns to enjoy penicillin, illiteracy consumes all the armies sent to fight it. No matter what we do about it – and we do a good deal, contrary to complaints from the literacy lobby – the condition persists. Depending on how you count them, adult illiterates make up anywhere from a tenth to a fifth of the Canadian population. We have no reason to think their number is shrinking, and some reason to fear that it is growing . . . social evil . . . illiteracy is caused . . . The remedy . . .

The metaphors are clear in this leader from the *Financial Times* of Canada on 4 July 1988. Ideas of disease and warfare come over in every word. The author of this emotive writing, Robert Fulford, then went on to make some interesting points about the *illiteracy* of the ghostwriting of speeches for politicians, thus stretching the term in a different direction.

Such metaphors are common in the media and in public discussion. In an interview on television the then Archbishop of Canterbury argued that the inner-city riots in Britain in 1991 were due to 'a matrix of illiteracy and delinquency and other wrongdoing'. Around the same time a leading British politician referred to a situation where there was 'not a high level of literacy so people were excitable and likely to be led astray'. Again the metaphors are clear, and especially revealing if you observe how literacy is juxtaposed with other negative terms suggesting weakness and crime.

The disease metaphor particularly is very pervasive. It can be used to damn the illiterate, as in the examples above, or it can be used to praise the literate. An example of the latter is to be found in Bruce Chatwin's novel *Utz*; referring to Prague in the mid-twentieth century, the narrator comments: 'The Soviet education system, I felt, had worked all too well: having created on a colossal scale, a generation of highly intelligent, highly literate young people who were more or less immune to the totalitarian message' (1988, p. 118). There is a great deal on literacy to draw out of this quote and I will return to it later on. For the moment, the idea that literacy is an inoculation, making one *immune* to brain-washing, is a further example of the disease metaphor.

Talking about a disease which has to be eradicated is also a common way in which literacy is discussed as a social issue. Powerful images can be built up with this metaphor, as in a recent newspaper headline: '12-year-olds caught in epidemic of illiteracy'. Further links are suggested by a cursory glance at other newspaper headlines: across the world illiteracy is often linked with criminality, with not being able to get a job, and with being a drain on the economy.

To move to another metaphor, a view of literacy which is at the root of much educational practice is that of treating it as a skill or set of skills. This has been very powerful in the design of literacy programmes at all levels of education. The acts of reading and writing are broken down into a set of skills and subskills. These skills are ordered into a set of levels starting with pre-reading skills and they are then taught in a particular order, each skill building upon the previous. Literacy is seen as a psychological variable which can be measured and assessed. Skills are treated as things which people own or possess; some are **transferable skills**, some are not. Learning to read and write becomes a technical problem and the successful reader and writer is a **skilled** reader and writer. As an educational definition of literacy, this view is very powerful, and it is one which spills over into the rest of society. It is often drawn on in government strategies for literacy.

It is important to realize that this idea of skills is a particular way of thinking about literacy; it is no less a metaphor than the disease metaphor. Everywhere there are metaphors for talking about reading and writing, some very graphic, others less so. Paulo Freire, for example, presented the idea of traditional literacy education as being **banking**, where knowledge is deposited in a person. It is a *thing*, almost an object which is given and received; shifting the metaphor slightly, empty people are filled up with literacy. He contrasts this deficit view with a view of literacy as a form of empowerment, as a right, as something which people do, a process rather than a thing.

Everyone has a view of literacy, and opinions on the subject are often held tenaciously. These views are expressed through metaphors. However, different metaphors have different implications for how we view illiteracy, what action might be taken to change it and how we characterize the people involved. For example, if illiteracy is a disease, then the people involved are sick, it should be eradicated, and experts need to be called in to do the job. If it is a psychological problem, then therapy or counselling are needed. Other metaphors call for training, empowerment, special education or social support. The participants might be construed as students, customers, clients or recipients. The blame, if it is blameworthy, might be attributed to fate, the individual, the school, the family, or the social structure. Note that some metaphors are within the education sphere, while others branch out into counselling, therapy and elsewhere. In all of them literacy has been socially constructed. Kenneth Levine discusses this (1985, p. 172) and has a tentative chart of different social ways of talking about illiteracy. Table 2.1 is an updated version of this.

Another approach is to view literacy in terms of access to knowledge and information. To be literate is to have access to the world of books and other written material. When viewed this way, the word literacy itself has become a metaphor which has been applied to other areas. This has happened with terms like **cultural literacy**, **computer literacy**, **information literacy**, **visual literacy** and **political literacy**. Here we see literacy loosely as understanding an area of knowledge.

The trouble with metaphors for literacy such as that of a disease or a set of skills is that they are limited in scope and do not capture the breadth of what is involved in reading and writing. I want to explore

Table 2.1   Some ways of talking about literacy

	Condition	Response	Means	Goal	Application
1	Sickness	Treatment	Clinical intervention	Remittance	
	Handicap	Rehabilitation	Compensatory aids	Alleviation	Dyslexia
2	Ignorance	Training	Instruction	Mastery	Orthodox literacy tuition
3	Incapacity	Therapy	Counselling	Adjustment Assimilation Autonomy	
4	Oppression	Empowerment	Political organization/ legislation	Rights	Conscientization
5	Deprivation	Welfare	Reallocation of material resources	Benefit	Positive discrimination
6	Deviance	Control	Isolation Containment Physical coercion	Correction Conformity	Negative discrimination

this, but first it is necessary to say some general words on metaphors and theories, in order to make clear the approach being taken in this book.

Theories and metaphors

In arguing for a different way of thinking about literacy, it is important to be very conscious and reflective about this activity. We need to be very clear about the language we are using. Throughout, I will be scrutinizing and deconstructing many of the concepts which structure and scaffold the ideas of literacy. This will include notions of **reading**, **writing**, **skill**, **illiterate**. The discussion will also embrace many ideas and concepts which do not appear at first to be directly related to literacy, such as when we examine what is meant by terms such as **learning**, **evolution**, **mainstream culture**. In addition, in slipping from discipline to discipline it will be obvious that terms are used in different ways. What I am trying to do is to find a way of talking about literacy which can bring together insights from these different areas. What is needed is not exactly a definition of literacy; rather we need a metaphor, a model, a way of talking about literacy. What sort of activity is literacy?

Before addressing this set of questions, it is necessary to say a few words about metaphors in general, how they work and what their role is. The notion of metaphors used here is broader than the everyday use of the term. I will describe what I mean by metaphor, then I will look at some definitions of literacy and describe some of the ways of talking about the subject which are developing in the field of literacy studies. When this has been done I will move on to another metaphor for literacy.

As part of living we all make sense of our lives; we can talk about what we do; we explain and justify our actions, our feelings and our intentions. We construct theories to make sense of the world. Our theories affect our action, just as our emotions and our intentions affect our actions. We adjust and change our theories in the light of experience. This applies to literacy as much as to any other part of life. Everyone has a view of literacy; everyone in some way makes sense of it. Everyone who uses terms like **reading** has a theory of the nature of literacy underlying their use of the word. I am going to call these views of literacy people's **everyday theories** of literacy. They are sometimes called **folk theories**. I prefer everyday theories, as folk already has the idea in it that they are not really true and is therefore pejorative in some sense.

These points about everyday theories apply equally to the theories of the specialist, the professional, the researcher. These people have theories which they (we?) are often more conscious of. However, these theories, which I will call **professional theories**, are developed and changed in a similar manner to everyday theories. The main differences between everyday and professional theories are that the latter are often more articulated and explicit; often they aim to be more general; they can be checked in more systematic ways; they are formalized into a seemingly impersonal body of knowledge and they are often passed on in an explicit way by teaching. These bodies of expert knowledge often have higher status and more authority, partly by getting into print. Particular theories can be backed by government policies and then promoted and supported by extensive funding. These official theories become dominant. They can be legally enforced and become the orthodox authoritative way of seeing an issue. Nevertheless, professional theories can be wrong, misleading and harmful and they are not necessarily superior to everyday theories. It is important not to give special privilege to professional theories as being inevitable right, or perfect, or as replacing everyday theories.

I distinguish everyday theories and professional theories but they are similar in kind. In people's actual lives they overlap. Social science and other theories *leak* into life, to use another metaphor. They provide the terminology and framework for talking about an area. For example, some of the concepts of Freud's theories about the mind and the subconscious have passed into everyday language. Another example would be views on child care, where the theories of psychologists and others influence everyday practices, including ways of talking about children. It is important to realize that professional theories can influence everyday discourse but in many areas, as far apart as nuclear energy, medical knowledge and general public understanding of science, there are questions raised about the role of professionals and the status of expert knowledge.

When talking about theories of literacy so far, one of the main professional theories underlying media, politicians' and parents' talk is that of literacy as a set of skills. It is a professional theory, embodied in textbooks and teaching materials, taught in institutions, supported by a legal infrastructure and guiding much literacy instruction in schools and colleges. It also leaks into life and forms part of people's everyday theories of literacy. The idea of skills and levels becomes the way parents talk about their children's progress; this approach may suggest, for example, that as a set of skills reading is best taught by a teacher, that learning to read should be isolated from other learning, and that the parents have no independent role in a child's learning to read.

The leak between everyday and professional theories works in both directions. As well as professional theories influencing everyday discussion, there is an influence in the opposite direction. Professional theories are articulated mainly in words from everyday life; words like 'intelligence' or 'evolution' are given more technical meanings, as researchers try to talk in a more precise manner. Nevertheless, professional theories are incomplete and are expressed partly in ordinary language. Inevitably, everyday usage fills the gaps left in these theories. The teacher of literacy at any level is partly guided by professional theories put over in training courses, but teaching is guided equally by everyday knowledge which fills out and completes the partial professional theories. This is inevitable and is part of the nature of theories; it is not some failure of professional theories. Another result of this mixing of different sorts of theories is that it is not clear whether common academic theories, such as 'the great divide' between oral and literate or the superiority of the alphabet over other writing systems, are mainly everyday theories or professional theories. This argument about the role of everyday theories in professional theories is relevant throughout the book and should be borne in mind in several of the discussions.

Another aspect of theories which is important for the discussion on literacy is that they are developed from experience in particular areas; they are then stretched to cover larger areas. The example of literacy as a set of skills will be given later as an illustration of this. Our knowledge is always partial and we need to generalize our experience to make sense of more of life. As a consequence, the backing for our theories is always partial. Mistakenly, we often look for one answer to cover everything, so that theories which are half true get extended too far to cover inappropriate areas.

Theories also differ in what they emphasize. This has its roots in the fact that theories differ in what they set out to do. Take, for example, the idea of individual differences in how quickly children learn to read. If you need to classify children in school and later in college, then grading and sorting become very important. Individual differences in how children learn to read, however small and impermanent, become highly salient. In another theory such differences might be completely irrelevant. Or to give another example related to literacy, issues of access and power are important in critical approaches to literacy, while in other theories they could hardly even be plausible concepts.

Metaphors and thinking

In the approach being taken here I am also making certain assumptions about the mind and thinking: crucially, there is an internal world, there is an external world, and there is some relation between the two. I will be taking a **constructivist** view of this, where people construct a mental model of the external world, with language at the centre of the construction. As a starting point, our theories are articulated in language, and in everyday language. One way of doing this is with metaphors, through the words we use, the labels we give things and the names we give to activities. This is a normal use of language and, in fact, there is no altern-ative to it. We use language to imagine what the world is like and what it might be like.

Most of language relies on metaphors, most words and relations between words are metaphors. One reason for this is that we need meta-phors for talking about things which are not concrete. A common start-ing point is the physical world. We use physical distance to talk about time, for instance, as in 'the week ahead' or 'from Monday to Friday'. Crucially, metaphors for the mind are often structured from the physical world too; this relates to literacy with such ideas as that of putting thoughts into writing. The skills metaphor, which posits a set of abilities which we either have or do not have, represents another very physical metaphor. We internalize the physical as metaphors for representing the abstract. I will not pursue this in any detail here. (And it is not essential for you to believe this in order to continue reading. I will just keep to the parts which are necessary for a discussion about literacy.[1])

Another shift between different areas is the way we use 'say' for 'read', 'see' for 'understand', 'talk' for 'write'. This is interesting in that since listening is aural and reading visual, they get mixed around: 'I don't see what this book is saying', or in this book where I write 'what I am talking about is . . .', or a letter I received which asked me to '. . . say in writing the things we discussed on the phone'. This is common everywhere, including the teacher talking to the young child in the beginning reading classroom, and we are usually oblivious of the fact that we mix these modalities. One researcher even reports the anecdote of the child who thought herself deaf because she could not hear the letters whispering to her – she could not hear what the letters said.

Something further to say about metaphors is that they themselves are part of larger systems; they fit together and form discourses, which are coherent ways of representing the world (Gee, 1996; Fairclough, 1992). Words are situated within the structures of other words. Metaphors are part of whole theories. They are like the tips of icebergs, in that the words we use bring whole theories with them. Using one aspect of the visual metaphor for understanding can imply others. Looking more broadly, concepts like **intelligence**, **evolution**, **society** and **the individual** are also used within the frameworks of broader discourses, although these might be more difficult to ascertain. These terms are important as **organizing ideas**. They organize a domain and stretch beyond a domain. Intelligence and evolution are two organizing ideas used in everyday thought. They are theories, they are metaphors of everyday thought. Simultaneously, they do two opposing things for the areas they are applied to – such as when talking about literacy. On the one hand, they enrich our everyday thinking; at the same time they constrain it. These other words inevitably have to become part of the discussion of literacy. Even seemingly innocent everyday terms when discussing literacy such as **mainstream**, **western**, or the insidious use of 'our' when discussing literacy practices assume that the reader and writer share cultural practices. (I am also guilty of this.) These terms need to be unpacked.

We need these organizing principles to help us make sense of the complex world we live in. A good theory or metaphor illuminates. It takes you further, it provides new insights and makes new connections. Concepts link with other concepts and we need to group them together. This view of metaphor will recur; it is an essential aspect of the constructivist view of language of chapter 5. It has implications for how people make sense of the world, how children develop, and what language is.

Definitions of literacy

Looking for a precise definition of literacy may be an impossible task; the idea that complex concepts are susceptible to dictionary-like definitions is probably a myth. Nevertheless, dictionaries codify some view of usage, and dictionary definitions can be a useful starting point on the way to a broader view of literacy, a theory of literacy. We need a way of talking about literacy which can encompass these definitions. In this section I will explore what can be learnt from dictionaries and the information they provide. It is a useful place to start as long as we do not confuse the meaning of a word with its etymology and we are not searching for some basic real or literal meaning. Although there is obviously a link, dictionary definitions also need to be distinguished from people's actual usages of words in their everyday speech.

The words **reading**, **writing** and **literacy** have many meanings. **Reading** can go from the mechanical uttering of the newsreader to the innumerable levels of interpreting any text. In the sense of understanding meanings, reading has always been applied to a wide range of phenomena, including the reading of barometers, tea-leaves and facial expressions.

The word has now been extended to include the different interpretations people – readers – might have of a poem, a novel or a film. Reading is deconstructing.

The English word **writing** has a systematic ambiguity so that a good writer is on some occasions a neat scribe and accurate speller, while on other occasions the term means a creative author, whether the texts are academic essays, novels or advertising copy. Which of these two meanings of writing should be dominant is a constant conflict in education, whether in the primary school or in the adult education class. We will return to these terms in the chapters on children's learning and on educational metaphors.

Literacy is a fairly recent English word and its meaning is being extended. I am using the term to cover new broader views of reading and writing, and that is how it is being used in several disciplines and in terms like emergent literacy, used in education. As already pointed out, it is extended in another way to mean competent and knowledgeable in specialized areas, with terms like computer literacy, economic literacy and political literacy. People talk of different 'literacies', so that different media can be discussed, and film literacy, for example, can then be contrasted with print literacy.

Tracing the historical changes in how dictionaries deal with such words is instructive. With literacy there are actually four words to consider: literate, illiterate, literacy and illiteracy and there can be both nouns, an illiterate, and adjectives, literate behaviour.[2] Going back to Samuel Johnson's first dictionary of English in 1755, only one of the terms we are interested in, illiterate, is to be found. I have examined 20 dictionaries published in the nineteenth century and early in the twentieth century. *Barclay's Dictionary* of 1820 also only has illiterate. Illiteracy is found in *Walker's Critical Pronouncing Dictionary* of 1839 with the caveat that it is an uncommon word. Literate, but only in the sense of educated or learned, sometimes appears too. There will be examples later of how in contemporary life the term is sometimes used to mean educated and how sometimes it is contrasted with education.

Literacy is not found in a dictionary dated 1913 but appears in dictionaries from 1924 on. There is also a change in the meaning of literate. A new meaning 'being able to read and write' is added. This meaning gradually grows in importance, so that in contemporary dictionaries, such as the *COBUILD English Language Dictionary* or the *Concise Oxford*, it is the first meaning, with 'educated' given as a subsidiary meaning.

The full-length *Oxford English Dictionary* has literate in the sense of educated right back in 1432, with a second meaning of one in holy orders coming later. I assume from the evidence of the other dictionaries that it was not a very common word. Illiterate dates from 1556 and is the only one of these four terms which Shakespeare uses; illiteracy dates from 1660. It is more than 200 years before literacy appears, in 1883 in a sentence from the *New England Journal of Education* about Massachusetts being 'the first State in the Union in literacy' (although the *Random House Dictionary* places 'literacy test' more than a decade earlier). Its origin is given as being from the word 'illiteracy'. Literate in the sense of being able to read and write, the opposite of illiterate, does not appear until 1894. Some of the quotes in the dictionary give a flavour of the historical connotations of the term. A quote from 1859 talks of putting 'the literate and the ignorant' on one level. A quote from 1628 refers to 'a weakling or illiterate'. The claim from 1894 could still be debated today, that 'literates contribute a larger percentage of their class to the criminal ranks than do illiterates'. In addition, illiterates are not cast totally in a negative light: there was a concern in 1865 that as a result of 'intellectual tests the army will exclude from it the dashing illiterates whose stout hearts and strong thews and sinews made it what it was under the Duke'.

Application of the term literacy to other areas such as economic literacy and computer literacy is much more recent. The *Oxford English Dictionary* has a quotation from 1943 referring to economic literacy. The idea of literacy in a communications medium is represented by a quote from the *BBC Handbook* of 1962 which refers to television and 'our skills in understanding the medium and our own literacy in it'. Other dictionary examples of the terms include musical literacy, sexual illiteracy and a house being described as having an illiterate design.

Linguists talk of unmarked and marked terms, where with pairs of opposites the natural, normal, default and common word is the unmarked, such as 'honest', and the other derived word is marked, as in 'dishonest'. One might expect literacy to be the unmarked term and illiteracy the marked version which is derived from it. But in terms of history and frequency of usage illiteracy, a fairly pejorative term, is the natural or unmarked term and literacy comes from it.[3] Illiteracy belongs to a class of words – disability is another example – where the longer word with an additional morpheme is the unmarked. Literacy and illiteracy do not have to be paired together, of course. Literacy is sometimes contrasted with **orality**, or with another neologism **oracy**. **Nonliterate** can be used as a less pejorative sounding alternative to illiterate; or the two can be used with different meanings, illiterate meaning not being able to read within a culture which is literate, while nonliterate covers people in a culture which has never had literacy. Even talk of a literate culture is an extension of the word beyond the idea of literacy being a property of individual people.

Literate is also contrasted with **numerate**, a word going back only to 1959 in the dictionary, where it was deliberately coined in a British report by the Central Advisory Council for Education, along with **numeracy** and **innumeracy**. The authors of the report are quite conscious of coining the words, unlike most new words, which slip into the language unannounced. In the report the words are contrasted with literate, literacy and illiteracy. A different and much older meaning of numerate as counted or numerated goes back at least to 1432, a similar age to literate in the *Oxford English Dictionary*.

Translation of these terms brings its headaches, puzzles and contradictions. Literacy does not easily translate into French, while there is no easy English equivalent of the French sense of *ecriture* as 'writings', and *illetrisme* as 'unlettered' is not common in English. Jean-Paul Hautecoeur (1990) points out that in the world of adult education *illetrisme* is used in France, whereas *analphabetisme* is more common in other French-speaking places such as Quebec. A word like 'unalphabetized' exists in other languages including Spanish, Italian, Greek and Danish. Note that it is a partisan word: in its make-up there is the idea that an alphabetic writing system is necessary in order to be literate. In several languages there is a verbal equivalent, like *alfabetizar* in Spanish, meaning to make literate. In English alphabetize is something you might do to a list or even to a writing system, but not normally to a person. English lacks any such verb for the act of making people literate.

I will give two examples where I have encountered problems with translation. These demonstrate the confusions which can result. Firstly in Angers, France a group of us from different countries planning an adult education conference argued amicably about the contents of the conference, about whether it should be generally on literacy or specifically on problems with writing. We then argued confusedly about the title. The English-speaking side felt the French wanted a general conference on literacy but then inexplicably wanted the title to be restricted to 'Writing'. After a morning of cross-cultural miscommunication, it was the patient translators who first realized that the problem was one of translating the term literacy.[4]

A second problem arose in a seminar when a group of us were dis-cussing a paper which compares print literacy and film literacy.[5] Firstly with Japanese, and then also with Greek and Danish, we discovered the difficulty (or impossibility) of translating a term like film literacy into other languages. Take Japanese, for example: it has a word for illiteracy equivalent to sentence-blindness and made up of the two characters *mon mou*, and the word for literacy means the recognition of letters. However, the word could not be used to mean film literacy or computer literacy. A general word for competence or knowledge could be used but it would not make the link with literacy. In Japanese one would say the equivalent of 'the ability to appreciate films', or 'the ability to manipulate computers'. Where computer literacy has been used the term has been directly trans-literated into Japanese.

Literacy studies

The meaning of the word literacy is to be found not just by examining dictionary entries. It has become a unifying term across a range of dis-ciplines for changing views of reading and writing; there has been such a growth of study in the area that it is now referred to as **Literacy Studies** or the **New Literacy Studies**.

The history of the term, and the field, can partly be seen in the way titles of key books have staked claims to the area. Prior to 1980 hardly any books mentioned literacy in the title. In the early 1980s there were one or two a year. This increased during the decade and 15 books pub-lished in 1991 had 'literacy' in the title. The titles reveal a great deal. One of the first key books in the field was *Language and literacy: the sociolin-guistics of reading and writing* (Stubbs, 1980). There is clearly a definition of literacy in that title. This was followed in 1981 by *The psychology of literacy* (Scribner and Cole, 1981) which at the time seemed a challenging title, claiming so much more than books entitled *The psychology of read-ing*. Already we knew that it relates to the 'social order' (Cressy, 1980) and that there is a 'literacy myth' (Graff, 1979). Although a short article rather than a book, a whole methodological approach was suggested with 'The ethnography of literacy' (Szwed, 1981). Others then asserted that literacy has a 'social context' (Levine, 1985) and is 'socially constructed' (Cook-Gumperz, 1986). It has theory underlying it as well as practice

(Street, 1984). It relates to 'popular culture' (Vincent, 1989) and it is 'emergent' in children (Teale and Sulzby, 1986). Other words in titles make links with literacy, including orality, empowerment, involvement, culture and politics, right up to interest in 'ideology in discourses' (Gee, 1996), or it simply goes under the heading *The new literacy* (Willinsky, 1990). 'Ecology' is one more link, one which can bring together many of these strands.[6]

More recently, a wide range of studies of literacy practices in different settings have been published. Literacy practices in a variety of different 'worlds' are presented in Hamilton et al. (1994) and in a range of different 'situated' settings in Barton et al. (2000). Community literacies have been studied in Australia (Breen et al., 1994) and South Africa (Prinsloo and Breier, 1996). The personal letter-writing practices of Pacific islanders are examined in Besnier (1993). Wagner studied Arabic speakers in Morocco (1993). American studies have often been of the literacies of minority communities, such as Moss (1994), Reder (1987, 1994) and Pérez (2004). Moll's work relates the school and community practices of Hispanics in the southern United States (1994, see also Gonzalez et al., 2005). Merrifield et al. (1996) studied two distinct communities, urban Appalachians and Californian immigrant Americans, exploring their literacies and learning in different contexts. Minority bilingual communities have also been studied in Britain (Saxena, 1994; Bhatt et al., 1996; Baynham, 1993; Gregory, 1996; Martin-Jones and Jones, 2000a). Some researchers have focused on particular social institutions, such as literacy in religious groups (Fishman, 1988, 1991; Kapitzke, 1995) or in the workplace (Gowen, 1992; Gee et al., 1996; Belfiore et al., 2004). A similar ethnographic approach has been taken by researchers investigating children's literacies at home and at school (Schieffelin and Gilmore, 1986; Mahiri, 2004, also in the case studies in Moje and O'Brien, 2000, and to some extent in Serpell et al., 2004), and children's nonformal literacies (Camitta, 1993; Maybin, 2006). Denny Taylor has produced a series of studies of literacy within families (Taylor, 1983, 1996, 1997; Taylor and Dorsey-Gaines, 1988). Fingeret and Drennon (1997) studied the impact of participation in literacy programmes on adults' practices outside the class. In chapter 4 I describe some of these studies of literacy practices in more detail.

In this book, I restrict myself mainly to print literacy. This means saying little about orality on the one hand, and on the other hand, different media. This is deliberate, and discussion throughout will make it clear how this is in many ways a practical decision to do with restricting the topic to a manageable one. I have taken print literacy as a starting point for understanding a much broader field; for me, there is something to say about written language in a fairly precise way which would not be possible in a broader, more diffuse and less focused discussion. Having said this, I also emphasize throughout the book that the borders of what counts as print literacy are becoming increasingly fuzzy and that one cannot isolate print literacy from other forms of meaning-making when trying to understand the complexity of people's lives or the demands of education and other spheres. Gunther Kress in particular talks of **multimodality** and how print literacy is intertwined with other modes, especially the visual mode, and how reading changes as society shifts from a reliance on the page to reading the screen. (See Kress and van Leeuwen, 2001; Kress, 2003; Snyder, 2002.)

A key to new views of literacy is situating reading and writing in its social context. In the books named above many people in different disciplines have been moving in the same direction. I will draw attention to just a few of them here, describing more in later chapters and drawing upon their ideas throughout. I will begin with three important academic studies, the work of Sylvia Scribner and Michael Cole, Brian Street, and Shirley Brice Heath. Their studies are well-known and have been extremely influential. In their different ways they provide three threads to weave together to represent the beginnings of literacy studies and they have become classics in the field.

They are part of different research traditions but they actually have a great deal in common. All three academic studies looked at particular societies in detail, examining separate groups within a society and how they use literacy. They start from everyday life and what people read and write. They observe closely and they are willing to make use of a wide range of evidence. Each study makes comparisons between groups in a society, teasing out differences, but they avoid making grand generalizations. Rather, they make points about the particular situations they have studied. They provide ideas for other people looking at specific situations. Equally importantly, they raise more general questions about what is meant by literacy. Part of what comes with these studies is a recognition of the complexity of the idea of literacy and the fact that much of our understanding of it is not obvious. This leads to new definitions of literacy.

Briefly, Scribner and Cole, working within traditions of cross-cultural psychology, carried out a fascinating study of the uses of literacy among the Vai of north-west Liberia. Their study was very detailed, covering the writing systems, how people learned to read and write, the uses of literacy. Their methods included interviews, observations and a whole battery of psychological tests. They provide detailed descriptions of different forms of literacy, including those which are learned informally and which exist outside the educational system.

Their book (1981) is a very readable account of their work. In it we can see how they shift their ideas from the notion of literacy as a set of skills with identifiable consequences. They are edging towards their alternative notion of a **practice account** of literacy, arguing that literacy can only be understood in the context of the social practices in which it is acquired and used. They conclude their study:

> Instead of focusing exclusively on the technology of a writing system and its reputed consequences . . . we approach literacy as a set of socially organized practices which make use of a symbol system and a technology for producing and disseminating it. Literacy is not simply knowing how to read and write a particular script but applying this knowledge for specific purposes in specific contexts of use. The nature of these practices, including, of course, their technological aspects, will determine the kinds of skills ('consequences') associated with literacy. (Scribner and Cole, 1981, p. 236)

There is a great deal to do with definitions in this quote and I will return to it. For the moment, we can see in their work that the move to attending to social aspects of literacy inevitably involves a shift in the ways of studying and researching the topic. It is a shift from a psychological paradigm to a social paradigm. In reading their book you can trace the development of their thinking as their research unfolds. They move away from traditional psychological thinking with the notion of discrete individual variables which can be added together towards other approaches. They begin to talk in terms of literacy practices, a term which will be central to the discussion of the next chapter. Their work has also been influential more generally in new work bringing together psychology with other disciplines concerned with locating individuals in their cultural contexts. These are loosely described as socio-cultural approaches.[7]

Heath and Street have a different starting point. They begin from more descriptive social and anthropological methodologies. Street studied Islamic villagers in Iran; he lived there as an anthropologist and carried out ethnographic fieldwork. Part of this included examining people's reading and writing. He describes his approach as an **ideological** approach to literacy, one that accepts that what is meant by literacy varies from situation to situation and is dependent on ideology. He contrasts his approach with **autonomous** approaches which claim that literacy can be defined separately from the social context. He describes how: 'the meaning of literacy depends on the social institutions in which it is embedded . . . [and] . . . the particular practices of reading and writing that are taught in any context depend upon such aspects of social structure as stratification . . . and the role of educational institutions' (Street, 1984, p. 8). Like Scribner & Cole he talks in terms of practices. His distinction between ideological and autonomous has proved to be a powerful one and has been taken up by people studying many areas, including potentially difficult topics for a social account such as assessment (see for example, Hill and Parry, 1994).

The third study is Heath's work in the south-eastern United States. Her book, *Ways with words* (1983) is another book which is very enjoyable to read. She developed close ties with three Appalachian communities in the United States over seven years and used ethnographic and sociolinguistic methods to provide detailed descriptions of people's uses of reading and writing in the home and in the community. Having a clear idea of the reading and writing done in the home and the community, she then turned to school, examining the relation between home literacies and school literacies. When defining literacy Heath comments: '. . . the concept of literacy covers a multiplicity of meanings, and definitions of literacy carry implicit but generally unrecognized views of its functions (what literacy can do for individuals) and its uses (what individuals can do with literacy skills)' (Heath, 1980, p. 123). This contrast between what literacy does for people and what people do with literacy has been taken up by several researchers. Heath's work has been important in getting people to focus on actual instances where people use reading and writing in their day-to-day lives, **literacy events**. It has been influential throughout education; it has made educators examine in detail the literacy in classroom activities, and it has made them think about what reading and writing goes on in the home and the community.

Here I have concentrated on what these three studies have to say about definitions of literacy. To round this out as a mini-history of literacy studies, two general collections of papers were published in 1985 (Olson et al., 1985; De Castell et al., 1986) and a reader not long after (Kintgen et al., 1988). Then the subject was on its way, with books and articles almost too numerous to keep up with. This has been a brief overview. Work by other people and references to a range of studies will be woven into the text in the next few chapters.

So far I have dealt with academic researchers. Another person who has contributed to social approaches to literacy, but from a very different direction, is the Brazilian educator Paulo Freire. His is a distinct approach to literacy going back more than 40 years. He has been very influential throughout the world in the area of adult literacy and I have already referred to one of his metaphors, that of education as banking; his work will come up again in several places, in relation to metaphors, in terms of literacy and thought, and when discussing adult literacy programmes. There is continuing interest in his approach, notably in work in the United States with adults learning English and in literacy programmes in developing countries. Some examples in the US are Auerbach and Wallerstein (2004), Shor (1987); and in Britain, Kirkwood and Kirkwood (1989). In developing countries, there has been a continuing interest in the REFLECT programme, developed on the basis of Freire's work (see Archer and Cottingham 1996, and see ch. 13).

In many ways Freire is starting from a different place from the other people mentioned so far; he has different aims, he is asking different questions and, crucially, underlying his approach is a different view of literacy. He makes explicit the fact that in practical terms literacy teaching takes place within a social context. Adults in the world today who cannot read and write tend to be the poorest, the least powerful, the oppressed. It is the inequalities in the world which foster illiteracy. Accepting this and examining it is the starting point of his approach. Literacy teaching begins with a critical examination of society and of the participants' relationship to it. Literacy education inevitably involves change and the first step is analysing and understanding one's own position in society. Inevitably, questions concerning the inequalities of power in the teaching relationship and more broadly in society have a central role. Like others, Freire is very aware that literacy can be used for different purposes, that it can have *domesticating* effects and that it can have *empowering* or *liberating* effects. It gets defined in very different ways. The link between his work and the academic studies is that he demonstrates from a different direction that there is not a monolithic 'thing' called literacy.

One way in which literacy studies is linked to more general shifts in thought is the way in which the topic is described as **critical**. Freire's is an explicitly critical view of literacy. Critical can mean several things.

There is a sense in which all education is critical, to the extent that it involves teaching people to reason, evaluate and think clearly. This is basic and important, but it loses some force when all educators claim to be critical and empowering. Another sense of critical is what I am doing here, subjecting the term literacy to examination, analysis and deconstruction, and coming up with a critical discourse on the topic. Such deconstruction can result in a critical examination of public usage, of media images, and of current educational provision – hopefully in a constructive way.

In addition, there is a further sense: critical literacy links up with critical theory, an umbrella term for much more general approaches to the nature of knowledge which emphasize how social structure affects individuals, and describe the inequalities in access and power which constrain what people can do in their lives (Giroux, 1983; Livingstone, 1987; Gee, 1996; Luke and Walton, 1994). In this sense links can also be made with critical approaches to the study of language such as Clark et al. (1990, 1991).

Literacy studies has the potential to have an influence at all three of these levels, relating to theories of inequality and searching for practical ways of empowering people, giving them a right to the possibilities of literacy. While social approaches to literacy are not inevitably critical, many people, such as Luke (2005), see a critical approach as an essential part of a social approach. As Mary Talbot puts it, 'Looking at language critically is a way of *denaturalising* it – questioning and making strange conventions which usually seem perfectly natural to people who use them. It can help *empower* them in the sense of giving them greater conscious control over aspects of their lives especially how language shapes them' (Talbot, 1992, p. 174).

Looking for a metaphor

Literacy studies covers a wide area, and I will deal with many different topics. It is hard to jump from children in schools, to adults at work, or to many different cultures and different historical periods, as well as describing in brief what language is and what learning consists of. I want to bring these diverse topics together, to integrate and expand upon them. We need a way of talking about literacy which can encompass all this. To keep it all in mind a metaphor would be useful.

So far I have called this a social approach to literacy. However, it is more than just adding the social as an extra dimension, a variable to be taken account of. Literacy has a social meaning; people make sense of literacy as a social phenomenon and their social construction of literacy lies at the root of their attitudes, their actions, and their learning. Nevertheless, in starting from the social, it is important to make clear that, as they exist at present, social approaches are not in themselves adequate. Adding the prefix 'socio-' to a word is not a magic way of conveying the meaning of good, or easy, or politically acceptable. One problem with social approaches is that they usually treat important psychological concepts like thinking, learning and memory as basic unquestionable and unanalysable concepts. In Jean Lave's terms (1988, p. 18), it regards them as 'unexamined primitive elements'. In addition, social approaches do not necessarily have a historical perspective and they may not be dynamic in the sense of viewing people as active decision makers.

It is important not to reject psychological approaches out of hand. There are certain psychological traditions which have been the basis of work on reading and writing. Alone they are inadequate. However, there are other traditions which are becoming more prominent, such as that drawing on the work of the Russian psychologist Lev Vygotsky, which aim to bridge the gap between social and psychological. Vygotsky was concerned with the social origins of thought. In particular he traced how children's 'internal' thinking develops out of their 'external' social interactions with other people. Reasearchers moving in the same direction use various terms to describe their approach including constructivist or constructionist, socio-historical, socio-cognitive, socio-cultural and activity theory. One metaphor which can be useful in drawing together the social and the psychological is the metaphor of ecology.[8]

The ecological metaphor

Originating in biology, ecology is the study of the interrelationship of an organism and its environment. When applied to humans, it is the interrelationship of an area of human activity and its environment. It is concerned with how the activity – literacy in this case – is part of the environment and at the same time influences and is influenced by the environment. An ecological approach takes as its starting point this interaction between individuals and their environments.

In the social sciences the idea of ecology goes back at least to Gregory Bateson, who linked up biological notions of ecology with anthropological and psychological concerns about the nature of human thought, referring to his collected works as *Steps to an ecology of mind* (1972). Two other early uses of the term are Bronfenbrenner's (1979) work on the ecology of human development and Gibson's work on the ecology of perception (1979). Some of these early uses may now seem simplistic, such as Bronfenbrenner's Russian dolls one inside the other, used as a way of visualizing how activities are situated in different layers of context: this is too static a model, making different contexts and environments seem very fixed. When applied to human activity more recently the idea of ecology has often been used to situate psychological activity, placing it in a more complete social context and a dynamic social context where different aspects interact.

An example of this development is Neisser's work on the ecology of memory (1982) showing the importance of studying how people use memory in natural contexts in their everyday lives. He is highly critical of the achievements of a hundred years of laboratory-based experimental studies of memory, and he argues for a more ecologically based approach, that is, a more naturalistic approach. His book begins with an article arguing point-by-point the importance of studying natural memory and criticizing the methods of experimental psychology; it is instructive to reread the article replacing the word 'memory' with the word 'reading'. Many of his criticisms of studies of memory apply equally well to studies of reading. Another use of the term ecology associated with psychological studies has been the idea of **ecological validity**. Researchers use the term to question whether experimental studies of psychological activity are valid reflections of natural everyday contexts. Other examples include work on the ecological basis of child development.

Within the sociology of language and sociolinguistics there is a separate tradition of using the term ecology. This dates back to Einar Haugen's (1972) work in the United States tracing the extent to which immigrants kept their own languages or changed to using the majority language, English. Another example is the work of Michael Clyne (1982) in Australia who uses ecology to mean the study of the environment which favours maintaining the community language. A more recent use has been Peter Mulhausler's (1992), who points out the need to focus on factors related to the ecology of a dominated language, rather than on the language itself if one is interested in its preservation.[9]

I want to use the ecological metaphor to summarize and integrate what is known about literacy today. One advantage is that it has been used in both psychological and social traditions. In addition, a biological or organic metaphor of some sort has been used by several people when discussing reading and writing. Freire refers to domestication; many people talk of the roots of literacy; Yetta Goodman (1984) refers to the soil in which growth of literacy takes place. I want to develop these fragments, using the whole metaphor, making it more explicit.

The ecological metaphor actually produces a whole set of terms which can provide a framework for discussions of literacy. Terms like **ecological niches**, **ecosystem**, **ecological balance**, **diversity** and **sustainability** can all be applied to the human activity of using reading and writing. Some of the ideas in books on biological ecology are worth exploring to see how far the metaphor can be taken: for example, that communities themselves are not self-perpetuating or reproductive, individuals are; that the structure and patterns in a community are the product of processes at the level of the individual. And that change occurs at the individual level: the consequences but not the mechanisms occur at the community level.

In recent years, some researchers have come to write about societies and ecologies as both having the properties associated with **complex systems**.[10] Complex systems are made up of many elements which interact with each other repeatedly. Over time, these processes of interaction lead to what is called the **emergence** of new patterns, features and structures, which are generated from the constitutive elements of the system but cannot be reduced to them. In the natural sciences, ideas of emergence have been used to explain how complicated and intricate structures, such as wasps' nests, ant colonies or slime moulds, can arise from the ongoing interaction of very simple processes (Johnson, 2001). In the social sciences, the emergence of a range of social structures including languages and literacies (see Sealey and Carter, 2004) has been explained in terms of similar processes. There are several ways in which literacy is also an ecological issue in the current popular sense of a political issue to do with the environment. First, languages are vanishing at a remarkable rate; they are disappearing at such a rate that most of the languages of the world are likely to disappear within the lifetime of today's schoolchildren. Literacy may be aiding this, but it can also have a role in changing it. For ecological reasons there is a need to protect these languages and the cultures they often embody. I will return to the issue of endangered languages and the role of literacy in sustaining them in chapter 13.

Secondly, dominating languages like English need to maintain their diversity and variety. There are several English languages, not one English. The dangers of a push to a monocultural view of any language are great. The edges are its vitality, and variety ensures its future. There is much diversity in language: there are different genres of language, different languages and different scripts. An ecological approach emphasizes diversity, and in the original biological senses of ecology, sees it as a virtue. Diversity is a source of strength, the roots of the possibilities of the future. This is just as true when applied to the diversity of languages and literacies. Again literacy has a role in maintaining diversity; it can be seen as the main force of standardization of languages, or it can have an important role in maintaining the range of variation in language.

Thirdly, there are communication technologies which can change the balance of languages and cultures, often in ways which have not been thought out. In the natural world there is technology available which means that whole forests can be destroyed and the earth transformed at remarkable rates, irrevocably and with unthought-of-ecological effects. The same is true of language and literacy. Large-scale communication, such as the internet, means that sudden and irreversible changes are taking place. Technology beyond a human scale is speeding up ecological change.

Ecology seems to be a useful and appropriate way of talking about literacy at the moment, and of bringing together its different strands. Using the term changes the whole endeavour of trying to understand the nature of reading and writing. Rather than isolating literacy activities from everything else in order to understand them, an ecological approach aims to understand how literacy is embedded in other human activity, its embeddedness in social life and in thought, and its position in history, in language and in learning. **Ecological** will be used in these several senses. If at this point a succinct statement of what is meant by an ecological approach is needed, I would say that it is one which examines the social and mental embeddedness of human activities in a way which allows change. Instead of studying the separate skills which underlie reading and writing, it involves a shift to studying literacy, a set of social practices associated with particular symbol systems and their related technologies. To be literate is to be active; it is to be confident within these practices. The rest of the book will be devoted to amplifying this.

3 The social basis of literacy

Practices and events
Literacies and domains
Broader social relations
Literacy as communication
Literacy as thought
Values and awareness
Individual history
Social history

Starting out from everyday activities involving literacy, in the first chapter I began to list the things which an integrated theory of literacy needs to include. To bring them together this approach starts out from three areas of enquiry: the social, the psychological and the historical. These are separate directions which people have come from in their work. They need to be interwoven in order to get an overview of what is involved in literacy. When bringing them together it soon becomes obvious that these are not really separable or distinct areas. For example, seeing literacy as a symbolic system immediately straddles the social and the psychological; it is a system for representing the world to ourselves – a psychological phenomenon; at the same time it is a system for representing the world to others – a social phenomenon. To give another example of how these areas are interlinked, an integrated historical notion of literacy has an individual sense of a person's history along with the social sense of history as the development of the culture: bringing together these two senses can shed light on the process of learning.

The aim is to be able to say similar things when talking about literacy in relation to areas such as adults, children, history and different cultures, and when evaluating what parents, politicians and newspaper editors say about the topic. At the moment these areas remain separate and if they were to make contact, people in these different areas would realize that they often have contradictory ways of talking. Introducing the ecological metaphor also raises a new set of questions; I hope that it will provide new insights and suggest new and unexpected links.

To repeat, this approach starts from people's uses of literacy, not from their formal learning of literacy. It also starts from everyday life and from the everyday activities which people are involved in. It is important to stress that education has not been used as a starting point and by the time the discussion gets to schools and learning there will be a different view of what literacy is and what learning is. The examples I will be using in this chapter are mainly taken from a study of reading and writing in Lancaster, England, which I have been involved in. It was a four-year study of the role of literacy in people's everyday lives, carried out mainly through interviews and detailed observation, reported in detail in the book *Local Literacies* (Barton and Hamilton, 1998). The study as a whole will be described in more detail in chapter 4.

Now I will give an outline of the approach, grouped under a set of eight headings. This view of literacy starts from everyday events. We need a social view of literacy which situates literate activities:

1   Literacy is a social activity and can best be described in terms of people's literacy practices which they draw upon in literacy events.
2   People have different literacies which they make use of, associated with different domains of life. Examining different cultures or historical periods reveals more literacies.
3   People's literacy practices are situated in broader social relations. This makes it necessary to describe the social setting of literacy events, including the ways in which social institutions support particular literacies.
4   Literacy is based upon a system of symbols. It is a symbolic system used for communication, and as such exists in relation to other systems of information exchange. It is a way of representing the world to others.

A literacy event is also embedded in our mental life; it forms and is formed by our awareness, intentions and actions. We need a psychological view of literacy:

5   Literacy is a symbolic system used for representing the world to ourselves. Literacy is part of our thinking. It is part of the technology of thought.
6   We have awareness, attitudes and values with respect to literacy and these attitudes and values guide our actions.

Any literacy event has a history, both at the personal and at the cultural level:

7   Literacy has a history. Our individual life histories contain many literacy events from early childhood onwards which the present is built upon. We change, and as children and adults are constantly learning about literacy.
8   A literacy event also has a social history. Current practices are created out of the past.

In the remainder of this chapter I will go through this list in more detail, explaining it and making it more tangible with examples. I will deal with some of the topics here and point out where other longer ones form the basis of the later chapters.

Practices and events

1 Literacy is a social activity and can best be described in terms of people's literacy practices which they draw upon in literacy events.

The two terms **literacy practices** and **literacy events** need to be explained. The first basic unit of analysis is that of event; there are all sorts of occasions in everyday life where the written word has a role. We can refer to these as **literacy events**. Talking in terms of literacy events is necessary to describe how literacy is actually used in people's everyday lives. An obvious example of a literacy event is when an adult reads a story to a child at night. This is an interesting literacy event in that it is often a regular event with repeated patterns of interaction. Such events are important in understanding children's and adults' learning of literacy. The term is broader than this though, and includes any activity which involves the written word; for some events, especially within education, the explicit purpose is learning, but for most literacy events this is not so.

In people's everyday lives they can be involved in a wide range of literacy events. One man we worked with in the Lancaster study went fairly quickly from discussing the contents of a local newspaper with a friend, to organizing his shopping, and taking a phone message for his son who does not have a phone: three quite different literacy events.

The notion of a literacy event has its roots in the sociolinguistic idea of speech events (which goes back at least to the work of Dell Hymes, 1962). It is used in relation to literacy by Anderson et al. (1980) in a study of young children at home. They define a literacy event as being an occasion when a person 'attempts to comprehend or produce graphic signs' (pp. 30–1), either alone or with others. Heath develops this, referring to literacy events generally as being 'when talk revolves around a piece of writing' (1983, p. 386). Elsewhere she defines literacy events as communicative situations 'where literacy has an integral role' (1983, p. 71). This is important in demonstrating that literacy has a role in so many communicative activities. In bringing up children at home and in teaching them in school there are often regular repeated events involving the written word, and it is useful to focus on these literacy events in order to understand more about how children learn to read and write. I will explore this in more depth in chapter 10, which is concerned with children's early literacy, and in the chapters following it. We will also see that in fact it is quite difficult to pin down what is and what is not a literacy event.

The point here is that in order to understand literacy it is important to examine particular events where reading and writing are used. Focusing on the particular is an integral part of an ecological approach; this is different from other approaches which place an emphasis on broad generalizations. An ecological approach to literacy is very cautious of the broad generalizations often associated with reading and writing. It starts out from a belief that it is necessary first to understand something within a particular situation before looking to generalities. This approach suggests certain research methodologies, such as ethnography, and rests on a particular theory of what knowledge is. Literacy is not simply a variable.

The second term which is useful is that of **literacy practices**. What do people mean by practices? There are common patterns in using reading and writing in a particular situation. People bring their cultural knowledge to an activity. It is useful to refer to these ways of using literacy as literacy practices. The term **practices** is used in several disciplines, and several researchers have applied the term directly to literacy, including the studies by Scribner and Cole and by Street which have been mentioned already. Scribner and Cole see the idea as central and they discuss how practices can be seen as ways of using literacy which are carried from one particular situation to another similar situation (1981, pp. 234–8). Another way of thinking about it is to start from more general notions of social practices and to view literacy practices as being the social practices associated with the written word. This can help us to see how social institutions and the power relations they support structure our uses of written language.[1]

Together events and practices are the two basic units of analysis of the social activity of literacy. Literacy events are the particular activities where literacy has a role; they may be regular repeated activities. Literacy practices are the general cultural ways of utilizing literacy which people draw upon in a literacy event. For instance, in the example mentioned earlier of a man discussing the contents of the local paper with a friend, the two of them sitting in the living room planning a letter to the newspaper is a literacy event. In deciding who does what, where and when it is done, along with the associated ways of talking and the ways of writing, the two participants make use of their literacy practices.

Literacies and domains

2 People have different literacies which they make use of, associated with different domains of life. These differences are increased across different cultures or historical periods.

There is not one way of reading and writing, there is not one set of practices. An adult at home may be helping a child with homework, trying to understand a tax form, scanning through a local newspaper, searching the internet. Each of these involves very different literacy practices. To take a particular example, Harry, a man in our research is involved in a range of different sorts of literacy: he writes shopping lists and telephone messages; he uses the local library; he reads and discusses the newspaper. At the library he participates in many different events and draws on a range of practices: as well as reading books he flicks quickly through the newspapers, sometimes renews books for friends he has recommended the books to, but claims never to read the notices in the library. He sometimes looks up old newspapers to read about himself and people he knows. In his home he has few books but he does have a collection of books on local history, which he seems to use regularly. Involving quite different practices from a different domain of life, he is asked to write the occasional letter of reference for former work colleagues in the fire service.

Where these different practices cluster into coherent groups it is very useful to talk in terms of them as being different **literacies**. A literacy is a stable, coherent, identifiable configuration of practices such as legal literacy, or the literacy of specific workplaces. In multilingual situations different literacies will often be associated with different languages or different scripts.

These literacies are configurations of practices and it is worth saying a little here about how they relate to each other. There is not a single dimension on which they can be placed from simple to complex or from easy to difficult. It is important to move beyond the idea, often implicit in literacy programmes for children and for adults, of there being a simple dimension from basic to complex forms of literacy. Literacies do not exist on some scale starting with basic or simple forms and going on to complex or higher forms. So-called simple and complex forms of literacy are in fact different literacies serving different purposes. They do not lead on from one to the other in any obvious way.[2]

Although we do not want to end up with a closed taxonomy of literacies, it may be useful to identify different categories of literacies. Various suggestions have been made, and although they are often presented in pairs such categories in fact are not usually polar opposites. To begin with, literacies are not equally valued. They vary in what purposes and whose purposes they serve. One distinction is between *imposed* uses of literacy and *self-generated* uses of literacy (see Barton, 1991). This emphasizes the importance of purposes: sometimes these purposes are self-generated; at other times, such as filling in official forms, they are imposed from the outside. This relates to a distinction used by Brian Street (1993) between *dominant* literacies and *vernacular* literacies. Dominant literacies originate from the dominant institutions of society. Vernacular literacies have their roots in everyday life. Another possibility is *indigenous* versus *imported* literacies, used by Irvine and Elsasser (1988), in their study of literacy teaching in the Caribbean. A different sort of dimension is that some literacies are *creative*, allowing possibilities for the writer, while others, like filling in forms and checking lists, are *constrained* literacies, although in fact all literacies probably have creative and constraining aspects. A further example is Freire's distinction between *domesticating* and *empowering* uses of literacy, mentioned earlier. There is no one clear set of categories for the recurrent configurations of written language. We will return to this when examining examples of texts in chapter 5.

Literacies are identified culturally as such. Different literacies are associated with different domains of life such as home, school, church and work. There are different places in life where people act differently and use language differently. In the ecological metaphor there are ecological niches which sustain and nurture particular forms of literacy. To take the example of home, school and work, typically people wear different clothes, talk differently, take on different roles, have different purposes. The social rules underlying people's actions in these three places are different. The physical space – buildings, and so on – are typically different and time is broken up differently. These are different domains and they give rise to different practices – meaning both the general social ways of acting and how people individually act on particular occasions.

The starting point for detailed examination of literacy practices is to realize that literacy may be different in different domains and that school, for example, is but one domain of literacy activity. Other domains may be just as significant. The home is a particularly important domain in that it is the site for a wide range of activities and it is where children typically first encounter literacy events. The home is 'the centre from which individuals venture out into other domains' (Klassen, 1991, p. 43). Within a domain such as the home one can look in more detail and examine the wide range of activities involving different literacies. I will return to this when discussing children's emergent literacy.

Having been precise about the link between literacies and domains, I must now point out that the reality is more fluid. When starting out it may be useful to identify home, school and work as separate domains with their own distinctive practices giving rise to particular literacies. In fact the home is a site, a physical location, for all sorts of activities. Different sorts of reading and writing from many sources, including school and work, are carried out in the home. The practices leak from one domain to the other and there is much overlap. Nevertheless, home and school remain separate domains where certain literacy practices are sustained, nurtured and legitimized while others are not. The same event might be valued very differently in the two places and have very different meaning to the participants.

As another word of caution, terms like **domain** seem to be flexible in size. **Genre** and **discourse**, which will be discussed in chapter 5, are other examples. They seem to lack a clear definition. How big are they? Are there three or four domains or are there hundreds? I am afraid that the idea of **literacies** is also like this. It is important not to lose sight of this when discussing a literacy. This can be very valuable where similar patterning is seen at different levels.

Broader social relations

3 People's literacy practices are situated in broader social relations. This makes it necessary to describe the social setting of literacy events, including the ways in which social institutions support particular literacies.

People may pass through many activities in a day, each making different demands upon them. They might have to be a parent, spouse, neighbour, customer, patient. In doing this people draw upon different aspects of their identity. Someone may be black, female, middle-class, a mother and a student and they will draw upon salient aspects of their identity in any situation. People are positioned by roles and the demands placed upon them, and in most situations they know a range of appropriate ways of acting; people generally know what to do if they are a parent, a patient or a customer. Nevertheless, roles are not fixed and unchanging things which people slot into. Rather, they are negotiated, accepted and sometimes challenged. In any situation people can have more than one role and there can be conflict between the demands of different roles. Given that many everyday activities can be literacy events, these ideas of roles and identity are a good place to start an examination of social variation in literacy and constraints on literacy.

It is in certain roles that people need particular literacies and use literacy. A simple example of roles in literacy events is that of gender in the home. As a newspaper headline reporting a survey put it, 'Wives write Xmas cards . . . Husbands write cheques' (*Daily Mirror*, 17 April 1989). This sums up a common role division, which we have observed in our studies, that often women write in the personal sphere, keeping in contact with friends and relations, and writing and recording Christmas cards, birthdays and anniversaries, while men deal with the business world of bills, mortgages and house repairs (see Barton and Padmore, 1991). These roles can be followed to the extent that men are unable to write a personal letter and women not know how to write a cheque. This is one of many examples we will come across where literacy activity is gendered, where men and women often act differently. However, this division is not by any means a hard and fast one and the roles are not always obvious. The roles are negotiated and they can involve conflict and change. Difficulties with reading and writing, for example, or particular skills can affect roles people have. And of course these roles can change as family structures change in society.

People's literacy practices do not reflect abilities in any straightforward way, but rather they are to do with what people feel is or is not appropriate. People learn that socially there are appropriate practices for specific roles and there are inappropriate practices. Viewing abilities like this represents an important shift in terms of how we think about literacy. The move towards describing people's actions as relative to the situation they are in is a significant step; it represents a move away from overreliance on the idea of a set of fixed abilities which is common in much discussion of reading and writing. In addition we should not lose sight of the fact that roles are related to power and that much literacy is learned in relationships of unequal power, those of parent and child, and teacher and student.

A second aspect of situating literacy practices within broader social relations is that in everyday life people act within various networks. These networks have broad functions covering work, child rearing and other areas of social activity and they are often networks of reciprocal support. Literacy activities are exchanged within these networks. For example Harry, who was discussed earlier, is part of several networks, including family, neighbours, and former work colleagues. His sister-in-law and his son provide a network of support for him. His sister-in-law does his shopping for him. His son helps him with official forms he has to fill in and also rewrites for him the odd reference he has to write for people in the fire service. This is a reciprocal relationship in that in turn he takes telephone messages for his son, who does not have a telephone. I will return to discussion of these networks and literacy in chapter 13.

Throughout I am starting out from how literacy fits into individual lives, how people experience literacy. The institutional framework is an important part of the context of people's actions. An alternative starting point for a study of the social basis of literacy could be institutional practices around literacy, examining religion, capitalism, advertising, and so on, as social practices. It is important to see how the state, the church and multinational corporations use literacy to plan, record, control and influence, and how people participate in these practices. Human activities including literacy are embedded in and get their meanings from such human institutions.

One way of examining different institutional settings is to regard them as different domains. When investigating different literacies, for each of these domains there are particular institutions which support the distinct literacy practices. Particular definitions of literacy and their associated literacy practices are nurtured by these institutions. Different institutions define and influence different aspects of literacy or different literacies; they become definition-sustaining institutions. School and the whole educational system, for instance, supports certain views of what literacy is and what it is for. Historically, different religions have developed distinct definitions of what literacy is and what it means to be literate. Taken together, the various institutions may support different literacies: it may be, for example, in a culture that religion influences ritual aspects of literacy; the family has an effect on habits of personal communication; while work and school influence public and formal aspects of communication. It follows from this that domains are not equal, and to some extent the different institutions may be supporting conflicting literacy practices. In addition to this patterning, there are larger concerns such as gender or national identity whose influence cuts across different domains. (See Street and Street, 1991, for example, on the influence of national identity and Collins and Blot, 2003 on issues of power.)

Literacy as communication

4 Literacy is based upon a system of symbols. It is a symbolic system used for communication, and as such exists in relation to other systems of information exchange. It is a way of representing the world to others.

Literacy is part of communication, of reporting the world to others. The relationship of reading and writing to other forms of communication needs to be examined. First, there is the relation to spoken language. Ideas about written language have moved on considerably from viewing it as *speech which is written down*. Written language has different functions from spoken language and any choice between written and spoken usually has other implications beyond a simple choice of medium. Writing enables us to go much further than with spoken language; we are able to fix things in space and time. Writing results in **texts**. Because it often is reproducible and open to inspection, written language can be a powerful form of language; we need to examine how writing extends the possibilities of language. It should be clear then that any view of literacy is part of a theory of language and it is necessary to set out a view of language, or at least the parts which impinge on literacy; this will be done in the next few chapters.

Although they are very different, written and spoken language are not easy to separate. In fact they are closely entwined, and in daily life people participate in literacy events where reading and writing are mixed in with spoken language and with other means of communication. Literacy events typically involve a written text and talk around the text. In many ways written and spoken language are not separable in literacy events and some researchers would go so far as to blur any distinction between written and spoken and call all forms of public communication literate. There will be examples of these approaches in the chapter devoted to school views of literacy, but I think it more useful to keep them separate for the moment. Writing is based on speech in some very real ways: spoken language is the basis for most people's learning of written language, for instance, and the very form of written language gets its inspiration from spoken language. Still, it is important to stress that the roots of written language lie only partly with spoken language. Written language has a life of its own. I will return to this in the chapter devoted to written and spoken language.

Other aspects of communication come into play with written language. Most significantly, it is visual; it is laid out in some way and displayed. The importance of the role of design, layout and other aspects of the physical context should be self-evident, and they form part of what is meant by writing. An ecological approach to communication needs to be dynamic and interactive too. This is a different view of communication from standard functional models which see it in terms of transmitters and receivers of messages, with writing and other technologies simply amplifying what spoken language can do. The point is that with written language you can do things you cannot with spoken. It does not just amplify spoken language. It extends the functions of language, and enables you to do different things.

It can be very useful to consider literacy as a technology, although this needs to be done with caution, and for people to realize that technologies are not neutral or autonomous. The idea of technology may seem to be bound up with a functional view which treats 'literacy', 'the individual' and 'society' as if they are independent entities that meet at some points, and which does not allow for the dynamic and interactive nature of these relationships. However, it need not be viewed like this and it is fruitful to retain some notion of literacy as technology, and to find ways of examining critically what this implies about the role of literacy and of technologies generally in society and in human cognitive activities.

It is different forms of technology which have provided the possibilities as well as the constraints for written language. Written language involves technology in a way that straightforward conversational spoken language does not. Whether it is a simple paper and pencil, or a spray can on a wall, or a complex word processor, written language always utilizes some technology. (Of course, much contemporary spoken language makes use of satellites, loudspeakers, microphones, tape recorders and other technologies.) Literacy is a good example to use when exploring the social basis of technologies. It can be viewed as a communications technology concerned with the production and reproduction of shared meaning or knowledge. This is the perspective taken by Raymond Williams (1981).

Literacy as thought

5 Literacy is a symbolic system used for representing the world to ourselves.

As well as communicating – representing the world to others – literacy is important in representing the world to ourselves. It is part of our thinking; it is part of the technology of thought. Language and literacy are used to define reality, not only to others, but also to ourselves. Literacy, then, has a role in the ecology of the mind.

Literacy is a symbolic system. Like other symbolic systems such as numbers it has both a cognitive and a cultural basis. As well as its external aspects, it contributes to the mind and to thinking; it enables people to do things which otherwise would not be possible. It is necessary to avoid the idea of the mind as fixed and given; at the same time we need to steer carefully round ideas such as that of there being automatic cognitive consequences of literacy. Like other aspects of human life, the mind is socially constructed within the physical constraints of being human. A practice account of literacy inevitably includes a practice account of thinking, covering how it is constructed and supported by social practices.[3]

Literacy is an ideal topic for linking the psychological and the social. Symbolic systems lie at the interface of social structure, technology and mind. A symbolic system such as writing *mediates* between individual cognition and social phenomena. I will return to the idea of mediation in chapter 5. What I mean by stating that writing is an individual system is that it has a psychological basis and that any piece of writing is an external representation or outcome of internal cognitive processes. At the same time, writing is 'out there'; it exists along with other social artefacts of culture and forms part of a broader social context.

It is not just the study of literacy but the study of language itself which has the potential to link the social and the psychological. Language is a symbolic system linking what goes on inside our heads with what goes on outside. It mediates between self and society. It is a form of representation, a way of representing the world to ourselves and to others. Language is a remarkable communication system enabling us to think and to talk about the world around us. More than other communication systems, it enables us to talk about things which are not present, and about things which are nonexistent, and to reflect upon, to abstract and to generalize our experience; we can create possible worlds; we are even able to reflect upon our internal states and upon language: we can talk about talk.

Psychological processes are usually thought of as being in people's heads. One way in which views on cognition or thinking have changed is that thinking has moved outside the head. Not only does the idea of processes change, but also what is meant by thought. The study of reading and writing should be part of a general shift of moving processes out of the head and 'outdoors', to use Jean Lave's phrase (1988). A shift which is taking place is seeing cognition, thought and mental activities as residing in cultural activities as much as in the head. These are ideas associated with Jean Lave, Barbara Rogoff and others in areas such as problem solving, memory and everyday mathematics.[4] The study of the processes of reading and writing can be fitted squarely into this approach. It can also help us see more clearly the 'effects' of literacy without falling down some great divide. All thought is socially constructed and it is the social practices around literacy, not literacy itself, which shape consciousness.

Values and awareness

6 *We have awareness, attitudes and values with respect to literacy and these attitudes and values guide our actions.*

People make sense of literacy as a social phenomenon and their social construction of literacy lies at the root of their attitudes towards literacy and their actions. Saying that literacy has a social meaning is going further than saying that there are social dimensions to it or that it exists within a social context. Literacy is embedded in institutional contexts which shape the practices and social meanings attached to reading and writing. Within these social contexts, the act of reading or writing becomes symbolic. The very act of reading or writing takes on a social meaning: it can be an act of defiance, or an act of solidarity, an act of conforming, or a symbol of change. We assert our identity through literacy.

Every person, adult or child, has a view of literacy, about what it is and what it can do for them, about its importance and its limitations. Everyone has a way of talking about literacy, they use a set of metaphors to do with literacy, they have what is in effect a theory of literacy. People can talk about reading and writing: their views are also expressed in their attitudes and their actions. To take some examples from everyday home practices, people often have strong views about reading at the meal table or writing in books. If they think reading at the meal table is socially reprehensible, they will forbid children to do it. Often books in themselves are thought to be of value, while magazines and comics are less valued. More generally, people's views of literacy are important in how and what they learn and a parent's attitudes and actions influence a child's behaviour at school. Attitudes are also at the heart of whether or not people think they have a 'problem' with reading and writing and whether or not they think it is appropriate to attend adult literacy classes.

Values are also clearly expressed in the relative importance attached to literacy as compared with other activities, such as practical and physical activities. Sometimes reading and writing are contrasted with work, at other times they are compared with leisure. An idea which we have come across repeatedly in our studies is that people feel that it is better to be reading than to be doing nothing, but it is better to be doing some 'real' work rather than reading. We have examples of this in our study of people talking about literacy at the turn of the twentieth century (Barton, 1988). We have further examples in our study of contemporary literacy. This ambivalence towards literacy seems to be a strong element in contemporary culture. As we can see, reading and writing are not just cognitive activities, feelings run through them.

Drawing attention to people's awareness and attitudes is also a way of bringing in human agency, bringing in intentions. An active view of literacy has people with intentions, meanings and values at its centre. The literacy practices we have today, the schooling we have today, the technologies we have today all result from active human decisions based on people's values. Related to this, all literacy activities have a purpose for people. People do things for a reason, people have purposes. In general, people do not read in order to read, nor write in order to write; rather, people read and write in order to do other things, in order to achieve other ends. People want to know what time the train leaves or how a new watch or video works; they want to make sense of their lives, or keep in contact with a friend; they want to make their voice heard. Reading and writing can be part of these social activities. Sometimes, as when filling in a benefit form, the various participants associated with the event can have conflicting purposes.

In later chapters I will deal more with people's perceptions, how they make sense of life and the role of awareness. I see awareness as a foundation stone of human intelligence and the ability to reflect on our activities as a crucial part of human activity. People's literacy practices are not necessarily obvious and it is often those of other cultures which stand out and which are subjected to detailed examination. It was when examining reading and writing in different cultural groups that people such as Scribner and Cole, Heath and Street observed practices. It is generally accepted that the practices of another culture have to be discovered by detailed observation; this is no less true of cultures we are close to. Often this is a difficult point to accept; even Heath's study seemed to take the middle-class, mainstream practices more for granted. They are probably closer to her practices, to my practices, and, maybe, to your practices. Nevertheless, we can reflect on our own activities and on those of people around us. We can become more aware of them, in order to understand, and if necessary, resist, challenge and change them.

Individual history

7 Literacy has a history. Our individual life histories contain many literacy events from early childhood onwards which the present is built upon. We change, and as children and adults are constantly learning about literacy.

There are two senses of historical change: that of the individual's growth and development; and that of the whole culture over a longer time period. We need a way of talking about literacy which takes account of these two notions, relates them and which is dynamic and can deal with change. In both of them current practices are created out of the past.

The first sense is the change in an individual person's life. Every person has a history, and for the discussion here, every person has a literacy history. This goes back to early childhood and the first encounters with literacy practices in home literacy events; it continues with involvement in community and school practices, and on into adulthood with its varying and changing demands. At any point in time a person's choices are based on the possibilities provided by their past experiences. Just as our view of literacy is dependent on our view of language, it is also dependent on our view of learning. Learning is something which takes place all the time; all activities involve learning; it is not limited to official sittings in a classroom, it is not something which only children do. We change throughout our lives, and as children and adults are constantly learning about literacy. This change is the key to learning.

There are several ways in which literacy is bound up with changes in people's lives. First, people read and write at particular times in their lives. The demands of life change: there are times in people's lives when they need to read and write more, and times when they need to read and write less. New demands can result from changes at work, or they can arise from changes in people's personal lives; for example, parents may experience changing demands when their young children grow up and go to school. In addition, people want to make changes in their lives, and reading and writing can enable them to make such changes.

A broad view of learning is needed which provides a way of connecting up pre-school literacy and adult literacy campaigns, and which also goes beyond these settings into everyday life. We need to account for how literacy is acquired, not just in schools and by children, but in everyday life; not just here and now, but in other cultures and in other times. It is important to link up learning by adults and learning by children and to have a clear idea of the importance and limitations of schooling. People learn in their everyday lives and not enough attention has been paid to this everyday or **vernacular** learning. The person I have mentioned already from our study, Harry, says that he could not read and write properly when he left school. He is not untypical in this. He learned new literacies at work, for instance in the fire service where he had to write regular reports, as he came across writing demands he had not met before. He also learned new literacies in his everyday life; he was secretary of the local working men's club for several years later in life, where he learned how to write such things as minutes of meetings and notices.

One implication of this view of learning is that children are not incomplete beings and adults complete. Literacy makes sense to anyone at any one time. Whether a four-year-old child, a person from another culture or another historical period, their literacy makes sense to them. Notions of incomplete literacy or restricted literacy do not make a lot of sense within this framework. There are not component skills which can be added separately like building blocks to make a complete building. Of course, it is still true that people may want to change and extend their literacies and this can be equally true for teenagers, adult basic education students and for professional writers.

Finally, in this view learning comes from social interaction, but it is also built upon foundations which are part of our human endowment, our intelligence, our innate potentialities. An ecological approach is neither innatist or environmentalist; it is about the dynamic interaction of the two, how people fit into the environment, how they form it and are formed by it.

Social history

8 *Literacy events and practices have a social history.*

The second sense of history is that of change in the whole culture. With literacy this goes back five thousand years to the origin of writing. There have been many developments in this long stretch of time. As I hope will become evident, the history of literacy raises many questions: about the scripts in existence today, about cultures without literacy and about the relation of literacy and thought. It can provide some insight into areas as diverse as the learning of literacy, levels of literacy in society, literacy and technological change and literacy and power relations. Recent history should make it clear how current practices are based on the past, and how they are not inevitable and unchangeable, but have developed out of past practices. Issues such as disputes about levels of literacy in schools, the importance of popular literacies, and the rise of elite notions of 'literature' and 'literary', can all be illuminated by examining recent history.

We need to account for the origins of literacy in the distant historical past, as well as understanding the closer historical basis of contemporary literacy. It is important to integrate these ideas, bringing together learning with an understanding of cognition and historical change. The two notions of history, that of the individual and that of the whole culture, come together at several points. One way is how from generation to generation people pass on a culture. In the local literacies study we compared different generations and we saw how practices are passed on from generation to generation. There are links with the past and with the future. Historically, there are connections with the earlier generations of people and in our contemporary study of everyday uses of literacy we have documented ways in which the people we have interviewed want life to be different for their own children (Barton, 1988). These people are passing on a culture in a changing environment, and this is an important way in which the culture and its associated practices change.

Another situation where the two aspects of change and history come together is with current rapid social change, where new technologies and political changes are changing the demands on people. New social practices give different possibilities and constraints, so that in the new workplace people have to monitor their work and keep records in new ways, as well as changing the ways they communicate. Some social changes increase literacy demands, some reduce literacy demands. Another example of this to do with modern technology is the choice between sending messages by email or by other technologies. The path to a choice in any particular instance is very complicated, involving availability, cost, technical ability, reliability and other factors. These possibilities are all changing the basis of communication in human relationships. Hopefully, examining examples from the past such as the spread of printing can illuminate current changes.

4 Researching literacy practices

A number of studies have examined literacy practices in different settings. This chapter reports on work that has studied literacy practices and outlines ways of going about this. It begins with an elaboration of the concept of literacy as a social practice, which was introduced in the previous chapter. It describes some research methods that can be employed to research literacy from this perspective, and outlines some examples of studies which have done this. A range of different examples is given. Examples of multilingual literacy practices show the complexity of the relationship between literacy and different languages. What it means to be literate differs in different languages with their own practices. I briefly sketch an example of how literacy is patterned in social life, that is, how literacy is gendered in society. I draw on studies of workplace literacy practices to show how these are patterned by the power relationships and structures of the workplace. These topics show the way that there are different literacies in people's lives, and how the use of these literacies is patterned socially.

Researching literacy as social practice

In chapter 3, I outlined some of the key features of an integrated perspective on literacy. This perspective has specific implications for the way literacy can be researched.

I explained how literacy can be seen as a set of social practices which people draw on in literacy events. From this perspective, literacy is located in interactions between people, rather than being a decontextualized cognitive skill – an activity, rather than just an internal attribute. Therefore, to understand literacy, researchers need to observe literacy events as they happen in people's lives, in particular times and places. The fact that different literacies are associated with different domains of life means that this detailed observation needs to be going on in a variety of different settings, and also that findings from one setting cannot simply be generalized across contexts. Research needs first to be specific to a given domain, before making any general claims about literacy.

The relationship between local literacy practices and broader social relations means that in addition to the detail of local observation, literacy research needs to extend its focus outwards, using other methods such as drawing on historical research or social theory to produce an understanding of the wider situation within which the literacy events are happening. The importance of power relations in patterning literacy practices means literacy researchers need to develop an understanding of the processes of power in the society which they are studying, and to take a critical approach, in the sense of making visible the power relationships which are often hidden.

Because literacy practices are situated in social relations, which are patterned by social institutions and power relations, some literacies are more dominant, visible, and influential than others. **Vernacular literacies** – literacies associated with people's private, home and everyday lives, outside the domains of power and influence – are often hidden. This account of literacy calls for research to make visible and valuable aspects of people's lives which have previously often been unseen and ignored.

Given that literacy is part of the way people get on with their lives, literacy practices are purposeful, embedded in people's broader life goals and practices. Rather than looking at whether people do or do not possess literacy skills, in order to develop a full understanding of what literacy means in people's lives it is necessary to look at how they use literacy as part of the process of making sense of their lives, representing the world to themselves, and working towards achieving what they want, using the resources available to them. Building up relationships with people over time enables the researcher to come to understand what people's broader purposes and life goals are, and how literacy figures within these.

As well as situating literacy in people's local contexts, this approach situates literacy in social and individual history. Current literacy events and practices are created out of the past, in an ongoing process of maintenance, development and change. Literacy practices are therefore not absolute and fixed for all time, either for an individual or for a society. In addition these changes often occur through processes of informal learning and sense-making, outside of a formal teaching situation. Therefore, research into literacy acquisition should not merely focus on classroom or school-based learning, but needs also to look beyond this to the way in which people acquire new practices in other domains, such as the home, the workplace and the neighbourhood association. This kind of literacy research involves getting to know people's histories and the histories of their communities, and how literacy practices have changed within these.

Research methods

All of the above demonstrates the value of studying literacy as it happens, looking both at specific literacy events and at how these events are embedded in social contexts. This can be done at various levels.

Large studies like *Local Literacies* (Barton and Hamilton, 1998) often involve researchers spending time in particular communities, using a variety of methods to develop as complete a picture as possible of the detail of people's lives and the place of literacy practices within them: a method called **ethnography**. Data collection in ethnography may include some or all of the following: observation of and participation in literacy events, which are documented using notes, audio recording and video recording; formal and informal interviews and conversations, which might again be recorded in a variety of ways; the collection of texts and artefacts created within the community, and of externally produced documents about the community where these exist; the use of photographs both as data in themselves and as a spur for interview discussions (Hodge and Jones, 2000); historical methods, including oral history interviews and working with archive material. It may involve methods such as question- naires, used as one method among others to develop an overall picture. Researchers are constantly developing and pushing at the edges of re- search methods and now work with information technology, using inter- active websites, mailing lists or chat rooms to interact with research participants and collect data.

Ethnography is a reflexive approach to research, meaning that it involves thinking about the position of the researcher and the research process itself, particularly in respect of its ethical implications. This approach sees participants not just as 'subjects' of the research but as active people, who will make sense of the research process and the results in their own way, and on whose lives the research will necessarily have an impact. Ethical implications must therefore be considered carefully. When you are spending time getting to know people, building up relationships of mutual obligation, and stepping into normally private areas of their lives with them, ethical obligations become increasingly complex and need a lot of thought. The ethnographic researcher of literacy must constantly be aware of the potential effects, positive and negative, that the research may have.

This sort of research usually generates a great deal of data of various kinds, and data analysis involves looking for patterns across the whole range of data. In *Local Literacies*, we described in detail a set of steps in the analysis process (Barton and Hamilton, 1998, chapter 4): storing and indexing the data in appropriate ways, reading and rereading data, and keeping notes of ideas about patterns, themes and exceptions. Gradually, a more systematic categorization will be developed as particular themes emerge as being significant and relationships between different categories become clear. The themes and focuses of the written-up research will emerge from this ongoing process of data analysis, with the writing of a research report, article or book being another stage of analysis, involving further interpretation and selection.

This approach is appropriate for a large-scale research project. Smaller- scale studies of literacy practices are also valuable, and can be one of the best ways for people to increase their understanding of literacy, by reflecting on their own practices and the practices around them. One good way of doing this is to explore the literacy practices in a particular area of everyday life. This would start with the identification of a particular topic – a place, an activity, or a group. This could be something very familiar, or something completely new. My students have studied literacy practices as diverse as those involved in celebrating Chinese New Year, buying a lottery ticket, using a shared college kitchen or going to church.[1]

After identifying a topic, the next step is to observe the visual environment, trying to get some distance from it and to see it in the way a stranger with no knowledge of the domain might. Getting down to detail is important here. Taking photographs is useful and can prove a very revealing part of the research. Having observed the visual environment, the focus shifts to identifying and documenting particular literacy events and the texts used within them. This might involve collecting or photocopying examples of texts. Interviews with people engaged in the literacy events can be used to help make their cultural knowledge clear and to make sense of the observations.

As with the larger-scale studies described above, the ethical implications of research activities and their potential impact on the lives of research participants need to be considered carefully. For instance, taking photographs in a public setting frequented by tourists may be relatively unproblematic, while taking photographs of a normally private activity might require negotiated and informed consent. People participating in the research should understand how the research is going to be used and to what extent it will be made public. They should have the chance to discuss whether their identities will be made public or whether they will be anonymized. Any research involving children or vulnerable people has particular ethical implications and needs to be negotiated carefully and openly.[2]

The data collected in this way can be analysed in relation to many of the concepts explored in this book: the different roles people take on in literacy events; the relationships between the literacies involved and other social structures, such as for instance gender patterning of literacy events; the different technologies that are being used and the possibilities and effects of these. In a class setting where several such projects are being undertaken, the patterns identified in different domains can be compared and contrasted. Such projects can be very instructive in really seeing the value of a social view of literacy, and in gaining new insights into the varied roles of literacy in people's lives.

Local and community literacy practices

I have already drawn on examples from the *Local Literacies* research. I will now give a fuller description of that study, as an example of the sort of research which can be carried out from this perspective, and of the potential insights this research can generate. This ethnographic research was conducted in Lancaster, a town in the north-west of England. It began with a survey in one neighbourhood, asking people about their ways of finding out local information. This was used as a lead-in to the topic of reading and writing.

Twelve households were then selected for case studies. The case studies consisted of extended visits in people's homes, beginning with audio-recorded semi-structured interviews, which were followed up with less structured interviews exploring each individual's own interests and practices. A variety of other research methods were also used in the case studies: some people used maps to plot where they went on a regular basis, others kept letters or junk mail, two people kept diaries of their literacy practices, one couple recorded bedtime reading sessions with their daughter, one man was accompanied to the library and to his local café, and researchers met people at social events, in the pub and at meetings.

This data collection stage was followed by transcription and analysis of the data. Then the researchers returned to 10 people more than a year later for a 'collaborative ethnography' stage, to share parts of the data and analysis, to check the validity of the analysis against the way people made sense of their own lives, and to collect further data.

In addition to this case study work, researchers collected a wide range of contextual information about the area, to give a social and historical profile of the city and neighbourhood. They also carried out interviews with people working in organizations with some relation to literacy, including schools, colleges and libraries, but also shops, travel agents, post offices, the tourist information office, advice centres, asking about the services provided, the literacies involved in attracting custom and dealing with the public, and the extent to which the organizations were aware of literacy difficulties. Researchers also documented local literacies in more informal ways, including taking photographs of literacy artefacts such as banners placed at a local roundabout to announce birthdays. They carried out case studies of community groups and organizations.

All this data was analysed and written up using processes similar to those described above, depending on the type of data collected, moving from historical descriptions of the town as a whole, to detailed descriptions of the life of the area, through to detailed case studies of several of the individuals researchers worked with.

A wide range and diversity of literacies were encountered in people's homes. The research identified six key areas of everyday life where reading and writing were of particular importance: **organizing life, personal communication, private leisure, documenting life, sense making** and **social participation**. Importantly, such vernacular literacies are different from more dominant literacies. They are learned informally, and this learning is integrated with practical application and embedded in people's lives. More dominant and visible literacy practices are more formalized, more standardized and defined in terms of the formal purposes of an institution, rather than people's own lives and purposes. Access to these dominant literacies is controlled through experts and teachers. Vernacular literacies are more likely to be voluntary and self-generated, and may also be a source of creativity, invention and originality, giving rise to new practices.

The research also brought to light the importance of social networks and relationships in these practices, with literacy being used for social communication, but also with people drawing on these social networks to help them with particular literacy requirements. All of the participants in the study were involved in some way with at least one self-organized local group or organization, and many had held officers' posts. Literacy is significant in terms of local democratic participation, with these local groups underpinning political participation at the local level, and also offering ways in to more formal political organizations (although literacy can also be used in groups to control and undermine democratic participation). This data shows the importance of people using reading and writing *in groups* to get things done, as one of a number of resources on which they draw. This view of literacy as a communal resource, rather than as an individual's particular skill, is therefore central both theoretically and in the data.

Literacy was used by people to make sense of events in their lives and resolve a variety of problems, such as those related to health, legal problems, employment-related problems and issues around schooling. Often this involved confrontation with professional experts and specialized systems of knowledge, and people often drew on their networks for support and knowledge, thereby becoming expert in a particular domain and becoming a resource for other community members themselves. Literacy was also used for personal change and transformation, both within and outside education-related domains, for accessing information relating to people's interests, for asserting or creating personal identity, and for self-directed learning. But despite their importance for people's everyday lives, vernacular literacy practices frequently have a low cultural value.

Some key themes and patterns were identified which linked people's experiences: the gendering of home practices, particularly in people's gendered literacy networks and their reading habits; the variety and importance of home numeracy practices, which are often integrated with literacy; and the significance of multilingual literacies in many of the homes in the area, which included a Gujarati-speaking community.

Further examples of local and community literacy research can be found in the later edited volume *Situated literacies* (Barton et al., 2000), which brings together a number of studies of reading and writing in a variety of different local contexts, informed by the same theoretical perspective outlined above. Many of the studies presented in this collection show how qualitative methods and detailed local studies can deepen a theoretical understanding of literacy. A study of literacy in prisons by Anita Wilson demonstrates the role of literacies in the struggle against institutionalization and 'losing your mind', the importance of literacy in attempts to maintain an individual identity within a bureaucratic controlling institution, and the use of literacy to construct a 'third space' between prison and Outside. This resistant use of literacy contrasts with work by Kathryn Jones with bilingual Welsh farmers at an auction market, where it is literacy which inscribes the people's lives into a transnational social order. Jones focuses on the process of filling in an 'animal movement form', showing how the individual farmers are incorporated into the agricultural bureaucratic system through a complex process of locally situated talk around texts. A study by Karin Tusting on the role of literacy practices within a Roman Catholic congregation shows how literacy is used to manage time in a variety of ways: how literacy artefacts are produced within a First Communion preparation class bothas tangible evidence of commitment through showing investment of significant amounts of time, and to serve as a permanent historical record of a fleeting set of events; and how the parish bulletin is used to synchronize events in time, both locally within the parish community and globally in relation to the Catholic Church as a whole, thereby maintaining community identity.

Multilingual literacy practices

Being literate is always expressed in a particular language. Whether it is English, or Japanese, or Vai, a specific language is implied. This may seem obvious but it worth pointing out to the extent that when measuring literacy in national surveys or when discussing literacy in schools and colleges, it is common to count only certain literacies. As an example of this, in a Canadian survey, only English and French were counted; this meant that in the survey results, and probably in education too, other literacies which people used, such as Spanish or Hmong, were ignored. That literacy assumes particular languages has always been true: in medieval times in much of Europe literacy meant being able to read Latin; vernacular literacies were ignored. Dominant cultures with dominant languages, like English today, tend to support monolingualism and to ignore or brush aside varieties, dialects, creoles and vernacular languages; they also tend to play down fluidity and change in languages and to ignore overlap and similarities between languages.

Most people in the world are exposed to more than one language. It may be that in their day-to-day life more than one language is spoken; there may be a different language used at home from that used in the school or in the wider community. Many different possible situations exist. It is also probably true that most people in the world are bilingual to some extent, that they use more than one language in their lives. These languages may or may not be written down. In earlier chapters I have talked of different **literacies** as existing within one language. Another sense of this term is the idea of different literacies being associated with different languages. This idea can be applied to bilingual or multilingual situations and it gives rise to another whole set of possibilities based upon whether or not the different languages are written down, and people's relative knowledge of the languages and the writing systems. In the 1990s, a wide range of research in multilingual literacies was being carried out in Britain, often using innovative methods. Much of this research is reported in Martin-Jones and Jones (2000a).

In the US, studies of literacies in multilingual settings are often related to improving the education of students from linguistically and culturally diverse backgrounds. The goal is to use ethnographic methods to better understand the different 'funds of knowledge' students bring from their homes and communities. Schools and teachers can then draw on this knowledge by relating school learning to home and community practices in more meaningful ways.[3]

A reasonably straightforward example of multilingual literacies would be Spanish speakers in Toronto, where English is the dominant language. Here we have two languages sharing a similar alphabet. Studying 'newcomers' to Canada, Cecil Klassen describes the different literacy practices associated with the two languages (Klassen, 1991). In a detailed study of people's uses of written language, carried out by interviewing people and observing them, Klassen identifies the domains of life where they come across written language: they are home, the street, stores, bureaucracies, work, schools and church. Within each domain he identifies the uses of literacy, so that within the home the list includes uses such as paperwork, correspondence, school work, religion, leisure. These can be further broken down, so that the paperwork in the home is associated with shopping, cooking, appointments, prescriptions, bills, notices, forms, documents and school communication.

Some domains are clearly linked with one language and its associated literacy, so that most written language encountered in streets, stores, bureaucracies and work is in English, while the literacy associated with religious worship is Spanish. Other domains are more mixed, noticeably the home. Home is probably the most complex domain in that literacy from all the other areas impinges upon it. Within the home, literacy associated with shopping, cooking, bills, forms, documents, school communication is in English, while that associated with correspondence, religion and leisure activities is in Spanish.

This study does not deal with the spoken language around these activities. I assume that much of the spoken language around literacy events such as understanding a note brought home from school will be in Spanish, even though the note is in English. The spoken language presumably involves a certain amount of switching between the two languages.

These lists of uses of literacy cover a wide range of literacies in situations which demand a complex set of practices. The strategies different people use to respond to these demands depend partly on their knowledge of the two languages and partly on their knowledge of the two literacies, as well as other factors. I will return later to the various strategies which people use to deal with these demands.

In the Toronto example we are just dealing with two languages, ones which share a common script and which are related. Both are world languages and it is clear that one of them, English, is more dominant in Toronto. In many multilingual settings, different scripts and language varieties add extra dimensions of complexity. In Jones's (2000) study of literacies in a Welsh hill-farming community described above, the people she worked with speak a regional variety of Welsh and a regional Welsh variety of English, as well as reading and writing standard English. Gregory and Williams (2000) and Blackledge (2000) report on studies in communities in which people speak Sylheti (spoken in one area of Bangladesh) and read and write Bengali, in addition to speaking the local variety of English in the areas of Birmingham and London in which they live.

The complexity of patterns of literacy use can be illustrated more graphically in an example of the literacy practices of Panjabis living in Southall, London which have been studied by Mukul Saxena (1994, 2000). Here more languages are involved and several different scripts. English written in Roman script is the national language. Three Asian languages are in common use: Urdu, which is usually written in Arabic script; Hindi, which is normally written in Devanagari script; and Panjabi, which is normally written in Gurmukhi script. The three languages are associated with Muslims, Hindus and Sikhs, respectively. Which language a person will use depends partly on their religious affinity, but it also depends on when and where they received their schooling, and on other social roles of the languages. So, for example, an older Hindu educated in pre-partition India might have been taught Urdu using the Arabic script. Someone who went to school in the Panjab after partition would probably have learned Panjabi in the Gurmukhi script, whatever their religion. For those Panjabi Sikhs who believe strongly in the Panjabi state, the Panjabi language written in Gurmukhi might well be preferred for its symbolic value.[4]

Many of the people living in Southall would know more than one of these languages and writing systems, and different generations of people within one family would have access to different literacies. The three languages are related, with Hindi and Urdu being virtually the same when spoken. What makes the situation more complex is the fact that all three languages can be and are written in any of the three scripts. People would often speak Panjabi in their day-to-day lives and would write it in Gurmukhi, Devanagari or Arabic according to need. So, for example, a Hindu might write a letter to a relative in the Panjab in Panjabi but in the Devanagari script. As Saxena says (1994, p. 202) this might be 'a matter of mutual convenience for writer and reader or a matter of symbolizing Hindu solidarity'.

Literacy events in Southall would contain all three languages as well as English. In their everyday life a person might encounter signs, newspapers, official and work-related literacy in English; newspapers and calendars in Urdu; magazines and religious books in Hindi; and letters and graffiti in Panjabi. Reading and writing of all four languages might be possible. Often a particular literacy event would draw on a more complex interaction of languages and literacies so that in planning a letter people might discuss the contents in one language and write the letter in another, even switching between languages or scripts within a letter.

It is important to emphasize the distinctiveness of literacy practices associated with each community which is examined. In Britain, for example, there is not one blanket 'Asian community'. Rather, people speak different languages, identify with different cultures and have distinct literacy histories. In another study, Tricia Hartley has studied Panjabi-speaking Muslims from Pakistan who live in a small town in northern England (Hartley, 1994). As in Mukul Saxena's study they are Panjabi speakers, but there is no tradition of writing the language where they come from in the Gujerat/Jhelum area of Pakistan. Reading and writing is in Urdu. Her study focuses on different generations of women and their literacy practices. Many of the older women had limited opportunities for education in Pakistan where they were brought up; they know very little English and are not literate in any language. Those who had received education in Pakistan were literate – including one woman who, having been through secondary schooling in Pakistan, knew five spoken languages and could write using four distinct scripts. Younger girls who have been educated in Britain have been taught English at school and have often learned to read and write Urdu in after-school classes.

As a consequence of differences like these, the children often had important roles within the family of explaining and translating written letters, notes and messages. They could act as links between the community and the dominant English-speaking community. Hartley observed that 'literacy skills were made available to family and community in the same way as skills in dressmaking and building' (p. 34) – they were not solely an individual's possession. She contrasts this with her own mono-lingual English upbringing where individual literacy skills were of para-mount importance. Another observation was that letters to Pakistan were not from one individual to another; rather they were from one family to another. The contents of a letter to be sent would be discussed and the person who did the actual writing acted as a scribe for everyone, not as the individual author of the letter. In these and other ways the distinct distribution of languages and literacies between different members of the community gave rise to particular literacy practices. Children may act as brokers for older members of the family where they have more facility in the languages and literacies of the dominant culture.

In other multilingual situations, different literacies may exist side by side with different functions. They may coexist or they may compete, with the powerful dominating the less powerful. Religious literacies are often associated with particular languages, with much of the work in Martin-Jones and Jones (2000a) reporting on settings where Arabic is used primarily or exclusively for reading aloud from the Q'uran, and other studies where Hindi and Sanskrit are used for reading from the Hindu texts associated with religious observance. In Scribner and Cole's well-known study, described in chapter 2, it is interesting that three literacies with distinct functions – English, Arabic and Vai – exist next to each other in a seemingly stable situation, with people being literate in one, two or three of the languages, or in none. The languages exist with their own scripts, with distinct uses of literacy and different ways of learning.[5] Hornberger's notion of 'continua of biliteracy' (1989, 2003) develops a framework for analysing settings like this, in which develop-ing literacy involves the use of more than one language. Her work draws out the power relationships to be examined in relation to the context of biliteracy, the biliterate individual, the content of biliteracy, and the media of biliteracy, and highlights the importance of such power relationships for language planning, policy making and educational practice.

What can we conclude from these multilingual situations? It is useful here to turn to more general bilingualism research. Bilingualism research has grown up with its own tradition distinct from the literacy research and developing independently. Nevertheless, the two traditions of research have been moving in similar directions, for example in taking account of context. One generally accepted conclusion from the bilingualism research is that within any one language people use different varieties of language appropriate to different situations and that being bilingual is in many ways similar to this. Different languages can be seen as different varieties with their own contexts of use supporting their own practices. Mono-linguals move between different varieties in different situations, bilinguals additionally move between different languages. The idea of there being different literacies with their associated practices fits in well here, and examining multilingual literacy situations can reveal clearly the social patterning of different literacies. And as Martin-Jones and Jones (2000b) point out, in a multilingual setting, language and literacy practices are inevitably bound up with issues of power relationships between linguistic groups. For instance, Blackledge (2000) shows how unequal relations of power between dominant-culture schools and minority-culture families dictated that Bangladeshi mothers of six-year-old children were unable to use their own literacies in the home–school learning context, constructing them as 'illiterate' despite the majority being literate in Bengali. What 'counts' as literacy in this context is socially constructed.

I will return to these language issues in chapter 13, when discussing adult literacy. For the moment I turn to another topic, as a clear example of the social patterning of literacy which permeates all aspects of everyday life, that is, an examination of differences in men's and women's literacy practices.

Literacy is gendered

Literacy is a highly gendered activity: by this I mean that in all the domains covered so far literacy activities pattern differently according to gender. In many ways literacy practices reflect more general gender differences in society, but they are not a simple mapping of them.

Beginning with children's first books, there are different ones for boys and for girls, often they are colour-coded for gender. Children are read to more by female adults than by males, and the teachers they come across in pre-schools and early schooling are more likely to be female. It seems that on average girls have fewer problems learning to read and more girls than boys start school being able to read. Throughout schooling girls score higher on average than boys on tests revolving around reading and writing. More boys than girls are diagnosed as dyslexic. There are some schools just for boys in Britain, and some just for girls. Some of the girls schools take boys up to around eight years of age. The subjects girls choose at school are likely to involve more writing and be more associated with arts. Boys and girls write about different things in schools. Most teachers of English are women, as are most teachers of adult basic education. Throughout childhood, there are books and magazines for boys and ones for girls; only a few are aimed at children generally.

Most people studying literature at universities in Britain are female; most lecturers are male. In adulthood most scribal jobs in Britain are done by women, and women are much more likely than men to have had training in shorthand, word processing and other scribal skills. Much of the fiction adults choose to read differs by gender. Women buy fewer newspapers than men and read different parts of the paper. In the home men and women carry out different literacy chores, with women usually keeping up personal contact through letters and cards.[6] This list could continue.

Historically these patterns have not always been the same, so that in Victorian Britain, for example, men were commonly secretaries; cross-culturally, there are some countries today where men commonly do the scribal activities. The status of a particular job varies in different countries. Internationally, the statistics on literacy levels throughout the world consistently show women to have higher levels of illiteracy than men, and to have less access to education generally. There are some literacies, such as Vai, which are traditionally only available to men and also a few examples of scripts only available to women, such as a secret script used by women in parts of China.

To some extent the above is obvious to everyone in the culture, but it is perhaps surprising the extent of the gendering of literacy in contemporary society; it touches every aspect of reading and writing. The depth of public acceptance of the gendering of literacy is revealed in a collection of images of literacy made by Fie van Dijk in Amsterdam (1994). She collected contemporary postcards and other images of people reading and writing, noticing differences between how men and women are portrayed visually. Looking through over five hundred postcards, there are striking differences in the literacy practices which the men and the women participate in, according to these images, with the men typically in more serious and dominating poses: the men and the women are literally positioned differently. Observing literacy events, even by photographing them, can be very revealing in this respect. The ways in which men's and women's experiences of literacy are different has been explored in many different areas, including studies of girls and school literacy;

and studies of the role of literacy in women's lives and the significance of returning to study as an adult.[7]

Workplace literacy practices

As pointed out earlier, literacy practices vary in different domains of life, such as the home, education and the workplace. This means that there may be different practices and that they may be valued in different ways. Detailed studies of literacy in different contexts have shown reading and writing being done differently in the home, in education and at work. The workplace is a particularly important site for the study of literacy practices. It is where many people spend the majority of their waking hours, and for many people work constitutes an important part of their identities. Literacies in the workplace have drawn increasing attention in recent years.

To give an example of how literacy practices can vary in different domains, consider some differences between the educational sphere and the workplace. The range of reading and writing activities in workplaces is often formulaic, limited and constrained, but at the same time sharing, copying and collaborating are typical in workplace literacies. In contrast to this, in education there is a broader range of activities but copying and collaborating are tightly controlled and monitored. Understanding the ways in which reading and writing differs in different contexts is an essential aspect of literacy learning.

There can be different theories of what literacy is in different domains. One idea which has become particularly powerful in discussing workplace literacies has been the notion that we are moving into a knowledge economy, and that many workers are deficient in the literacy skills needed to cope with the changing demands this places upon them. This has led to calls for more workplace education and training from Government and from large employers' organizations, often with the underlying implication that workers who refuse to 'upskill themselves' are damaging the business or the country's economic competitiveness.

Ethnographies of workplace literacy practices show a more complex picture. Certainly, in some workplaces which have introduced new management practices such as Total Quality Management, flat hierarchies and increased teamworking, the communication and literacy demands placed on workers have changed. The rhetoric of so-called 'fast capitalist' texts – the management literature which promotes such developments – is that these changes will improve workplaces and empower workers. But Gee et al. (1996) show how these changing demands call for new kinds of workers, requiring different sorts of education and preparation. Through case studies of workplaces such as an electronics assembly factory in Silicon Valley, they show gaps between the rhetoric of the management texts and the realities on the ground. Far from fully 'empowering' workers, many of the new literacy practices workers were expected to engage in were experienced as disempowering, such as when already overworked front-line workers were expected to engage with ever-increasing numbers of new texts, particularly when their first language was not English. Many of these new practices reinforced existing hierarchies, rather than challenging them.

This is a common pattern in ethnographies of literacies in the workplace. These demonstrate that 'literacy skills' in the workplace are not decontextualized competencies that individuals have and can put into action anywhere. Rather, literacy in the workplace depends on who people are, their backgrounds, cultures and opportunities, and the contexts in which the literacy practices are taking place. This means that people's identities in the workplace, the ways workplaces are organized, and the incentives or disincentives people perceive for displaying skills all influence the literacies that people engage in.[8] For instance, studies of literacies and technology in tourism and hospitality workplaces showed that the specific features of reading in one site did not necessarily transfer to another, and that the uses of literacy in these contexts depended on workers' knowledge and understandings of the work as a social setting (Searle, 1999, 2002).

What is seen by management as a lack of literacy skills may, from the workers' perspectives, be seen as resistance to unreasonable requirements or disciplinary controls. For example, a study of a company manufacturing workstations in Silicon Valley exploded managers' assumptions about workers' lack of skills; it showed how workers' experiences of incentives and disincentives to invest in the programme, along with opportunities or lack of opportunities to take part, suspicions about managerial intentions, and management responses to their actions all played a part in whether or not they chose to exercise the skills management wanted them to (Darrah, 1997). In a collection of studies of literacies in four workplaces, Belfiore et al. (2004) found that managers and supervisors commonly attribute failure in the workplace to lack of literacy skills, abilities or confidence, and propose training solutions. However, by getting to know workers well and observing their literacy practices outside the workplace, they found that workers who appear unwilling or unable to engage with text in one setting often get along very well with texts they encounter in another.

One detailed ethnography that demonstrates all of these points is Gowen's (1992) *The politics of workplace literacy*, a study of the introduction of a functional literacy programme in a US hospital, which describes how the social tensions and power relationships of the workplace were key factors in tensions and conflicts which affected the effectiveness of the programme.

The social patterning of literacy practices

These different areas in which literacy practices have been studied – in relation to local and vernacular practices, multilingualism, gender, work – in different ways all demonstrate one key point: literacy practices are socially patterned. Despite ideas of universal literacy and free access to education, it is obvious that literacies are not spread equally through society. Secretaries, newspaper publishers and benefit claimants are involved in quite different literacy practices; literacy is valued differently by them, their relation to the power of literacy varies.

To understand the role of literacy in society it is necessary to examine the social patterning of literacy practices, and the way this relates to power in society. This can involve people having access to particular literacy practices restricted in some way. Looking at historical examples or examining other cultures, restrictions have always been apparent. Jack Goody and colleagues identify this issue with the notion of **restricted literacy** which is used to characterize some societies. To explain the restrictions on literacy in society, Goody looks to such factors as religious 'restrictive practices' and mismatches between the language of literacy and vernacular languages. The idea of restricted literacy assumes some opposite of **full literacy**, which, according to Goody, was found only in early Greek literacy (Goody and Watt, 1963).

However, people who talk of restricted literacy do not follow through all its implications. The notion of restricted literacy draws attention to important aspects of literacy but the topic should not be regarded as a peripheral one, something found only in some situations. Rather, literacy is socially patterned and restricted in all societies. All societies control access to the written word in some way, because literacy involves information and idea transmission and is practised in a context where its uses may both maintain and challenge existing social institutions. In looking more closely into the mass literacy of ancient Greece, which Goody took to be the best case of unrestricted literacy, the obvious point can be made that exclusion of women, foreigners and slaves, all classed as noncitizens, constitutes a massive restriction on access to literacy.

Restrictions on literacy can take many forms.[9] First, in all societies literacy has developed only to function in specific contexts. This is clear in a society without a long tradition of literacy where reading and writing may be restricted to religious uses, for example, or external commerce and administration. In the Vai example each literacy has specific uses. This is also true of some of the invented Native American writing systems which have been described (see Walker, 1981 for examples). In a complex western society with many uses of literacy, the uses are constantly changing, with literacies coming and going. However, it would be a mistake to see contemporary western uses of literacy as *the* uses of literacy. There is not some finite checklist of literacies, so that at some point a society has complete literacy. Literacies come and go in society and exist in response to specific social practices; old literacies die out and new ones are created.

Within a society there can be a range of restrictions, including overt political restrictions. Some societies place deliberate restrictions on the access to literacy skills and the written word, creating an elite group of scribes, readers, interpreters or intellectuals. These restrictions can be enforced via secrecy and penalties.[10] An example of explicit control of the access to literacy is documented by Clammer in his study of the coming of literacy to Fiji, where missionaries introducing religious literacy controlled access to different literacies (Clammer, 1976).

There are many explicit controls today. Literacy campaigns have been opposed by governments; literacy workers have been harassed and killed in various parts of the world including Southern Africa and Central America. The legal framework of literacy, with laws affecting copyright, photocopying and royalties restrict in other ways. The power exercised by governments is imposed on schools by laws and financial control. Newspapers and communications technologies are similarly controlled, as are photocopying and copyright. Most restrictions, however, are less explicit. In any society the distribution of literacy skills is still patterned by the social structure, even if no-one is specifically excluded from reading and writing. Restrictions can take the form of access to education and jobs, or to particular literacy practices. Restriction of writing can be more significant than restriction of reading, because of its creative aspects, giving the possibility of expressing ideas and points of view that may challenge existing social institutions. In literacy programmes for children and adults it is worth noting the extent to which they focus on writing rather than reading, and what sort of writing, whether for instance they aim to provide people only with a narrow literacy related to work.

The control and manipulation of literacy is pervasive and depressing in terms of what it means for people's rights and development, and their sense of personal power. The ray of hope in all this is that despite attempts at restrictions, literacy has a life of its own. People taught to read a religious tract are also able to read an opposing view; given a glimpse of the possibilities, people will teach themselves and extend their reading and writing. There have been self-taught readers and writers throughout history. The printing press has ensured that burned books are hard to eradicate and, as the quote from the novel *Utz* in an earlier chapter suggests, maybe people can become immune to a totalitarian educational system.

A final form of restriction on access to literacy is probably one of the commonest, that is, restriction resulting from language choice. Literacy is always in a language and the introduction of literacy, and particularly mass literacy, is generally accompanied by the standardization of language and the establishment of official languages or dialects. This can be more or less consciously planned. Such a process frequently involves marginalization, even elimination, of vernacular languages and dialects, along with the cultures which they support. Restriction by language is not confined only to developing countries establishing language policies. In contemporary Canada the national testing of functional literacy which only accepted English or French literacy and did not count literacy in any other languages has been mentioned already.

Examining restrictions on literacy is a first step in understanding the social patterning of literacy. Many questions can be posed: who reads and writes, and what literacies and literacy practices do they participate in, what are imposed literacies, which are taught, which are accessible through education? What are the social institutions which support and sustain particular literacies? There are then social restrictions on people's reading and writing. There is room for detailed studies of how particular institutions such as schooling or the contemporary workplace sustain particular literacies, and the way in which they do this through the legal framework and other pressures. In the next chapter, we will be looking at questions about texts: who would write a particular text, who it is aimed at, how it constructs the reader. All of these are questions about the social patterning of literacy.

5 Literacy embedded in language

Literacy and language
  From registers to genres and discourses
  Texts and intertextuality
Taking meaning from texts
Language mediates

Literacy and language

In the next three chapters I examine the relationship of literacy and language from various perspectives. In this chapter I explore how literacy is embedded in language. I first discuss general ideas about language, making points about how language is used in different ways and how it is always part of a discourse, and how discourses result in texts. Examples of texts are discussed, underlining that texts are bound to each other through intertextuality; that people are positioned by them; and that the study of literacy, as of all language, is the study of practices and the study of texts. The next section discusses an aspect of what is meant by reading: reading is best seen as taking meaning from texts. Finally the point is made that there are several senses in which literacy mediates human activities. Chapter 6 deals with the many ways people have characterized the differences between written and spoken language and it is followed in chapter 7 by a discussion of different writing systems and other forms of notation.

Anything which is said about literacy presupposes a view of language in general; it rests upon a theory of language. It is important to examine these views of language and to sort out the relationship between views of language and views of literacy. The approach here rests upon a constructivist view of language, as mentioned earlier when discussing metaphors and thought, which sees language as playing a central role in the mental models people construct of the world. There are further senses of **constructive**. Language has been constructed historically, it is also constructed when the child learns it, and it is constructed whenever someone uses it. This view of language is becoming an increasingly dominant view. In general the study of language has undergone a revolution in recent years, with the dominant views moving away from investigating a system which is described solely in terms of its structure towards viewing language as a dynamic social activity which serves people's purposes. Here I want to provide a brief introduction to aspects of language which are necessary for understanding the ecology of literacy. The key ideas are that there are different forms of language, which can be referred to as discourses; that these result in written texts; and that these texts mediate people's experiences.

From registers to genres and discourses

To start from spoken language, people have a range of ways of talking and they use appropriate ways of talking in any situation. This is actually one of the meanings of the word 'language', when people refer to the language of advertising, or the language of the law. Identifiable different ways of talking in different situations are often called **registers**. People choose an appropriate register for talking to a baby, a bank manager and a beloved, each very different ways of talking. The idea of there being different registers has grown up from the study of spoken language but it is also applicable to writing: when writing a business letter or an email message to a friend, people choose an appropriate register.

Those studying written language rather than spoken, especially literary language, have more commonly identified different forms of writing as different **genres**. A novel, a poem and an academic article are all different genres: they are each identifiable forms of written language, so that if you see just a couple of sentences from one of these, you would probably know what it was. Many language specialists have found the concept of genre very useful, although there are various disagreements about the way both terms, register and genre, have been used. These words have also become emblems of particular theories. The important point for studying literacy is that in both written and spoken language the idea of there being different forms of language is central.

One issue which arises in discussing registers or genres, and which I have already mentioned, is that of how widely or narrowly to apply the terms. Working at a very broad level, linguists have talked of informal and formal registers, or even the spoken register and the written register, with the idea that moving from spoken to written involves a change of register. There are various identifiable registers which have been described in detail such as **teacher talk**, the language of classrooms, **baby talk**, used to address babies, or **foreigner talk**, when addressing speakers of other languages. A possible problem with this approach is that one can make finer and finer distinctions, for instance identifying distinct ways of talking used by teachers in staff rooms, secondary school teachers, science teachers, teachers at parents meetings, and so on. Are each of these separate registers? Similarly with written texts, one can talk broadly of novels and poetry being different genres, or one can get narrower and narrower, so that Mills & Boon romances are a genre, as are Thomas the Tank Engine stories. As another example, scientific writing can be divided up into biology, physics, chemistry and so on; alternatively, people can examine differences between scientific and popular physics writing, or even between physics articles and student essays.

Genres are socially constructed conventions of writing; they are the accepted conventions for doing things, connected with writers' purposes. For teaching it is useful to be able to identify and describe the conventions of particular genres. However, it is very easy to become prescriptive and normative about such conventions, listing the properties of different genres; this is something which was an issue in the 'genre debate' which began in Australia. Influenced by the work of Michael Halliday and others, a genre approach to the teaching of writing became the centre of a heated argument about how to teach writing in schools.[1] Whatever they are called, there are identifiable forms of writing associated with specific domains of social life. Part of the aim of the study of literacy is to identify the patterning of written forms of language.

A broader concept which is essential when discussing different uses of language is that of **discourse**. Registers and genres contribute to broader ways of using language which are referred to as discourses. The language of advertising or the language of law, mentioned above, differ from each other not just in terms of different grammatical structures: they are different ways of using language. Obviously new specialized vocabulary is one thing which has to be learned in a new discourse, but it is surprising the extent to which new discourses are reorganizations of existing components of language: things you can do already put together in a different way. Discourses differ in *how* the language is used. This is much of what advanced literacy learning is, or learning new subjects in school or college. Frequently the root of what we cannot understand lies in the way the language is put together, rather than in particularly complicated vocabulary. This is true where new discourses are being created, and much of learning is learning to participate in new discourses.

Discourse is an important concept here as it can be used to emphasize that language is only one part of any social interaction, so that talking to a baby or a bank manager involves not just appropriate language but also appropriate behaviour in appropriate settings. This broader view of situating language in a social context and of including 'ways of being', to use James Gee's phrase (1996, p. 127), as well as ways of speaking and ways of writing, is to see language as discourse. The idea of discourse still suffers from the two problems mentioned above in relation to registers and genres: of having very general senses and much narrower ones; and implying certain theories. The term discourse is used by different people in different ways and is sometimes used interchangeably with the terms covered already. What I want to take from this approach as being useful for the study of literacy is the idea that what must be covered is broader than just discussing the linguistic form of particular registers or genres, and that particular ways of using language are ways of structuring knowledge and relationships.

The point is that when using language, people are drawing on the resources of a particular language, such as English, but they are always doing this within a particular socially constructed discourse. There are various discourses and they only exist if they are recognized by people as identifiably distinct, as for example with academic discourse, a particular way of using language which is generally recognized. Academic discourse exists because it is recognized by the people who use it – and often by people who do not use it – as distinct. Rather than saying 'people who use it' it is probably more accurate to say 'people who are part of a discourse community'.

A **discourse community** is a group of people who have texts and practices in common, whether it is a group of academics, or the readers of teenage magazines. In fact, discourse community can refer to several overlapping groups of people: it can refer to the people a text is aimed at;

it can be the people who read a text; or it can refer to the people who participate in a set of discourse practices both by reading and by writing. People's preferences in how they wish to define it are dictated partly by their purposes. Someone examining teenage girls' magazines, for instance, might focus on the readers the text is aimed at. Teachers of academic writing in colleges might be more interested in how learning to write makes one part of an academic discourse community. More generally, discourse communities are defined by having a set of common interests, values and purposes. Centrally, members have agreed common knowledge – what you can take for granted. Members of a discourse community by definition have a common discourse, in the narrow sense of common ways of using language, and in the broader sense of common ways of acting in relation to knowledge. Discourse communities also have ways of inducting new members (see Swales, 1990 for more on this). The term is important in that it makes it clear that much written language is for relatively small groups of people. The phrase is also useful to us in that it emphasizes the ways language, including written language, can bind groups together.[2]

Texts and intertextuality

Whatever terms people use, the idea which is important for the discussion here is that there are different forms of language, not one homogeneous whole. These forms of language result in texts, and in a wide variety of texts. Some genres are more precise and well defined than others, and genres may be more obvious in written language, which is often more standardized and codified than spoken language anyway. Nevertheless, once anything is written it becomes a text which can be referred to, and this inevitably includes spoken language, since speech can be written down in some way. We can comment on and analyse texts, whether the texts are written business letters, poems, forms, or written transcripts of spoken conversations. Once they are written, texts can be inspected, dissected and analysed in various ways. Analysing a text, any piece of language, is done by sociologists, psychologists, linguists and others, and is variously called **discourse analysis**, **text analysis**, **conversational analysis**, according to the analyst's purposes and theoretical persuasion. The point I want to make in this section is that understanding literacy involves studying both texts and the practices surrounding the texts.

So far I have only given fleeting examples of different texts. There is a danger in giving any examples: since different texts are so different from each other, one can mistakenly assume that one's pet example is representative of all texts, whether it is the novel or the academic essay – two forms which have been widely studied – or anything else. There are so many different forms of text: diaries, love letters, notes to oneself, poems to a friend in hospital, web pages, text messages, newspaper articles, advertisements, graffiti, bank statements, company reports, prayers – to name but a few. The wide range of texts is obvious to anyone who looks around in contemporary society. It is fair to say that we live in a textually mediated world (Smith, 1990; Barton, 2001). This book itself is a text. Within it, the examples such as the quotation on illiteracy as a germ at the beginning of chapter 2 can be treated as a text, as can the examples of children's language and other quotations which come later.

There is not space to analyse the texts in detail here.[3] However, it is still useful to give further examples of texts here to illustrate points about literacy. I have chosen examples from one domain, that of everyday local life; had I chosen another domain such as academic work life, the examples would be very different. Here is a text:

> Notice is hereby given under Section 70(3)(a) of the Local Government (Miscellaneous Provisions) Act, 1976 that the City Council of Lancaster has determined to vary the fees chargeable for certain Hackney Carriage and Private Hire Vehicles and Operators' Licences as shown in the schedule hereto (such proposed fees being in excess of the amount chargeable without notification under Section 70(2) of the above Act).
>
> Any objection to this proposed variation must be made in writing by the 5th February, 1993 to the Chief Solicitor at the address given below . . .

This is part of an advertisement in the *Lancaster Guardian*, a local weekly newspaper. It appeared early in 1993 on the same page as advertisements for trips to an Eric Clapton concert, for jumble sales and discos, details of a forthcoming meeting to 'maintain the ancient orders of bishops and priests in the Church of England' and small ads, one proclaiming:

> SLIM HANDSOME silver haired solicitor, owns Silver Shadow Rolls, two prawns short of a cocktail but sincere, seeks lady, lasting relationship. Box No. 3269 . . .

and another:

1079 my heart has never been far from you, please lets try to get ours
right this time. Box No. 3251 . . .

On the opposite page of the newspaper an article on dieting, surrounded
by advertisements for local health clubs, includes the following:

> . . . have we got news for you! This year, couch potatoes are OUT!
> . . . With all the leisure facilities in the district, there's really no excuse for
> lounging about in the armchair or propping up the bar every single night
> of the week. Now is the perfect time to get stuck into a healthy exercise
> and diet regime – taking care of your body . . . Avoid crash diets like the
> plague. They may be all right for extremely fit people like athletes who
> may have to shift a couple of pounds quickly. But your metabolism can-
> not handle crash dieting . . .

These examples of texts have all been taken from one British local newspaper. These are some of the texts of contemporary life: the official notices,
the advertisements, the advertising copy purporting to be informational
prose. The first point to make about them is the wide range of genres
which are present even within one or two pages of a local newspaper.
The official notice and the article on dieting, for example, use language
in quite different ways and to achieve quite different purposes. Legal
notices, advertising copy and small ads are different genres, each clearly
identifiable. In terms of literacy practices there is a whole set of questions
one can ask of any text, to do with how it is produced and how it is used.

Let us look first at the question of the production of texts. Presumably
many people were involved in producing the official notice, it did not
have just one author. Texts vary in the extent to which they are authored.
The official notice is signed, in fact in capital letters, by the Chief Solici-
tor of the city. It is unlikely that he actually wrote it in the sense of
authoring the text and he may never have seen it. The text probably
went through a hierarchy of scribes; it then continued on its way through
advertisers, subeditors and printers until it reached the newspaper page.
(The idea of a signature is interesting. It is a special form of writing; no
one else can do it for you; it cannot be typed and it is consciously learned.)
Many people with different roles are involved in producing the texts of
contemporary life and it is possible to trace the life of texts at they are
moved from one context to another.

The official notice appears in the paper presumably as a legal require-
ment before taxi licence fees can be increased; given the language in

which it is couched, it is unlikely that it appears in the paper so that taxi drivers can be given a chance to discuss in depth the proposed fee increases. If it had been intended to inform it could have been written in plain English. The article on dieting which has a quite different style has no author mentioned and may well be a piece of syndicated writing used in many local papers. It has a function to persuade and to support the advertisements on dieting which it is surrounded by. The two small ads, assuming they are genuine, were presumably written by individual people.

A useful concept when thinking about texts is that in any text the reader is **constructed**. There is only a range of possible options which the reader can take up; a newspaper article or a love letter assumes certain knowledge, values and beliefs in the reader. There are limited **subject positions** for a reader. This is clearly illustrated in the article on dieting where the reader is positioned as being an unhealthy, overweight adult. The reader is also assumed to drink regularly and, elsewhere in the article, to eat meat, to have eaten too much over the holidays, to be in employment, and to have little will-power. The positioning here is explicit, with the reader even referred to as 'you'. Often it is more implicit and texts vary in the extent which they position you or attempt to position you. The small ads and the legal notice position people in different ways; one of the small ads is aimed at a specific reader, and other readers are onlookers. All these texts can function to include – and to exclude – people. Being positioned by texts is clearly bound up with how one sees oneself, one's identity; in these examples it is possible to identify the various ways in which texts constrain the potential ways of being at one's disposal.

There are some uses of language which make more assumptions about the reader and demand more. Forms which people have to fill in are an interesting example since they combine both reading and writing: reading someone else's categories and then, by filling in the form, committing yourself to the categories. The form defines the range of possibilities and the person filling it in then has to choose from within them. The advertisement for the Eric Clapton concert in the newspaper has a simple form with it. A more revealing example of forms, in terms of learning about literacy, would be the ones which unemployed people are confronted with when claiming benefit and looking for work. On one such form, known as the 'Helping You Back to Work' form, people are presented with this seemingly innocent question 'Can you start work as soon as you find a job?'. There are then two boxes, marked YES and NO, one of which has to be ticked. Unlike the official notice on taxi licences, this form has been 'plain Englished'; nevertheless, it may still present difficulties. While all the words are common and well-known ones, and the sentence structure is straightforward, this question gives many claimants problems. The claimants have to know the intentions behind the words. Experienced claimants know that they have to answer 'yes' to questions like this, that benefits are dependent on people being available for work immediately; experienced claimants also know they should avoid suggesting any restrictions in terms of how far they are willing to travel to work, what hours they are available, and how much they are willing to work for.[4] In coping with the discourse of forms, problems are often not to do with the complexity of vocabulary or layout of the form. Rather, what is more salient is familiarity with and acceptance of the institutional framework in which the questions are located. Often form filling involves constructing a new view of oneself, one which fits into the categories provided by the authorities behind the form. Job application forms are a good example of this. It is a joint construction, although not necessarily a co-operative one.

Once again, I am keeping to a narrow sense of literacy as print literacy, and so to a narrow sense of text as writing. I have not brought into the discussion the importance of layout and other aspects of the texts. The legal notice was set out in a particular way. The small ads were displayed in the narrow columns and small font typical of their genre. The paper they were all printed on was that typical of a broadsheet newspaper, thin newsprint paper of a certain size. Note that reproduced here in a book they are no longer the texts they were. They have become different texts: they are now examples in a book on literacy. They are in a different context, and their meaning has changed. You, the current reader, have no opportunity to object to the increased taxi licence fees, nor to answer the small ads.

In several senses, texts can become fixed points. It is in texts that assumptions are displayed, what you can take for granted becomes important. This is done in many ways: in choice of words, in specialized vocabulary, in the background knowledge which is assumed, as well as in particular forms of writing. An important aspect of the assumed knowledge is that texts refer not only to the external world and to common knowledge, but they refer to other texts, both implicitly and explicitly, and this is known as **intertextuality**. Intertextuality is the way texts refer to other texts. This can be very explicit, in precisely quoting from a text which is clearly identified, for example in the way in which someone writing an academic paper refers to earlier work. Alternatively, it can be by the use of other's phrases or more oblique reference, right across to using stock terms and phrases appropriate to the discourse. I am using the term loosely here to point out how texts depend on other earlier texts.[5] I believe the idea has some relevance in explaining the chunks of language in which we speak, comprehend and think. The formulae of political rhetoric or oral story-telling are intertextual, as are the unanalysed chunks which children build their language upon. Such an approach is also a useful antidote to the idea that people select individual words from some dictionary or lexicon in their brain whenever they speak or write. The important point here is that texts are made up of other texts.

In the examples above, it is quite probable that the person who first wrote out the official notice about taxi licences drew upon previous official notices to help them. Such legal notices may have a long history; and the schedule of fees in the notice includes details of the fees for horse-drawn carriages, a form of transport not seen in Lancaster for many years. I imagine the layout of the notice is similar to the layout of legal proclamations from the Middle Ages. Similarly the other examples, including the forms, small ads and advertising copy, are all drawing on previous examples of the particular discourses, either implicitly or explicitly.

Some texts become fixed points and have a degree of permanence in people's lives. People can structure their identity around a text, whether it is a religious book, a prayer or saying hung on the wall, or a constantly reread academic article or love letter. It is the fixedness of texts which allows them to be analysed and dissected. They can become reference points for individuals and for societies. Other texts are more transient, such as the junk mail of a household, or online chat, or daily newspapers which are thrown away: here particular texts may have little significance, but the overall effect is a consistent one positioning people and structuring their identity.

The examples from the newspaper are all concerned with communication with others. There are many other sorts of texts which are more for the self. These include **drafts**: and as well as drafts of student essays and academic articles, people make drafts of personal letters, difficult telephone calls and job application forms. Another type of transient text are **scratch notes**: these are telephone messages written down quickly, notes from books or lecture-notes which are later written up. They have in common the facts that they are written for the self; that they are in note form, often with idiosyncratic abbreviations, spelling and grammar;

and that they only make sense to the writer for a limited period of time. Drafts and the scratch notes of work and home domains can have a very short life span.

Textual analysis of all sorts can lull people into believing that texts themselves do things, and to forget the people behind the texts. It is useful to think of the ways in which texts act in place of people but it is a mistake to think that texts in and of themselves do things.[6] For instance, it is not so much the texts themselves which structure subjectivity, but how they are used. Practices structure subjectivity. In thinking about the people behind the texts there are the people who constructed the texts, and there are the people using them. Texts can become disassociated from the people who produced them. Often their origins are lost and texts take on a life of their own. The people behind them may be hidden, whether it is graffiti, a government form, a mathematical proof, a short story, a textbook, or a newspaper blowing in the wind. Nevertheless, every text has a history. Similarly a practice account needs to know details of how texts are used in life. Texts do not just exist, but they are used. To understand literacy more fully we have to know more about how texts, whether they are novels, timetables, or newspaper advertisements, are actually used. What do people do with newspapers, advertisements, textbooks, instruction manuals? What does it mean to be lost in a book? There have been studies of how people use texts.[7] It is important to see what actually happens with different texts as the intentions of the producers are unlikely to be an accurate guide to how texts are really used. The text, then, is one part of what a literacy is made up of, but it is only one part: there is more than the structure of the text, there are the practices. Texts cannot be isolated from practices and understanding literacy involves analysing practices as well as analysing texts.

Taking meaning from texts

The discussion of texts has already suggested a great deal about what is meant by reading. There have been developments in the way both reading and writing are characterized. The standard view of reading has been as a psychological process; there are whole textbooks on this which act as if that is all that there is to reading, and it is this view which we are stepping beyond. The standard psychological view of reading may be thought appropriate if one were interested in designing a computer to analyse language; one might treat language as a set of words with a meaning (a lexicon), which can be assembled in any way subject to a set of rules (a grammar). However, if one is interested in what people do with language, it is probably more useful to see meaning as the uses which a word or phrase has had up till now – and every use of a word corroborates or changes its meaning.

What is an appropriate view of reading? From what has been said so far about the constructivist nature of language, and about topics such as intertextuality and mediation, it should be clear that taking meaning from a text is not a straightforward matter of simply knowing the meanings of words and combining them in grammatical categories. A constructivist view of reading and writing is that, like all acts of con- structing meaning, people are active, not passive; they engage with texts and they carry out operations such as selection, organisation, and con- necting to make meanings (see Spivey, 1990). This is still a psychological view of reading but it is a more complex one, one which should be more compatible with social views of reading.

Reading involves knowing, bringing knowledge to a text. It is not simply applying a skill. The process of reading involves interacting with the text, not taking *the* meaning from the text. What we can say about reading is tied up with what is meant by understanding. Understanding is partly the intertextual links the reader makes. In addition comprehen- sion is active: we can read if odd words are missing, or not known. In fact the learning of new words is dependent on the redundancy of written language. This is a significant way of learning the meaning of new words for both children and adults.

There are very different ways of reading. Standard ones are those such as skimming and scanning. But there is much more to it than this, there are very different ways of taking meaning from a text. Different social practices will involve different forms of reading. Reading a horoscope is different from reading the instructions for using a new video recorder, or reading a threat. There are very different speech acts represented in language, such that the actual words themselves will be comprehended in a different way. One needs to know the speech act, whether for exam- ple something is a threat, a promise or an instruction, before one can understand it. (Although they are called speech acts, they are also present in written language.) Different texts are read in different ways. The same text, such as a verse from a religious text, can also be read in very different ways. It can be taken factually, as an instruction, as something to provoke meditation and thought. Often texts are reread to take further meanings. There is the possibility of oppositional readings. This is very different from reading to relax, to pass the time, or when someone is lost in a book.

The idea of reading as being concerned primarily with meaning is itself socially constructed; taking meaning is the particular interest of contemporary educators. But learning by memory or chanting or singing a text may not involve taking meaning from the text. I have already said that discourse communities are bound together by their use of language. The important point for literacy studies is that different discourse communities use texts in very different ways. These give rise to very different meanings of 'to read'. The meaning of 'to read' is also changing, as reading screens is now entwined with reading books and the relationship to other forms of meaning-making, such as images, is changing.

Different ways of reading will be apparent in the examples of the previous section. A detailed example of interaction with the text will be presented in the chapter which discusses reading to children. For the moment, I will turn to the idea of mediation to examine what it can contribute to what is meant by reading.

Language mediates

Language mediates our experience, and written texts can do this in a powerful way. In its most basic sense **mediate** means to bring two things closer and this is done by means of a medium. The idea of language as a medium has many senses. I will go through three different senses of mediation, each one building upon the others. The first idea is that language mediates our experiences. All experience is mediated, in that we construct a view of reality. One of the most important mediators of experience is language itself. The view of language which we construct internally is influenced by the language we have available. The words we use to name an experience provide a way of coding it, organizing it, remembering it. Language mediates thought and it contains the metaphors we live by, to use Lakoff and Johnson's phrase (1980, chapter 2).

Following on from this is the most common sense of language as a medium in that it is a medium of communication. Facts, ideas, hopes and threats are communicated to other people through language. Language is used for communication; it is also central to the way we structure and organize our knowledge. Language mediates what goes on inside our heads and what goes on outside, and it is in this way that the study of language has the possibility of uniting the psychological and the sociological.

In real-life situations where language is used, there is a further way in which mediation is important. Another person making sense of, describing, interpreting an event or an experience is mediating that experience for us. Story-tellers, priests, actors, politicians all mediate our experience when they tell us something, offering a structure, a way of making sense of reality; each is offering particular possibilities for taking meaning from an event. This is also true of others who may not be setting out to tell us a story or give us a message: doctors, police inspectors and school teachers all mediate our experience. An important example for the way in which we learn about the world is when the adult mediates the child's experience by describing, interpreting and making sense of it. There are particular roles where people make sense of the world for others.

If we turn to the written word, then it follows that what is written in novels, textbooks and newspapers also mediates our experience in a powerful way. In a story the text influences and structures how we experience reality, and it has the possibility of controlling what we know and how we feel; a story can affect whether we feel sad, or happy, angry or expectant. This can be even more true of other media such as film and television. Invoking other senses with sound, graphics and colour, the mediation is much greater. A film can control how long we see something and from what angle, and it can influence with what disposition we make sense of the experience, for instance by using background music and colour saturation to frame a woodland scene as 'threatening' in a horror film or 'idyllic' in a romance.

With writing and other media it is important not to lose sight of the active nature of mediation. It is not so much language which mediates as people using language who mediate. People actively mediate by the language they use, and with other symbolic systems. If we engage with a book or a film, we are letting the story-teller or film maker mediate our experience. This can get quite complex in life: for example, in schools textbooks are mediators of experience, but they are not usually just read from end to end, rather, teachers mediate the textbooks.

The active nature of mediation exists also for the listener, the reader or the viewer. This also provides more insight into what reading means. Reading is a form of mediation. If attending, the reader can take the reading offered by the text, or rather the writer of the text; alternatively the reader can do many other things, according to their purposes. As human beings we can have many possible reactions or reading to a proffered text. First, if we are reading a book, whether it is a complicated novel such as James Joyce's *Ulysses* or a complicated academic book such as Noam Chomsky's *Syntactic structures*, we can search for the author's intended meaning. We can read it in order to agree with the author. However, the reader is always bringing their own meanings and these will also mediate their understanding of the text. There is not in fact a meaning *in the text*, only the meanings which a reader *takes from the text*.

In addition, very commonly the reader has their own purposes and is looking for something specific in the text. This may bear some relation to what the author intended to offer on the nature of Ireland or the nature of language. The writer has offered preferred readings or natural readings, a range of possibilities. This relates to the idea of the reader being constructed or positioned, which was mentioned above. However, there is also the possibility of the reader doing something quite different. The reader has the power to ignore the offered readings of the text and to make some oppositional reading. One could search *Ulysses* or *Syntactic structures* for evidence of sexism in the text, for instance. There are all sorts of critical readings which either text could be subjected to. Nevertheless, in whatever way we read it, the written word is mediating our experience.

To summarize, I have used mediate in three related senses. First, from a constructivist view of the world, all our experience is mediated, nothing is direct, and language is a central form of mediation. Second, by the way they structure reality for us in social interactions, people can mediate our experience; and thirdly, texts, whether they are books, films or advertisements, mediate our experience.

6 Configurations of language

Written and spoken language are different
Continua from written to spoken
Configurations of language
Decontextualized and explicit?

A central question in understanding literacy is the relationship between written and spoken language. In chapter 3 we began to see ways in which written and spoken language are intertwined. When examining the origin of written language or children's development of literacy, the importance of the spoken language will become obvious. As an example of this to be pursued in a later chapter, in the telling of bedtime stories the written story is located in spoken interaction, and one of the important aspects for learning to read is the spoken language around a written text. While there are other influences on writing and it is situated in general communicative activity, it is important not to lose sight of the roots of the written word in the spoken.

The question of the relation between written and spoken language has received a great deal of attention from linguists since the 1980s. From examining what was written in that decade there is a very clear sense of progression in people's ideas about the topic. In order to understand current views I want to document these changing ideas. This chapter then will take the form of a history of ideas about written and spoken language, showing how later ideas are built upon earlier ones and that there is now greater attention to the diversity of literacies and to the embedding of language in its context.

To give the briefest summary of developments up to 1980, there have been several shifts in emphasis. The academics of two centuries ago studied the past and dealt with written text to do this. Literary academic life was largely the study of the written word. Linguists at the beginning of this century were doing something distinctly different. They were structuralists who described languages, documenting and analysing as many languages of the world as possible. They concentrated mainly on the sounds of the language and the grammar. Written language was ignored as an unimportant derivative of spoken language, to the extent that in 1933 the influential American linguist Leonard Bloomfield could deny that writing was language. It was 'merely' a way of recording language. Real language was spoken, and linguists were encouraged in their training to ignore the written form (see Stubbs, 1980, p. 24).

This was the dominant approach to studying language until the revolution in linguistics in the 1960s associated with the work of Noam Chomsky. Part of this new view was to treat language as being more abstract and independent of modality. In this period there was little talk of differences between written and spoken language: one talked of language in general. In reality nearly all the work on processing, on how we understand and produce language, was concerned with the processing of spoken language. What happened between the ear and the mouth was what concerned the **psycholinguists**. This period is important as during it many of the current psychological approaches to language were begun. At the same time as studying spoken processes, the grammatical products which were studied, analysed and evaluated were, in retrospect, the products of writing. Questions about sentences being grammatical and well-formed were questions about written language.

Encouraged by Chomsky's critique of earlier behaviourist psychology, the psychological study of language had a decade's start over investigation of social aspects. It was the sociolinguistic critique of Chomsky's linguistics which drew attention to differences between written and spoken language. Sociolinguists made tape recordings of 'real data' and used these to question the judgements of linguists which were based solely on intuition. Sociolinguists talked of utterances and acceptability instead of sentences and grammaticality. Data was 'attested' rather than based on intuitions, that is, actual examples of real language use were collected. To me this was a confrontation between data from two different sources, written language and spoken language, and it led to people examining these differences between written and spoken. It is instructive that one of the first general books in this new field of literacy was entitled *Language and literacy: the sociolinguistics of reading and writing* (Stubbs, 1980). The title signals that the starting point for much discussion of written and spoken language was sociolinguistics (although the field of sociolinguistics is still concerned primarily with studying language variation in spoken language).

From the point at which attention was focused on written and spoken language, I would identify three phases which this research went through in less than a decade. First, there was a phase of accepting that the two forms of language are different and attempting to identify the differences. The second phase was more cautious in identifying the differences and began to examine overlaps and to talk in terms of a continuum or continua from written to spoken. The third phase accepted there are not just two forms of language; rather there are many complex configurations of language involving both writing and speech. I will deal in turn with each of these three phases of thinking about written and spoken language, as each has added to our understanding of literacy.

Written and spoken language are different

The first phase of examining written and spoken language started from differences in **modality**, meaning here the medium in which they are produced, and then examined differences in structure between written and spoken language. The differences in modality are striking. Spoken language exists in an aural medium in real time, it is continuous and is accompanied by hesitations, errors, pauses, false starts and redundancy; there are paralinguistic features like voice quality, and kinetic features like gesture and body language. It decays or disappears immediately and so must be understood or remembered in real time. The hearer is present, giving a shared context between speaker and hearer which can be referred to implicitly, with words like 'that', 'here', 'now'; the context provides the possibility of interruption, feedback, monitoring.

Written language is characterized as the opposite of spoken language in terms of all these features. It exists visually and is more permanent than spoken language. Being visual, a linguistic analysis into sentences, words and segments is provided in the text. Many sweeping generalizations about written language are made. There is no speaker present; hesitations and errors have been removed and there is no shared context nor the possibility of feedback or interruption. Written language is 'out there', prepared, formal and decontextualized.

In many ways spoken language has the advantage over written language. Stubbs (1980) lists the superiority of speech in many areas. It came first in history, long before writing; it is first in individuals' learning. It is acquired naturally, has a biological basis, exists in all cultures of the world and has more functions than written language. However, contrasted with this long list of the advantages of spoken language, written language has a 'social priority' in that it carries greater social status in many societies and often carries legal weight.

Given these differences between spoken and written language, people then examined structural differences between the two. They did this either by comparing some spoken text such as the transcript of a conversation with a written text such as an academic article, or they set up experiments where subjects had to respond to a situation either with a spoken account or with a written account. The actual texts could then be compared. Structural differences at all levels of language were found. At the broadest level spoken texts were organized in a different way from written texts. Written texts were more likely to have deliberate organization with an overall 'thesis', paragraphs and other forms of discourse structure. Written language had clear and complete sentences. Within sentences the grammatical structure was likely to be more complex, with complex noun phrases and subordinate structures, so that the information in written language is packed in densely with many words like 'which' and 'that'. Spoken language had a simpler grammar with sentences co-ordinated – linked together with words like 'and' and 'then'. The vertical, layered syntax of writing contrasts with the horizontal, linked syntax of speech.

It is fruitful to view written and spoken language as having different grammars. The basic unit of written language was undoubtedly the sentence, clearly marked with capital letter and full stop, while the unit of spoken language was more murky, either the vague **utterance** or **idea-unit** or some artificial variant of the clause such as the **T-unit**. Within a written sentence certain grammatical structures were preferred. There would be more passives, subjunctives, relative clauses and nominalizations in written language. Writing would also have more definite articles, participles, attributive adjectives and auxiliaries.[1] Overall a written text was likely to be shorter with longer words and a wider variety of words.

Spoken language meanwhile had more imperatives, questions and exclamations, more active verbs and more deictic terms (those words like 'here', 'now' and 'that'). Written language was more dense, more deliberately organized and contained more new information. It is important to emphasize that spoken language still has its own structure; some grammarians have mistakenly viewed spoken language as failed language with deleted parts of speech and badly formed sentences.

The list of differences between written and spoken is long and impressive. What is surprising in retrospect, given that the seeming extremes of conversation and literary text were compared, is how slight the structural differences are. For each of the two forms of language there is more of this structure or less of that one, but overall there are no clear differences. There is no structure found only in written language or only in spoken. For every difference between the two, one is forced to say 'typically': in writing there is typically more of this structure than of that structure. Nothing is absolute. There is a great deal of overlap between these two extremes and it appears that writing has developed no syntactic structures which are not also found in spoken language.

A similar conclusion, that there are not great differences, comes from examining differences in the processing of written and spoken language. There are many studies of the differences between how people understand, remember and recall items which are written and ones which are spoken (such as some of the studies in Olson et al., 1985). What strikes me in these studies is how small and relatively insignificant are the differences between how people understand written messages and how they understand spoken messages. To some extent it may be that we construct a meaning, which we keep hold of, and we throw away the medium. Once more, there is no great divide.

Continua from written to spoken

A second stage in understanding differences between written and spoken language came with the acceptance that casual conversation and literary texts were two extremes and that maybe letters to friends and lectures to classes came somewhere in between. The idea was that any example of language lay on a continuum from written to spoken language. A continuum has the idea of a straight line drawn between two points.

When people tried to place letters to friends and lectures to classes on a continuum it very quickly became clear that there was not one continuum but, rather, there were several continua or dimensions from speech to writing, each dimension being different. All sorts of dimensions were proposed, some referring to the way in which the language was produced, some referring to structural features of the text or to other aspects. One dimension was formal–informal; written language is more formal than spoken language, both in its production and in terms of the resultant text. Connected to this was the dimension of planned–unplanned; written language had considerable planning behind it so that the text was more organized and had the false starts and hesitations removed, while spoken language was in some sense unplanned. The idea of spoken language being unplanned was confusing to psycholinguists who had studied the planning involved in speech, taking much of their evidence from the false starts, hesitations and pauses of speaking. With just two dimensions one can see how they are linked – formal language tends to be more planned – but at the same time one can see that in situations requiring formal language, whether they be written or spoken, the language can be more planned or less planned.

Another set of proposed dimensions clustered around the idea of the explicitness of written language and the meanings which are conveyed by the two modalities. The meaning in written language was explicit while in spoken it was seen as being more implicit. In the written text the meaning was in the text – **sentence meaning** – while in speech the meaning lay more in the intentions of the speaker – **speaker meaning**. Related to this, spoken language had a context, while written language was seen as being decontextualized. Written language was concerned with conveying information and logical meaning; spoken language conveyed affect and interpersonal meaning. Each of these differences could be seen as a continuum on which any example of written or spoken language could be placed.

The structural differences could also be described as a continuum. Rather than the earlier characterization of written language as being more complex in structure than spoken, there was considerable work on the discourse structure of spoken language, arguing that the way spoken language cohered, or held together structurally, was different from written language but equally complex. Written language was dense and integrated while spoken was looser and more fragmented. Written had syntactic complexity, while spoken had discourse complexity. One way of visualizing this is as the hierarchical organization of written texts compared with the horizontal co-ordinated organization of speech, another continuum.

Which of these are crucial? Which of these dimensions are basic and which derive from other dimensions? One answer to this, suggested by Wallace Chafe, started from a modality difference between written and spoken language and saw this as the basic difference which others are derived from. Chafe pointed out (1982, p. 36) that 'speaking is faster than writing, and slower than reading', and he argued that other differences are derived from this. While speaking and listening go on together at the same time, at the same pace in a shared context, writing and reading pull in different directions. The physical act of writing takes a long time while the act of reading can be very speedy, quicker even than listening to spoken language.

The two dimensions which he saw as crucial and which derive from this basic difference in how written and spoken language are produced and understood are the dimensions of detachment and involvement and of integration and fragmentation. Involvement and detachment refer to the stance of the participants. Speakers express more involvement, with themselves, with the hearer, and with the subject matter, than do writers. Integration and fragmentation are more descriptions of the text, reflecting differences in the structure of written and spoken texts described earlier.

This is as far as the idea of continua between written and spoken has gone, although one development has been to examine large corpora of data and to derive dimensions statistically (e.g. Biber, 1991; Aijmer and Stentström, 2004). Some of the people who have studied differences between written and spoken language throughout the 1980s, such as Deborah Tannen, realized some of the limitations of this approach and began to search round for alternative ways of talking, such as there being oral and literate strategies, which can be used in both speaking and writing (see Tannen, 1985).

Configurations of language

The idea of one continuum or several continua separating written and spoken language is too simplistic a view of the relationship in several ways. First, when focusing on the supposed extremes of conversation versus the literary essay, what has happened is that other forms of writing and speech have been ignored. When other forms, such as personal letters, are examined in detail, it is clear that, in fact, they do not lie halfway along some straight line between conversation and essay. In addition if we look at other technologies beyond the pen and paper we find quite different forms of language which, again, do not lie between conversation and essay. Also in many literacy events, the written and spoken cannot be disentangled. Finally, we find written and spoken so intertwined that good writing contains oral strategies. I will give examples to illustrate each of these points in turn.

Niko Besnier, an American anthropologist, has studied the personal letters written by people on the Pacific atoll of Nukulaelae who speak – and write – Tuvaluan, a Polynesian language (Besnier, 1988, 1989). He studied five spoken registers and two written registers, analysing the linguistic features used in these different forms of language. The features he looked at included those which have been mentioned earlier as appearing differentially in written and spoken language, such as relative clauses and complex noun phrases; 42 such linguistic features were counted in each of the registers. When analysed statistically onto dimensions, it is possible to see their relative importance. There are many lessons for those studying differences between written and spoken language. I want to focus on just a few. First, the two written registers were not at one end of the dimensions with the spoken registers at the other end – rather, they were all mixed in. Second, the personal letters were at the extreme end of one of the dimensions, one roughly corresponding to the informational versus interactional focus which was mentioned earlier. However, it was not at the end predicted by the continuum research of the last section: personal letters were not at the information end of this dimension, they were at the interactional end. What this means is that in terms of linguistic features which can be easily counted and analysed, personal letters display more affect, emotion and interpersonal feeling than conversation and the other spoken registers which Besnier studied.

Several more general points about differences between written and spoken language can be made from this one example. First, letter writing, or any other form of language, is not something which can be described just in terms of its mode of production. What letter writing is and how it is defined is a social issue; different kinds of letter writing are defined within any one culture and may vary from culture to culture.

Examining letter writing in another culture draws our attention to this, and if we return to personal letters in mainstream western culture, I am sure we will also find that they do not fall neatly halfway between everyday conversation and literary essay. In fact, these are probably forms of emotion and affect expressed in personal letters which are not expressed orally.

The approach of examining different forms of language can be extended by considering the possibilities provided by different technologies. The different configurations of written and spoken make any comparison of the two very problematic. Conversation on the telephone, to start with, is clearly spoken language, but it has some of the properties associated with written language, of less shared context and few possibilities for feedback. The answerphone has in addition no hearer present. A radio broadcast has a different configuration of features and a news broadcast may be spoken language which is being read from a written text. The radio phone-in brings further possibilities, as does the tape-recorder. New technologies such as email, the World Wide Web and mobile phone texting bring different forms of communication, some of which, such as email and text messaging, seem to give rise to different forms of language, while others, such as the fax machine, may be less likely to; they all change communication practices. People approach new technologies by applying their existing practices to the new medium, so that as has happened with email, they may at first encounter problems of interpersonal communication.

Something which is obvious in these forms of language associated with new technologies is that we cannot readily disentangle the written aspect from the spoken aspect. As technologies are developed even the link between reading and writing on the one hand, and speaking and listening, on the other hand, breaks down: computers can write down what is spoken to them and speak what is written. The relative speed of these four functions which was at the basis of Chafe's dimensions breaks down today; he very much had the idea of paper and pen in mind. This point about the difficulty of unravelling the written word from the spoken is made obvious when we consider these different technologies. This can be seen elsewhere in this book, when attempting to unravel literacy events in people's everyday lives: two people puzzling over the instructions for a new digital watch, or trying to decipher a train timetable together are using written and spoken language totally tied up with each other.

A further layer of complexity is added by a general shift from page to screen which Gunther Kress has identified as the most significant change in contemporary forms of communication (Kress, 2003). This move has brought in far greater possibilities for combining written communication with other modes, such as images, video and sound effects. Kress claims that this shift to a predominantly 'multimodal' form of communication has led to a revolution in communicative practices. The logic of writing – a linear, sequential form of communication – has been replaced by the logic of the image, a spatial and simultaneous form, where layout and position are as important as sequence. This changes the nature of the literacy involved quite significantly. Some have suggested (e.g. Lankshear and Knobel, 2003) that this shift has led to the development of a 'new mindset'. Those who have grown up with and are at ease with these new literacy practices understand and engage in them in a very different way from those for whom they are something new.

The original investigations of differences between written and spoken language were based upon the idea that a literate culture shakes off the seeming inadequacies of oral culture and develops distinctly different ways of making meaning and of communicating. Consequently the role of spoken language and oral traditions in literate culture were played down. However, the enduring importance of many aspects of spoken language in contemporary society has become more and more apparent. People have identified oral traditions in literate culture and found no contradiction in accepting them alongside written language. These can be identifiable oral traditions such as urban myths and stories; it is also true that oral transmission is a major influence in the maintenance of most social practices, whether it is child rearing, learning a new job, or the conventions of legal and educational institutions. Even in the most seemingly literate of environments such as a law court, a school room or a university office, most of the conventions of how to act, and what to do are passed on orally.

In fact, the whole idea of distinguishing written and spoken language begins to break down. They are not actually separable in real life since spoken language is an important context for most literacy events. As Michael Halliday has observed when discussing differences between written and spoken language: 'They are both language: and language is more important than either. It is a mistake to become too much obsessed with the medium' (1985, p. 92). We will return to this issue of the relation of written and spoken later when discussing language events, as an alternative to literacy events.

Finally, I have been assuming that it is sensible to talk about language in general, that there is something called English which covers both written and spoken forms. However, it is worth pursuing the idea that written language is a different language from spoken language, with its own forms, conventions and grammar. While it may not be so easy to see this for English, there are many examples such as Greek and Arabic where it is accepted by linguists that a gulf exists between standard, classical written forms and everyday spoken ones. If one knows one of these forms, whether it be the written or the spoken, one nevertheless has to learn the other as a different language. An example closer to English is that of French, where through language change over time, the written and the spoken languages are quite different. There are some quite basic ways in which they are grammatically very distinct. In spoken French, for example, adjectives and nouns are not marked for number, that is singular and plural forms are normally pronounced the same as each other. In the written language, however, they are always distinguished. Similarly, written French has far more different forms of the verb than spoken French. It is differences such as these which linguists would point to in order to argue for treating two languages as different from each other. The relation between written and spoken is specific to a language, then, and is different for different languages. It is also a dynamic relationship, one that can change over time.

Decontextualized and explicit?

Two ideas which have been associated with the written and spoken debate are that written language is **explicit**, and that it is **decontextualized**. These properties of written language are then linked with specific reasoning abilities which are explicit and decontextualized, and the connection is made that the reasoning abilities have their source in learning to read and write. It should be clear now from the discussion of written language that neither of these is true: written language is not explicit and it is not decontextualized.

It is central to the notion of an ecological view of literacy that it is always contextualized; human activity always takes place within a context. With a text, the shared knowledge, which all human understanding depends upon, is part of the context. This is knowledge concerned with the content of the text; it is also knowledge of the genre, the conventions of the discourse. To some extent the confusion arises because learning spoken language as a young child is so tied up with the immediate context; learning is also gradually moving away from the immediate context, and children do this with spoken language as well as with written.

Of course language varies in the extent to which it relies on the immediate context to be understood. A distinction made by Frank Smith is useful here (1984, p. 147). He refers to situation-dependent language and situation-independent language. Situation-dependent language makes use of the environment for clues to meaning; this can be done in many ways, for example with deictic words like 'that' and 'there'. Both written and spoken language can be situation-dependent. Situation-independent language can be discussions, explanations, stories which do not refer to the immediate context, and, again, they can be written or spoken. Nevertheless, even when not relying on the immediate situation, written language still has a context.

The idea of written language being explicit, containing all the meaning in the text so that no reference to the context is needed for comprehension, is related to this. It has been the aim of some forms of written discourse which have been developed historically to be more explicit and self-contained. The language of law is the most striking example of this, with the idea that all people interpreting the law will interpret it in the same way. More precisely the idea is that other lawyers in court will interpret it in the same way, since laws are written in a language which excludes ordinary readers. Rather than seeing all the meaning being in the text it is probably more useful to think of lawyers as a discourse community with shared notions of context. It is interesting that as legal arguments move further up the courts, for example where an appeal is taken to the highest court in the country, the legal discussion is more and more likely to revolve around language. They are discussing interpretations of the text. Much of the discussion in the highest courts concerns the meanings of words and the intentions of the original law-makers. The idea of intertextuality, how lawyers get current meanings by referring to earlier texts, is also relevant here. Language falls down when total precision and one single meaning are needed. That is why throughout the history of literacy new notations, like algebra, calculus and formal logic, have been invented. Decontextualized language is an aim which cannot be achieved with ordinary human language. This is because of the very nature of language. Explicit notations have had to be invented.

The belief that written language is explicit and decontextualized has been used to argue that there are great differences between oral cultures and literate cultures. However, to assume that, since expository texts are explicit (if in fact they are so), they are the only source of explicitness in a culture, and that cultures without expository texts lack a certain form of reasoning, is a false argument. It is a form of the 'deficit' argument: its reasoning is as follows. We (i.e. literate cultures) have something – literacy – which leads to something else – explicitness. Another culture lacks the first attribute, therefore it lacks the second. This is the falseness of the argument: it is totally possible, and in fact true, that there exist other possible sources or causes of explicitness. This error in arguing comes from examining only our own language or culture in detail and then identifying certain aspects which other cultures lack. This is done without investigating these other cultures in detail, and, crucially, not examining how they might use different means to achieve the same ends.

The language of oral cultures has not been studied to the extent that the language of written cultures has been. However, it is essential to dispel the myth that people in oral cultures sit on their haunches all day in the sun chatting to each other and that idle conversation is their main form of speaking. Rather, people in oral cultures, as in all societies, have a range of discourses available to them. Oral cultures can have schools, legal systems and political structures, and these institutions demand particular forms of language. Those who have examined ways of speaking in oral cultures have demonstrated that people use other means to achieve the effects attributed to writing in literate cultures. Several examples of this can be given. One claim is that writing enables the originators of a message to distance themselves from the content of the message. This may be true, but it is incorrect to imply that oral cultures do not have ways for speakers to distance themselves from the messages they carry. This may be achieved by form of words, by tone of voice, by stance or by costume, but it is certainly a feature of the discourse of oral cultures. To take another example, the suggestion that oral cultures lack metalinguistic terms, that is, words for talking about language, is easily countered by several anthropologists who have examined in detail the language of various cultures. Each of these studies of very different oral cultures demonstrates that nonliterate people can talk about talking in very sophisticated ways. Further, oral cultures can have forms of speech which are as distinct from everyday conversation as expository text is in our culture. They have a wide variety of spoken genres and there have been studies of oral poetry, oral literature and ritual communication. The final point which comes from such studies is that it probably does not make much sense to lump all oral cultures together as if they represent one sort of culture with one sort of language.[2]

7 Writing systems and other notations

Writing systems

Writing systems

This chapter continues the discussion of written language by examining some of the writing systems used for languages of the world. It extends an ecological understanding of writing by showing how writing systems relate to the structure of the languages which they represent, by comparing the various social demands on writing systems, and by locating writing as one of many symbolic notations which people use in their lives.

Starting with writing systems, there are two principles upon which writing systems can be based. These two principles reflect the commonly stated fact that language can be analysed on two levels: it can be analysed in terms of **sounds** or in terms of **meanings**. Either of these principles can be used to express language in a written form. In practice, writing systems make use of both principles. In reality, describing a particular writing system involves much more than specifying the units that are its building blocks, and it includes punctuation, layout and script. However, the units represent the principles underlying the construction. Inevitably the description which follows is an oversimplification, and fuller descriptions can be found in books devoted to writing systems (e.g. Gaur, 1984; Harris, 1986; Sampson, 1985; Daniels and Bright, 1996; Coulmas, 1996).

The **logographic script** of Chinese is usually cited as the modern example of a language which relies on meaning. The basic unit of the writing system is the **character**. The character is a unit of meaning, so that the simplest characters represent individual **morphemes** (the minimal units of meaning in a language). There is a traditional classification into six distinct types of character in terms of how they are constructed. Some characters are purely anchored in meaning in that they are visual abstractions of the meaning of the word. For example, the character for tree is an abstraction of a picture of a tree. However, most characters are more complex than this and contain some clue to the pronunciation of the word as well as a clue to their meaning. The most common type of character is made up of two parts, a radical, which contains a 'clue' to the meaning, and a phonetic, which contains a 'clue' to the pronunciation. There is a relatively small fixed number of radicals (around two hundred) and they are used as components of a large number of characters. Such characters are known as phonetic compounds and it is estimated that around 90 per cent of characters are composed in this way. Thus the great majority of Chinese characters have internal structure. The Chinese writing system has a history of being misunderstood in the West. A common misconception is the image of Chinese people having to learn by memory 40,000 unrelated squiggles. This idea is constantly repeated but is totally incorrect.[1]

Japanese is interesting in that it uses both sound-based and meaning-based units. Japanese is the oft-quoted example of a **syllabic writing system**. The spoken language is straightforward in that it is fairly simple and regular in its syllable structure and only a small number of syllable symbols (around 40) are needed to write it. However, the writing system is far more complex: Japanese uses two distinct syllabaries to write the language – words of Japanese origin and grammatical morphemes are written in *hiragana*, while words of foreign origin are written in *katakana*. In addition, up to a third of all words are written using Chinese characters. Finally, despite the common descriptions of Japanese as utilizing three scripts, it is important to emphasize that in fact it uses four: Roman letters, *romaji*, are also used, for example in newspapers. There are also common abbreviations in *romaji*, and even mixed systems within a word. These four systems coexist in any one sentence and the reader of a text is in fact contending with four different systems at the same time. The proportion of Chinese characters in Japanese writing declined in the first half of the twentieth century, but now appears to be stable (see Coulmas, 1991).

English has an alphabetic writing system where the symbols bear some relation to the sounds of the language. It is not a direct relationship and, as with Chinese, the symbols – the letters – may best be described as providing a clue to the sounds. That English utilizes both principles, sound and meaning, is also true, although it may be less obvious: first, written English may contain logographs, such as *&*, 6, @, and second, many idiosyncratic spellings, such as right, write, rite, act as logographs. As in Japanese and Chinese they serve to keep potential homophones (words that sound the same) apart in writing and have to be learnt individually. Similarly, the morpho-phonemic information in our spelling system (the relatedness of words like sign and signature, for example) often provides a clue to meaning.

Describing writing systems in this way should clarify some potential problems with the different writing systems. With English we should realize that the aim is not solely to provide a phonetic representation and that English is not necessarily inadequate where it fails to have regular sign–symbol correspondences. The logographic nature of our words may be demonstrated by the tenacity with which many English speakers resist any changes to the spelling, however minor.

Comparing writing systems

The relation of languages and writing systems needs to be clarified. First, spoken languages differ widely in the ways they are constructed and a writing system cannot be discussed in isolation from the language it is being applied to. Different writing systems may suit different languages, so that a syllabic system may be totally appropriate for a language such as Japanese which has a simple and regular syllabic structure, while such a system would be very cumbersome in another language such as English.

The Chinese writing system suits the Chinese language in certain ways because of particular facts about the way in which Chinese is constructed. Chinese has very few inflections to add to the ends of words; it also has a large number of homophones. These two different facts about Chinese contribute to a logographic system suiting that language fairly well. This is one example of the distinctiveness of different languages.

To give another example, this time from Arabic: most words are based upon triliteral roots, that is, words which have three consonants. Words with related meanings are then made from the root with different vowels between the consonants. The root for words to do with writing is k-t-b. For example, 'he wrote' is *katab*, the word for books is *kitab*, for writer it is *katib*, and the word for koranic school is *kotab*. Prefixes and suffixes can be added to the root, so that *maktab*, the word used by Brian Street for one of the forms of literacy in Iran, is also the word for office, and *maktabeh* the word for library. As with other related languages, writing the vowels is often optional and words can be understood with only the consonants; when vowels are needed to make writing comprehensible, vowel symbols can be added, attached to the consonant symbols as diacritics. This is a different way of making words from English.

We can go further than this and point out that different languages themselves vary in terms of how easy they are to write down: spoken English, for example, has certain properties such as the ubiquitous reduced vowels, in about, unless, photographic, photography, which the writing system has never adequately captured, and which make English a fairly messy language to write down. With alphabetic systems there are also problems dealing with suprasegmental phenomena (those which extend over more than one segment) such as tone in tone languages.

That certain writing systems suit certain languages is not to suggest that writing systems are adopted for a language solely on this basis. Writing systems are adopted for political reasons; maps of the spread of writing systems and maps charting the extent of Chinese-based writing, or Arabic-based writing, or English-based writing are maps of economic and religious domination. The choice of writing system is first a political decision and within that constraint further decisions are made (see, for example, Wellisch, 1978). There are also examples of languages, such as Hindi and Urdu, which have two different writing systems and two different names according to religious or political divisions.

A point which needs to be made if we are to evaluate different writing systems is that there is not one simple dimension on which to base such an evaluation. Writing systems serve many different purposes and these will impose different and sometimes contradictory demands (see Berry, 1958, 1977; Venezky, 1977). Two demands to begin with are those made by someone learning to read and those made by a fluent reader: do writing systems differ in how easy they are to learn and do writing systems differ in how quickly or efficiently they can be read by the mature reader? As we will see, neither of these demands is itself a straightforward matter. They are distinct demands as there is no obvious reason to expect that the characteristics that aid the mature reader are the same ones as those which make it easy for the learner. Things get more complicated when we consider that the learner can be adult or child and the language can be their first or their second language. Most focus has been on the child learner,[2] and this makes a good example.

Although fluent reading need not be in relation to spoken language, learning to read typically starts from the spoken language. Different writing systems require the learner to attend to different aspects of the language, the meaning or the sounds, and at different levels of detail, syllables or segments. A logographic system is probably the easiest to master at the very beginning stages of learning to read and a child recognizing whole words in English is effectively treating English words as logographs. Syllable-based systems such as Japanese demand less detailed analysis of the spoken language and it has been claimed that with such systems children learn to read more quickly and do not experience reading problems such as dyslexia.[3] It seems that at the very beginning stages of learning to read, alphabetic systems such as English are overly complex.[4] Pure alphabetic systems have the advantage that once one has 'cracked the code' one can read any word. This is also true with a syllabic system; there are more symbols to learn but once one has mastered them any word is readable. With logographs the learning continues into adulthood with parts of each new character being learned separately. There is a parallel here with English spelling – we are never sure of the spelling of a new word we hear until we have seen it written down; we are often unsure of how to pronounce a word we come across in reading until we hear it spoken.

There has been considerable interest in what is referred to as the **efficiency** of different scripts (see, for example, Taylor, 1981; Henderson, 1982). At the surface level of dealing with the visual information, the processes involved in reading a text will differ with different writing systems. The question posed is whether a skilled reader can read more efficiently, that is, more quickly and accurately, in one system than another. Most of the research on reading processes has concentrated on English.[5] While comparisons between scripts are difficult to make without bringing in a host of other factors, probably all researchers would agree that there are not global differences in efficiency attributable solely to the type of writing system. Certainly there is no support for the idea of alphabetic scripts being more efficient in this sense than other scripts.[6] Within a writing system, individual scripts may lead to more confusion than others, so that German written in Gothic script and modern script and different people's handwriting can differ dramatically in legibility.

Different forms of layout and different fonts can of course have great effects on readability.

Just a few of the demands on a writing system have been covered here. The lists of demands that can be made on a writing system can easily be extended beyond ease of learning to read and efficiency for the mature reader. One could discuss ease of learning to write and efficiency for the skilled adult writer. Writing involves a whole set of different skills from reading and places different demands on a writing system. Another demand is the ease with which it can be incorporated into forms of technology. Japanese and Chinese have proved cumbersome for printing and typing. However, computing presents a new configuration of factors and with this new technology Chinese characters present fewer problems of storage, retrieval or printing (see Stallings, 1975; Becker, 1984). (At first the alphabet was thought to be particularly suited to the computer; to some extent design was geared to the alphabet.) One could easily continue with this list of demands. For our purposes here, we have demonstrated that each writing system has advantages and disadvantages, and that they have to be discussed in relation to the specific language which they are expressing.

Other notations

So far I have been talking of writing and writing systems in terms of scripts and continuous prose texts, and of their relationship to English, but there are many other things which are written. There are other symbol systems which are part of writing or which are closely linked with it. Literacy is so much more than encoding spoken language into writing. It is important to mention some of these other symbol systems and to get an idea of their breadth. Beginning to explore these symbol systems is part of the idea of examining how writing extends language.

Numbers are a good starting point for this discussion. Numbers have many different functions: they can be used to count things, to order things, to measure things, and more. Much mathematics is dependent on the fact that it can be written (see Hurford, 1987). I will give examples here from algebra. In algebra, letters, numbers, words and ideographs (like =) are often mixed, as in

if $x = 3$, and $y = 4$,
then $3x + 4y = 25$.

In fact the letters and numbers are also ideographs in this example. Also the words are often unnecessary:

$x = 3$, $y = 4$,
$3x + 4y = 25$.

Here, everything is ideographic. Note that it also has been freed from being English and can be understood in several languages. Speakers of many languages who know a little mathematics can read it and understand it. Interestingly, if they read it out loud they might say very different things. (There is a parallel here between this and the way speakers of different dialects of Chinese understand each other in writing but not in speech.) This example still has Roman letters, but it need not; as when Greek symbols are used.

Mathematics is relatively self-contained, and it is often useful to see these symbolic systems, algebra, geometry, computer languages, as separate languages. (This has been discussed within linguistics, for example with Chomsky's work many years ago on mathematically different types of languages.) However, viewing them as literacies means discussing different issues. There is a sense in which they are self-contained. Nevertheless, they are each taught, designed, discussed and used within the context of a human language such as English, or Korean, or Urdu. Their ecology is that they are embedded within particular human languages, and are associated with particular language practices in writing and in the talk around them.

An ecological or practice account of other symbolic systems draws attention to the same issues which are arising in the discussion of print literacy. With numeracy, for instance, it emphasizes its cultural basis, how it is located in particular practices, how it is spread differentially through society, how there are numeracies as well as literacies, and more. The cultural aspects of numeracy have usually been eclipsed at the expense of the cognitive aspects. Many questions come up. How are they used in everyday life, that is, what are people's everyday practices, and how does this relate to the ways in which they are formally taught? In any numeracy event, what is the mix of oral and literate? What happens in bilingual situations, whether it is the infant classroom or the international conference?

What roles do different people take? How are the activities gendered? Some of these questions are being addressed by researchers mentioned already.[7]

There are many other notations which, like writing systems and algebra, make use of sequencing; this is commonly left-to-right ordering. These include chemical equations, computer programs, knitting patterns, musical notations, linguistic rules, dance notations. Each has their own history: some are very recent, while dance notations have been around since the 1500s and musical notations are older. Some, like musical notations, are written continuously and wrap around at the ends of lines like prose writing. However, most of them make use of separate lines, like poetry. This is an additional use of physical space and is a dependence on layout. Note that computer languages, such as C++, Java or HTML, also have different dialects and issues of standardization arise. There are questions about which of these notations are still in a particular language. Notations for sign languages for deaf people are an interesting example in that they are currently being developed with different conventions developing for British and American Sign Language (see the introductory chapters in the British Sign Language dictionary, Brien, 1992).

To take one of these examples, music, again there are many parallels with print literacy. There are many different musical systems throughout the world. Western musical notation was designed for particular purposes, for certain narrow sorts of music; it was developed and added to as the need arose throughout the centuries. Nowadays there are additions to solve particular problems, for example when writing down steel band music or other forms which were previously unwritten. In the historical development of music there are strong parallels with the development of writing systems in the way innovations moved from one system to another, with people sometimes inventing systems without knowing other systems. There is one dominant system, the western system, and there are some things it is good at representing and others it represents less well. It fits some music well, but not others. There are particular problems it cannot solve easily. The western system has become naturalized, in that people often believe it to be superior in all aspects to other systems, or even to be the only real system. A practice account of musical literacy would be very revealing. It is probably true that, for example, the great majority of people who play musical instruments in the world are not literate. Such an account would show that the actual use of musical systems is part of cultural practices. For instance, western music is commonly read while people play the music, for many forms of music at least. Most other systems are not read in this way, but are used for learning and for recording – in the sense of keeping a record.

A second area where written language goes beyond the spoken is in layout. This can be in a highly structured way, such as with telephone books, many lists, forms, train timetables, flow charts (see Goody, 1977; Gaur, 1984). Another sort of highly structured layout is nonlinear, with maps, mental maps and plans. Elsewhere, layout is used, but in a less structured way, as in advertisements and signs (see Swann, 1991; Kress and van Leeuwen, 1996). Layout is important in poetry, in note-taking, in title pages, but less so in continuous prose, which is the form of literacy which has been studied the most. In all these other forms a significant part of the meaning is in the layout. Layout is an area where intertextuality is important and where we understand the new in terms of what we know already. Much visual layout is a borrowing from what we know already, putting it together in novel ways. Like algebra, design and layout vary in whether they need words of a particular language with them in order to be understood. Many of these systems are dependent on printing for their exact reproduction, just as other new ones are becoming dependent on computing and new technologies for their existence.

An instructive example on the role of layout is that of maps. Maps bring their own set of issues, with technical questions of how to represent contour, a third dimension, and issues of different projections. Different projections are used according to people's purposes: local maps, a whole country, or the whole world require different projections and, as the chaos theorists have pointed out, deciding on the length of the coastline of Britain, for instance, depends a great deal on the scale used. The very special problem of representing the almost spherical world on a flat piece of paper always involves some compromise, so that Mercator's projection dating from the sixteenth century, the most common for maps of the world, solves some problems, but cannot cope with others. It is good for sea navigation, for instance. However, it is inaccurate when comparing the size of different countries, as it makes land masses further from the equator larger than those near the equator. Another projection, Peter's projection, developed in the twentieth century, solves some of these problems. Quite different maps exist according to people's purposes, whether it be travel, geological exploration, or espionage. A practice account of maps as a literacy raises all sorts of additional questions. Queries about the maps people themselves draw and how people use maps, who draws the national maps, and what gets included and what gets left off have not really been dealt with; nor has access and how people learn to use them. Maps are a central part of literacy and there is a map dating back to the origin of writing on clay in Mesopotamia, but very few examples of maps remain until much later. Literacy partly originated in such design and layout, and is still embedded in it; and maps also exist in some form in nonliterate cultures today.

The previous chapter introduced the argument that a shift from page to screen in recent times has led to a predominantly multimodal form of communication becoming dominant. This makes questions about layout and the interaction between different modes increasingly significant, as written texts interact with images, video, and sound, and different fonts, sizes, backgrounds and styles interact as resources for making meaning in texts. Recent research in multimodality examines how people use this wide variety of resources to make meaning in new ways in a range of social contexts (Kress and van Leeuwen, 2001; Kress et al., 2001). This changes the role of the written text involved, which becomes one part of the communicative event rather than dominating it.

There is room here only to raise issues and ask preliminary questions. Discussion of literacy and notations could be extended, for example, to signs in train stations and airports. See Scollon and Scollon (2003) for an analysis of 'discourses in place': they explore the importance of a range of issues such as placement, layout and language choice in the sorts of meanings which are created by signs and other multimodal texts placed in public positions. There could be debate as to whether or not to include earmarks on animals, monastic sign systems, board games, body painting, each raising its own set of issues, and each adding a new form of complexity. Once again in the discussion here I want to stop at print literacy, and not try to cover the whole of semiotics, the ways in which we make meaning.

8   Points in history

Introduction

The historical study of literacy can be used in two complementary ways. We can approach it in a broad way to understand more about the origin of reading and writing. At the same time, we can use the history of literacy to raise questions and provide insights as to what is meant by literacy, and about what an ecology of literacy should be like. Inevitably in a short amount of space I cannot do justice to such a broad subject and this is not intended to be an overview of the whole history of literacy. It is necessary to be selective and I have chosen topics which are illuminating for the study of how literacy fits in with other activities in life. This chapter will concentrate on just a few points in history which seem important for an ecological understanding. First, the origin of writing is important in that it involves being clear about what is meant by writing; discussion of the beginnings of writing also makes it clear how writing draws upon a range of other forms of symbolic representation. The development of printing is another place to pause in that it represents an important example of the development of a technology within a social context which has been well documented. Finally, a brief overview of the development of a literate culture makes the point that every aspect of literacy has developed and has a history.

The archaeology of literacy

A history of literacy needs to start before the supposed origin of writing, by examining the precursors of writing. The evidence about the origins and early uses of writing is very sparse and it is difficult to piece together existing information into a coherent account of the development or diversification of functions of reading and writing.[1] The evidence for the earliest uses of writing usually comes from materials which survive well, such as stone, baked clay and bone. But it seems reasonable to assume that there would have been earlier work which has perished over time.[2] The term archaeology is used here to emphasize how little is known about the origins of writing and how indirect much of our knowledge is.

What is writing?

To add to the discussion of definitions of literacy in earlier chapters, there are views which come from the study of the origins of writing. To go back to the beginning, intentional semipermanent marks have existed for a very long time. Paintings and etchings on rock surfaces began to appear during the Upper Paleolithic period around 32,000 years ago. If we assume that the first inhabitants of the Americas crossed the Bering Straits 10 to 15 thousand years ago, and that the shape of the Lakeland hills of north-west England were formed 'only' 10 thousand years ago as the last ice age ended, then we can get a feel for how long ago this is. These markings are found worldwide. They are not found just in one place and they do not appear to have spread out from a single origin. They consist mainly of representational pictures of human and animal figures and geometrical markings (combinations of lines, circles, dots, etc.). This was also the time period by which Homo sapiens had emerged in Europe and the Near East with their specialized tools, clothing and ritual worship. The explosion of visual representation at this time is in fact used as one marker of the qualitatively different achievements of our species. Many and varied examples of cave paintings and other marks continue throughout history. However, the emergence of what people regard as a true writing system dates back less than 6,000 years from the present. There is, then, in years, a greater gap from the earliest cave paintings to the emergence of writing, than from the emergence of writing up to the present.

Between cave paintings, the earliest known symbolic representation, and computer graphics, a recent manifestation of it, lie many varieties of visual symbolic representation that any study of writing must situate itself within. Activities that we may wish to call 'writing' extend far beyond the use of an alphabetic script written with a pen on paper: typing symbols onto a screen, carving Mayan hieroglyphs onto a stone sarcophagus, incising cuneiform characters onto a clay tablet, stamping Chinese logograms onto silk fabric, are all writing activities. There are many ways in which etching a mythic map on birch bark to transmit a narrative within a tribal culture is a form of writing, and, as we have already seen, the alphabetic writing system is frequently mixed with other symbols and forms of layout, for example in advertisements or statistical reports. It is not clear what the boundaries are and where the metaphors begin. To the historian, which of these activities involve literacy? Which are writing systems?

When discussing the origins of writing, the definitions historians offer vary mainly in how inclusive they are. The dilemma centres around the connections between the system of visual representation and spoken language, which may be more or less tenuous for a given system. As an example, Gelb (1963, p. 12) suggests a broad definition which encompasses, but does not restrict writing to, systems based on linguistic forms: 'Writing is a system of human intercommunication by means of conventional visible marks'. Diringer (1968, p. 8) however, offers a more restricted definition that emphasizes the correspondence of a writing system with spoken language: 'Writing is the graphic counterpart of speech. Each element, symbol, letter, hieroglyph, written word, in the system of writing corresponds to a specific element, sound or group of sounds such as a syllable or spoken word in the primary system.' A basic distinction is between writing and purely expressive forms of visual representation, such as pictures, carvings and sculptures. In contrast to these forms, writing is seen as having a main purpose of communicating messages from one human being to others. The marks of a writing system therefore are, to some degree at least, stylized and conventional so that they can be understood by several people. Crucially, the writing system is composed of a sequence of conventional marks. It is distinguishable from the static representation of a single picture.

A second distinction is between writing as a carrier of symbolic meanings and other vehicles for such meanings. These range from the use of objects or sets of objects to convey messages, such as notched sticks and knotted ropes, to the other extremely complex and abstract systems of notation of the previous chapter which have developed from writing: mathematical and logical notation, chemical or alchemical formulae, musical notation, spatial representation in maps and diagrams, and codes of various kinds. Although these systems are formally distinguishable from writing in that they have separate sets of symbols to communicate distinct kinds of information and relationships, in practice their use and development is closely tied in with writing itself. As several people have pointed out, a major task for understanding writing systems is to document and integrate these aspects of visual representation and their significance for human symbolic thought.

The distinction between writing proper and other notational systems seems to centre around the type of information being communicated. It may be possible to make the distinction clear by restricting 'full' writing to those systems which are based on some correspondence with the spoken language. 'Writing' then becomes one restricted variety of notation for conveying linguistic information comparable to other notational systems. Ideographic systems without a linguistic link are thereby relegated to a category of 'proto-writing' or 'forerunners' of writing. This is, in fact, the solution favoured by Gelb and others. Such a solution partly reflects a central preoccupation of these authors with spoken language as a starting point for investigating writing. If one's starting point is the development and variety of visual manifestations of human symbolic thought, however, such divisions are less pivotal. Gaur (1984) has pointed this out, challenging traditional approaches to the history of writing by looking at writing primarily as one means of information storage, which facilitates human communication through space and time.

Earlier forms of symbolic representation

The coming of writing is associated with the development of towns and a certain level of complexity in a society. Writing originated in at least three separate cultural areas: in the fertile crescent of Mesopotamia and Egypt, in China and in pre-Columbian America. A further possible source, in the Harappa civilization of the Indus valley (now Pakistan) has uncertain origins and is as yet undeciphered. Of these systems, only the Chinese has maintained an unbroken tradition to the present. Use of the pre-Columbian scripts and the Indus valley script ended with the demise of the civilizations of which they were a part. The earliest evidence of writing occurs in Mesopotamia around 3500 BC, with the cuneiform writing of the Sumerian people. For the other Middle Eastern scripts it is not clear how far the societies traded with each other, and people may have known about the existence of writing, even if they did not copy the writing systems. The early Sumerian script was originally pictographic, but exact details of where, when and by whom it was invented are unknown. The Mesopotamian and Egyptian scripts went through a chain of transformations from pictographic beginnings to the development of alphabetic forms spreading through different cultures and languages, so that most current writing systems can be traced back to them.

Early societies had a wide variety of uses for the systems of representation which were around before writing. Examining different cultures today, as well as the historical evidence, reveals no one precursor of writing. Rather, several distinct types of visual representation can be linked to writing (Barton and Hamilton, 1996). The cave paintings and early pictographs described above as the first evidence of intentional semipermanent marks contained abstract and conventionalized forms of human and animal figures. These markings are distinguishable from writing in that there is no sequence to the pictures or symbols: they appear to be static and self-contained impressions rather than being narrative in intent. We can only speculate about the reasons why these early markings were made and about their symbolic meanings, if any. It is certainly possible that many of them were made for *expressive and aesthetic purposes*, rather than deliberately communicating messages or recording meanings. It is hard to get the evidence but it is argued that some had *ritualistic or magical significance*, as the markings appear in areas of caves that must have been quite separate from living quarters.

The use of *visual memory aids* has been widespread in past and contemporary societies and likewise occurs in both oral and literate societies. A variety of devices has been used and they are often extremely complex, ranging from the use of notched sticks for calendars and reckoning, to the wampum beaded belts of the North American Iroquois. They have had diverse functions, including narrating stories and carrying messages. These devices continue in literate societies (e.g. the Catholic rosary), and they illustrate a widespread function of symbolic representation as an amplification of human memory. Similarly, it seems likely that some of the geometrical markings found in caves and elsewhere were *tallying devices* for counting and reckoning time, acting as rudimentary lunar calendars. Tallying devices appear frequently in cultures without systematic writing systems. The development of tallying systems for reckoning time and objects seems to have preceded other aspects of writing by thousands of years. In fact this tallying may have been a major impetus toward developing more complex systems of symbolic notation, both mathematical and linguistic.

Markings which are *symbolic of ownership or personal identity* are extremely common in both oral and literate societies. Such markings range from branding of livestock, craftsmen's hallmarks, tattoos and totems indicating community or kinship identity, to the symbols of heraldry, seals, badges and flags. There are many historical examples including Scandinavian runes which were used to identify personal weapons, and Egyptian ceramic craftsmen's marks. As Gaur points out:

> Property marks are in many ways already a utilitarian form of writing – they can act as 'signatures', establishing authority, indicating ownership. They are closely connected with elements congenial to the development of systematic writing: a growing awareness of the importance of personal property, a realization that in a differentiated society property can bestow status; a desire to protect and/or exchange such property and the realization that property must be administratively identifiable. (Gaur, 1984, p. 23)

For related purposes, all sorts of *tokens* have been developed for recordkeeping and exchange, used to unambiguously identify and reckon commodities in a commercial context. Recent investigations have suggested that the original Sumerian cuneiform writing system developed directly from the use of such tokens, some of which were in use as early as 10,000 years ago (Schmandt-Besserat, 1992).

There have been many pictographic or purely ideographic narrative forms consisting of more or less stylized sequences of pictures which have the clear intent of *communicating a message*. Examples can be found in Inuit/Alaskan peoples, North American Indians, and Australian aboriginal 'churingas' which are narratives of a mystic Dreamtime expressed via abstract symbols on wooden tablets. These are examples of spatial and narrative representations that can be extended in complex ways (see Goody, 1981). As the pictographic signs become more and more abstract and systematic, the structure verges towards a system like Chinese writing and can provide a bridge between these early forms and actual writing systems.

Early uses of writing

In each of the societies identified above as sources of writing, literacy was used for different purposes. In ancient Mesopotamia the original impetus for developing writing appears to have been trade and commerce, and the earliest users were merchants and accountants. By 2300 BC there is evidence of a very wide range of uses, including letters, records, lexical lists, literary texts, legal documents such as records of land sales, and general administrative records (see Trolle-Larsen, 1989, pp. 138–9; Postgate, 1984, p. 8). In Egypt, the considerations were also economic, but in addition they involved the development of a calendar for predicting the floods of the Nile, and the writing was done by priests and administrators. Even then there were scribes, people who wrote for others.[3] In these societies it seems that writing had a function primarily in the economic sphere but also in other areas.

In China, the first written 'documents' that we know of include examples of divinatory uses and administrative uses. The Chinese developed extensive historical and literary records, maps and astronomy early on, but the development of writing does not seem to have been primarily due to commercial needs as in the fertile crescent. In the Indus valley, the surviving (but largely undeciphered) records seem to be of seals or tokens, indicating commercial and administrative uses. In later Indian civilizations, writing was first used for commerce and administrative purposes and gradually established itself as a carrier of religious tradition after initial resistance. Historical records were not highly developed. In pre-Columbian America, the commercial and administrative uses of writing appear to have been less important than the religious and divinatory uses, involving the development of a calendar and astronomical science. However, religious uses overlapped with administrative ones and it is not really possible to separate them (see Hammond, 1986, p. 106).

Looking at each of these societies in turn, the picture suggests that we can identify a pattern of development in any given society, as for example, Baines (1983) has done for Egypt, but that there is no single or necessary order that applies to all societies. There is not one key original use with all others developing from this. What is important is that what was going on in these societies at this point in history gave the possibility of literacy. Literacy arose with the coming of urbanization and more complex forms of social organization.

With so little evidence remaining from the period of the first writing, we know very little about who wrote, who read and levels of literacy at the beginning. Nevertheless, with scribes from early on, there were obviously particular social roles associated with literacy; there were formalized ways of teaching, and institutions such as libraries in existence. There are also examples of early bilingual literacy with translations of texts etched into stone.

In conclusion, the evidence suggests that writing has been used in early societies and civilizations for many of the broad functions that we can identify today, although in detail and complexity there are still huge variations. From the beginning many materials and techniques were utilized as they were available; seemingly ephemeral uses of literacy such as graffiti were present from early on. It should also be clear from this section that there was a great deal of continuity from other forms of visual representation to actual writing in terms of form and uses.

Literacy and historical change

There is a whole cluster of ideas which hang together and which provide an alternative to the ecological view of literacy which I am describing. This alternative has been termed an **autonomous** view of literacy by Brian Street (1984) and was referred to in chapter 2. It is the idea that literacy can be described autonomously, separate from any context; that there is a psychological variable called literacy which can be measured and which remains the same in different social contexts and at different historical times. The autonomous view has been broadened to suggest that there is a 'great divide' between literate and nonliterate, both at the individual level and at the cultural level, and that there are cognitive consequences associated with literacy itself. In terms of historical development it is assumed that contemporary Western alphabetic literacy with its roots in Greek civilization is superior to other forms and it has evolved naturally to this superior position.

These ideas have been subject to widespread criticism and it is tempting just to refer readers to other works and to ignore the autonomous view of literacy. However, this view of literacy is still being supported, and more importantly it is a common strand underlying public debate about literacy and popular images of reading and writing. This is evident in some of the press quotes about literacy earlier. There are alternative models of what literacy is and there is a struggle as to which models are to have precedence; there are competing ideologies of literacy struggling with each other for dominance. In this section I want to concentrate on the autonomous view, examining its intellectual origins in discussions of early Greek literacy and its view of historical development.

We have to deal with the significance of Greek literacy because it has been an important source of views on literacy, sometimes clarifying and sometimes clouding our vision. An influential paper on this which can act as a landmark is one by Jack Goody and Ian Watt first published in 1963 and republished in several places since then (see also Havelock, 1963). They discuss the idea of a great divide between oral and literate, both socially, in terms of cultures, and psychologically, in terms of how people think. An important aspect of the great divide proposal is the notion that modern literate societies are fundamentally different in many aspects of social organization from earlier simpler societies and that these differences are ultimately attributable to literacy. Aspects of modern societies that are said to hinge upon the existence of literacy include the development of democracy, certain forms of political organization and the possibility for technological advance.

All these proposals are identified in Greek society from the sixth century BC onwards, the foundation stone upon which western civilization has apparently been built. To summarize their argument, Goody and Watt see the Greek example as crucial, arguing that the rise of Greek civilization was the prime historical example of the transition to a really literate society, offering not only the first instance of this change, but also the essential one for any attempt to isolate the cultural consequences of what they refer to as 'alphabetic literacy'. Although accepting that any claims are extremely tentative because of lack of evidence, they do suggest a causal link between the development of alphabetic literacy and cultural developments in Greece at that time. This is the idea which has been taken up by others and which underlies much discussion on the effects or consequences of literacy. It is therefore important to stress that Goody later accepted that two of the phenomena he was juxtaposing did not in fact have their roots in Greek culture. The Greeks did not 'invent' the alphabet – it was in existence a thousand years before. And they did not 'invent' the new forms of logic which are seen as the key to western thought – some of the forms of proof and argument attributed to the Greeks existed far earlier in Babylon (Goody, 1983).

A particularly bizarre aspect of the 'Greek' argument, to me at least, is the notion that the alphabet itself, rather than writing, or even the development of printing, is directly responsible for certain aspects of abstract thought. This position is found in Goody and Watt's argument and is attributable to the work of Eric Havelock.[4] It is also to be found in the work of Marshall McLuhan.[5] To some extent the claim rests on the alphabet being constructed on more abstract units than other writing systems. However, as shown earlier, this is an oversimplification. In addition, if abstractness were the most significant criterion then we would look to Korean, with its writing system based on distinctive features of the sound system, rather than to the alphabet. Beyond claims in Havelock's work, it is difficult to find any more direct historical evidence that the alphabet, rather than writing itself, is crucial. As pointed out earlier, differences between writing systems are not as clear-cut as they might at first appear and they need to be discussed in the context of specific languages.

Writing as evolution

A common view of the historical development of writing places it within an evolutionary framework of development, from pictographs, through logographs, to syllabic systems and on to the alphabet, that is, as a development towards our own writing system. Evolution is a metaphor, a way of conceptualizing a phenomenon. I see the term **evolution** as being embedded in a whole metaphorical system, as explained in chapter 2. Like any metaphorical system, use of the term will play up certain aspects of the phenomenon it is describing while at the same time playing down other aspects. When applied to the history of writing, I believe it hides

more than it reveals. It is not a particularly good metaphor for understanding the historical development of writing, and probably not for
other human symbol systems, including spoken language. In this section
I point out some problems with the standard histories of writing when
expressed in an evolutionary framework. There are several problems: in
particular, I discuss those associated with views on the superiority of the
alphabet. I argue that in an evolutionary framework important aspects of
literacy get left out. There are three issues: it feeds a misunderstanding
of the relation of languages and writing systems; it is difficult to compare
writing systems; and it makes it hard to identify mechanisms of language
change.

Evolution is one way of talking about change. In our society today it is
an easy metaphor, the default metaphor, one which fits in with other
social concepts and which can be used across different domains without
question. Implicitly it brings with it a whole system of beliefs. Evolution
is an everyday word and it can be used in a casual sense, for example
in a book on fashion I came across called *The evolution of hats*, or when
someone describes the evolution of their ideas. In such examples one might
replace the term evolution with the words 'development' or 'change'.
However, use of the term implies something more than development
or change. It implies a certain sort of change: it brings along a whole set
of notions, ideas such as that change is unidirectional, natural and inevitable. Passive and impersonal adaptation is implied and it also carries with
it notions of improvement, superiority and progress. This cluster of ideas
makes up the term evolution and it is this framework which is invoked
by using the word.

The roots of the current everyday concept lie in Darwinian biological
evolution of the nineteenth century. However, there is little consensus,
especially when the term is applied to cultural phenomena. Graham
Richards, in a thorough review of theories of social evolution (1987,
pp. 206–34), identifies and describes nine clearly discernible positions.
These positions take opposing views on the most basic questions of the
relation of the biological and the cultural. It is another area where the links
between the psychological and the sociological are not clear, and crucially
this is an argument where current social values strongly affect people's
positions (as Bowler, 1986; Lewin, 1984, and others point out). All this
makes it very difficult to pin down what is meant precisely by evolution
when it is applied to the development of writing. A particular theorist
may intend to use evolution in a more precise way when applying the

term to writing, and the extent to which everyday notions of evolution are invoked is never clear. Nevertheless, as we will see in the examples below, evolutionary thinking generally has the biological framework underlying it.[6]

Evolution towards the alphabet?

Built into this description is the idea of the alphabet as evolutionarily superior. This is then linked to notions of progress and the idea of some natural evolution towards the best system, to the extent that the history of writing has been the history of the alphabet (see Harris, 1986, p. 37). The roots of this idea are found in the work of Gelb (1963) and Diringer (1968), the two most widely quoted documenters of the writing systems of the world, mentioned earlier. Gelb's book begins with a family tree which has our own English alphabet right in the middle at the bottom as if all changes were an inexorable development towards this point. Diringer proclaims that 'alphabetic writing is now universally employed by civilised peoples' (1968, p. 13) and he turns up the most extraordinary explanations as to why users of what he regards as lesser writing systems have failed to adopt our alphabet (p. 127).[7] These views on the alphabet seem to have originated as part of a post-Second World War ethnocentrism, such that in 1958 Berry was able to claim that 'it is generally accepted on all grounds an alphabetic system is best' (p. 753).[8] Another popularization of 'the technologizing of the word' (Ong, 1982) is cast in this same evolutionary framework.

What gets de-emphasized in the evolutionary account is the fact that the two principles upon which writing systems can be based are to be found to exist in *all* types of writing system, as explained in the previous chapter. These two principles reflect the commonly stated fact that language can be analysed on two levels: it can be analysed in terms of sounds or it can be analysed in terms of meanings. Either of these principles can be used to express language in a written form. Logographic systems rely primarily upon meaning, while syllabic and alphabetic systems rely on sound. In practice all writing systems make use of both principles and the earliest writing systems contain instances of both principles.

A whole cluster of ideas surround the concept of evolution. At the heart of it is some notion of a natural linear progression toward the best. However, development is not 'natural'; rather it involves individuals in social settings making decisions. Development is not 'linear'; it involves little understood mechanisms of contact. As we have seen already, there is not one 'best' system; different writing systems suit different languages and there are broad and conflicting demands on writing systems.

Contact and change

There are different ways for a society to acquire a writing system. Literate individual people or organizations from outside the language and culture may design a writing system. Alternatively, insiders with 'the idea of writing' may work out their own writing system. There have been examples throughout history of indigenous peoples inventing writing systems after exposure to merely the idea of writing; often they invent syllable-based systems. There are well-known cases in West Africa and in North America.[9] These different paths have not been explored in detail but what needs emphasizing here is that the most common way for languages to get a writing system is through people having contact with another language which already has a writing system. The writing system is borrowed and adapted to new circumstances. It is by means of this process of adapting to the demands of a new language that most of the significant developments in writing systems have taken place. Each development is small but significant and is explicable in terms of the context in which it occurs (see Goody, 1981 for examples). This applies throughout the spread of writing systems and it helps us, for instance, to clarify the development of the alphabet. The alphabet was developed gradually and awkwardly as writing systems were adapted to suit different languages. In fact, it probably does not make sense to try to pinpoint the actual emergence of a distinct alphabet.

The idea of contact and change is more accepted in discussions of spoken language. Spoken languages change in various ways and for various reasons.[10] One of the most important influences on language change is contact between languages. Contact is important in all cultural change, including written language. The spreading branches of an evolutionary tree do not capture this form of change, and a different way of visualizing it is needed.

Different ways of talking about change are needed. Change is embedded in a social context and involves active human decision making. Some socio-historical account is needed where writing is embedded in its cultural context. Change is not purely linear. We need a more complex and richer account of change if we are to address questions such as how writing systems spread to different societies, or describe the role of literacy in language change, or understand contact as a mechanism of change. An ecological notion of change, showing the importance of context, is needed rather than an evolutionary one: that it is developing, but not that it is evolving.

A social history of literacy

The development of printing

The uses of reading and writing have varied considerably from society to society and in different historical periods. To some extent this has depended on the materials available for writing and the methods of manufacture and dissemination. The manufacture of paper, the development of printing and of electronic media are some of the most visible technological milestones in the spread of literacy. Here I will concentrate on the technology of printing. It is a powerful example of the restructuring of literate activity through technical invention incorporated into the social organization and production of knowledge.[11]

Printing goes back thousands of years. In one sense the existence of printing predates writing, in that the use of seals as stamps goes back seven thousand years. As an example of printing, techniques of stamping can be traced back to the ancient use of individual stamping seals, through to block printing which was in use in China by 600 AD, and on to movable type printing which was widespread in China by 980 AD. Movable type printing was developed in Europe in the mid-fifteenth century, giving the possibility of mass copying of texts.[12] Prior to the coming of printing there was a scribal culture where books were copied by hand.

In Europe printing was accompanied by the explosion of knowledge which occurred during the Renaissance. Many hypotheses have been put forward about the impact of printing by means of the wide dissemination of texts, both in terms of the breadth of ideas suddenly available to people and how printing may have shaped those ideas. Eisenstein (1979, 1981) integrates a great deal of scholarly material to suggest that printing had complex and contradictory effects in terms of productive knowledge and the secularization of thought. She also suggests that many of the effects claimed for literacy, discussed earlier, may be due to printing and the wider circulation and preservation of texts that mass copying made possible. Printing gave rise to a distinct literate culture and the earlier scribal culture had many of the same limitations often attributed to oral culture: individual copyists produced texts with idiosyncratic formats and conventions and were subject to mistakes, whereas printing allowed a large number of identical texts. The existence of a few copies of a given manuscript made for restricted publicity and high incidence of loss or destruction of a text. Scribal culture was also highly selective, since it could not sustain advances in knowledge on many fronts at once.

Printing supported two opposing tendencies at the same time – cultural diffusion and standardization. In terms of cultural diffusion, the availability of multiple copies of a text allowed many people to read the same text at any one time. It also gave the possibility for one given person to read and compare many different texts, thus encouraging the cross-fertilization of new ideas. This diffusion could be of new knowledge or the reinforcing of old. Printing facilitated the wide circulation of new knowledge and in this way contributed to the breaking down of old religious traditions and authorities. It could also have some opposite effects: not only were secular and 'enlightened' writings circulated widely, but alongside them were medieval religious, occult and mystical writings which reinforced past traditions.[13]

In itself, printing may not be selective in the kind of ideas it exposes readers to. More important are the social uses it is put to, and the social restrictions such as laws and censorship mentioned earlier. In another sense, however, printing may be highly selective and contribute to the channelling of certain messages and the emphasizing of particular stereotypes. Eisenstein describes how it can be used to amplify and reinforce existing ideas by constant repetition. These amplified messages are channelled by fixed linguistic frontiers so that different stereotypes develop in different vernacular literatures, though other frontiers, such as religious ones, cut across them. The reverse side of this amplification is of course the effective suppression of other ideas and messages by neglect or deliberate putting aside when things fail to reach print or go out of print. Such elimination is all the more effective because of the weight of truth and authority accorded the printed word.

The process of standardization has perhaps been the most widely recognized effect of printing: the elimination of scribal errors and idiosyncrasies, in repeated copies, the fixing of linguistic maps and conventions and the mass reproduction of texts that are particularly difficult to copy accurately by hand such as pictures, maps and diagrams. Maps had been around since the beginning of writing, but they were boosted by printing, and probably came to serve very different purposes, with a new-found accuracy dependent on this technology. It should be stressed that printing does not just give us narrative texts, it gives us repeatable layout and form: items such as maps of the mind and of the known universe were an important early product of printing. In a different area of standardization, printing aided the establishment and spread of standard languages as Illich (1981), for example, demonstrates for Spain.

Eisenstein (1979) emphasizes the powerful role that early print-shops played in the systematization of literate knowledge. They were 'laboratories of erudition' in their own right, compiling and producing reference manuals and guides, indexes, devising notation systems, arranging contents, running heads, and footnotes, and so vastly changing the shape of what was a book and the practices associated with it. It is important to remember that each of these parts of the book developed and has its own social history. And new sorts of books such as chapbooks, cheap popular volumes, came into existence.

The coming of print in Europe at this point in history, then, appears to have played a very dynamic role in the way people think about and read texts, a role that is not simply the effect of mass circulation of new ideas, but more complex and contradictory than this. Printing certainly fostered a 'systematic' approach to learning, by means of the opportunities it presented for someone to scrutinize a variety of ideas side by side and to compare historically different versions of the same text for inconsistencies and developments, and also through the efforts of printers themselves in classifying and cross-referencing existing texts. As a result of the increased preservation and accumulation of texts and fixed records, Eisenstein suggests that the pursuit of truth itself took a new direction. It became the discovery of new knowledge rather than the constant effort to recover and preserve traditional knowledge. This gave rise to the idea of the steady advance of knowledge with fixed records to mark its stages of development.

The development of a literate culture

The development of a literate culture has many aspects starting before the coming of printing and continuing to the present. A first point to be made when examining history concerns the levels of literacy in a society.

Historians are constantly surprised by their discoveries of the large amount of reading done by ordinary people, men and women, and by the role of books in their lives. For example, in a fascinating book about daily life in a small sixteenth-century Italian town, Carlo Ginzburg comments in passing: 'It's astonishing that so much reading went on in this small town in the hills . . . Books were a part of daily life for these people' (1982, p. 31). More than half the people there borrowed books from each other; there was a 'network of readers' in contact with each other. There was a wide range of books; around half of them were religious, half were not.

Other historians make similar points. Examining an earlier period, the eighth and ninth centuries, Rosamond McKitterick comments on the number of ordinary people who were literate in France and Germany and sees evidence of a literate society then. She comments that its use was not just for religious expression but for 'the conduct of daily business and entertainment' and that it continues 'a considerable way down the social scale' (1989, p. 270). Michael Clanchy, studying the shift towards reliance on written records in the development of a literate culture in twelfth- and thirteenth-century England, also points to widespread literacy (1993).[14] The ups and downs of levels of literacy in history have also been noted in India and China (Gough, 1968). Another historian, in documenting the rise of compulsory schools in Britain, also demonstrates how widespread literacy was in earlier periods back to Anglo-Saxon times (Kelly, 1970). He points to the amount of education available in the Middle Ages with a range of schools and other institutions providing literacy instruction. He documents the number of foreign languages available in classes, along with navigation, mathematics and astronomy. This would be in addition to the informal teaching and learning which took place.

Using the evidence of whether or not people signed the marriage register, Vincent claims (1989, pp. 52–4) that two centuries on, in England in the 1750s, more than half the population were literate, that the figure had passed 60 per cent before the introduction of compulsory schooling and 90 per cent by 1870, the year of the first Education Act introducing compulsory schooling. We should be careful of using signatures as measures of literacy, because it is this measure which also allows Vincent to state that by 1914, illiteracy in England had vanished and that the country could be treated as homogenous in terms of literacy, a claim which needs closer examination. Being able to sign one's name is only one definition of literacy. Additionally, a general problem of applying dates to the measures is that the person signing at age 20 may be alive 60 years later, and in this time their literacy might have stayed the same, or it might have changed.

Before the coming of compulsory schooling there was still a great deal of literacy teaching. There were parents, grandparents and siblings all involved in the activity of teaching, with teaching aids for parents in existence. There were Sunday schools and day schools, with teachers from the local community, unqualified and unsupervised; it is estimated that in 1851, three quarters of all children in England attended Sunday schools. Additionally, there were dame schools run by individual women in their own homes. In terms of methods of teaching, Vincent writes, 'the most striking characteristic of the procedures adopted to teach children their letters up to the imposition of universal and compulsory education was their sheer variety' (1989, p. 67).

Much of the basis of contemporary literacy is in compulsory schooling. Schooling took over the teaching of reading and writing in the nineteenth century, and it is only recently that families are claiming some of it back. Compulsory schooling in Britain dates from the laws passed in the 1870s, although it took a further 40 years to consolidate. The first laws gave the right for all children who wanted it to have free schooling, but the formation of school boards in an area was not compulsory. They came into existence gradually and universal secondary schooling came much later. Primary schooling had as one of its clear and explicit aims that of teaching children reading and writing. In fact, once children have been taught to read and write, the purposes of education are often unclear and disputed. Compulsory schooling gave the possibility that everyone could be literate, although the idea of this was not accepted as a right until well into the twentieth century.

It is important to remember that every aspect of literacy practices has its roots in history and has social implications concerned with relationships of power. The institutions of literacy have gradually developed, such as the library, bookshop, printhouse, photocopy shop, as well as government printing houses and official forms, along with the postal service and other means of communication. The legal framework of literacy mentioned under restrictions, such as copyright and royalties, all has a history which can be traced. Literacy roles such as that of author, secretary, copy typist all have a social history, some dating from the beginnings of writing and others developing more recently. Most importantly, formalized ways of teaching with schools and an educational system have all developed, along with methods of teaching and ways of training teachers. Many of the developments have been documented, including a history of libraries, the development of the teaching of reading, and even a history of the pencil and of ink.[15]

It is also true that every form of writing, every sort of text, developed and has a social history. Specific forms of writing, specific literacies such as expository text, were developed over time. Charles Bazerman has traced the history of the research article as a genre, for example, and others have examined the development of scientific writing more generally.[16] For each text of chapter 5 – the advertising copy, the official notice, the small ad – we can ask questions about its historical development. Particularly interesting is the official notice of increase in fees for taxis with its roots in legal literacy, and which now can be seen as restrictive in its use of language from the past. Books for specific purposes have been gradually created, such as for children learning to read, text books for studying particular subjects, instruction books, grammars, dictionaries, catalogues and timetables. It is not just books which have developed, but other literacy texts such as tickets, bills, paper money, travellers cheques, and so on.

Everything has such a long period of development, often spanning the whole time period that writing has been in existence, as has already been noted for maps. The development of signatures, a special form of writing with unique properties, is another good example; individuals' written signatures appeared in the sixteenth century, even though seals, with much the same function, went back seven thousand years. Conversely, the idea of everyone having a signature, or even a surname, is much more recent, and arises from official demands on individual lives.

Practices around texts also develop and change. Sacred religious books have been around for over a thousand years but the practices around them have changed with the centuries; there are different ways of taking from the text at different periods. Looking at the past from the present, the social position of a text may change and we need to examine its social position at the time of writing, so that at a certain point in history if the parish register is used in collection of taxes, for example, it has a fairly central role, and would be more important than today. It would be a mistake to project contemporary values onto history.

Finally, to make the link with the present, every person has an individual history. Everyone has a literacy history, an individual continuous strand from their first exposure to literacy as an infant right up through schooling and their adult life. Children today are often in contact with people who have memories going back up to 70 years; if these grandparents remember parental anecdotes, stories can go back a hundred years. Schools, libraries and other institutions in Britain are often a hundred years old, with a shape and layout reflecting Victorian values, both in the very real physical sense and in the practices they support. Cultural images of identity and purpose can be imbued with two hundred or two thousand years of history. All of these are ways in which the past structures the present and influences contemporary literacy.

9   The roots of literacy

Introduction

In a literate culture the preparations for literacy begin at birth; literacy is embedded in the oral language and the social interaction of the child's surroundings. In this chapter and the following one I explore the origins of literacy in children's development, keeping to the preschool years. Once again, the route to understanding the social basis of literacy has to take several detours. The chapter begins by looking at different types of learning, especially those which emphasize the role of the environment; then it briefly cover the early development of spoken language which acts as a root for literacy development; then in the next chapter we come on to written language, exploring reading to children and examining the reading and writing which children are exposed to in the home.

Immediately it is necessary to address the question I raised before as to what culture we are referring to. I pointed to the problems in talking of 'our culture' and in concentrating exclusively on Western mainstream culture. Child language acquisition is a good example of a field of research where the majority of studies have been of children growing up in the dominant culture of white middle-class English-speaking families in Britain and North America and where generalizations of how children learn have been taken from this mainstream culture. One important aspect of this culture for the discussion here is the obvious one that this it is highly literate. Work in child language development starts from this culture; it then moves out to other western literate cultures, to nonwestern literate cultures and cultures where literacy is not a central part of everyday activities. As will become obvious, the few studies of other cultures, both within western countries such as the United States, and beyond, such as work on Kaluli and Samoan, paint a very different picture and challenge commonly held beliefs about literacy and child language acquisition.

Approaches to learning

What follows in this section is not a complete theory of learning, but some parts which are important for a social view of the development of literacy and which are often not covered when learning is discussed. These ideas form the basis of ecological learning. The approach I describe here grows out of work in child language acquisition and in everyday learning, particularly the work influenced by the ideas of the Russian psychologist Lev Vygotsky. His insights on how to link society and the individual have spawned a whole tradition of socio-cultural research on learning, which has been referred to earlier.

The first point to get across is the complexity of learning. Some people interested in child development have talked of a 'language acquisition device', something internal which is an innate part of our human language learning apparatus. This is too simplistic if it becomes the dominant metaphor and is taken as being the one means of learning a language. Within a constructivist framework, measuring out the percentage contribution of innateness is not really a very sensible approach. Internal factors and external factors are too intertwined; they are not mixed in some simple way which allows one to identify constituents – in fact the constituents do not exist as entities which can be isolated and compared qualitatively.[1]

It may seem obvious to state that there are several ways of learning, some more complex than others, but this has not always been accepted and the search for one single way of learning has been an extensive one. There are also many things which need to be learned in order to master something like literacy, and this is likely to involve several different forms of learning. At one extreme, simple conditioning exists and probably it has a part to play in literacy learning. Activities like literacy also make use of more complex ways of learning. These activities are part of the acquisition of what have been called higher psychological processes. It is these complex ways of learning which we need to explore. A useful quote, identifying four types of learning involved in socialization, is the following:

> Socialisation is the means by which culture . . . is transmitted. The agents of socialisation are primarily parents, teacher, peer-group and the media. There are four processes by which socialisation occurs. First skills, habits and some types of behaviour are learned as a consequence of reward and punishment. Second parents and others provide models for roles and behaviour which children imitate. Third the child identifies with one or both parents, a process which is more powerful than imitation, through which the child incorporates and internalizes the roles and values of the parent or other significant adult. Fourth, there is the part played by the growing individuals themselves. They actively seek to structure the world, to make sense and order of the environment. The categories available to the child for sorting out the environment play an important part in this process. (Weinreich, quoted in Henriques et al., 1984, p. 19)

In this quote note the complexity of this one thing we call learning. In the different forms of learning there are varying contributions of individual and social aspects. Getting away from learning as an individual pursuit is essential. Learning does not relate to just an individual, but it includes the situation, the activity and the participants in it. Also learning is not a passive activity, as many simple views of the reading process imply; rather it is an active one (as the word 'activity' itself suggests!); the child learns by being involved in an activity, by being part of the interaction. Learning is a social activity and it often involves children changing the ways they participate in an event.

Learning does not just take place in situations officially designated for learning such as the classroom but it is a component of all activities. Nevertheless, there are some situations particularly conducive to learning and which are common in children's experience. Learning takes place in situations which for the child are often repeated: there are many common activities which consist of regular repeated routines. The situation supports the learning. This is where an analysis of events becomes important, one type of such regular event being the **literacy event**.

We now turn to the participants. There are common power relations in much learning. In Western mainstream culture a commonly encountered situation for young children is when they are with one adult, although, obviously, several people can take part in an activity, and older children can have significant roles. Adults are knowledgeable; adults know the culture; adults initiate the child into the culture. One way of looking at this is through the notion of **scaffolding**, where the adult supports the child's activities and provides a framework within which the child acts. This is a support which is gradually withdrawn as the child develops. We can see what this means in routine activities such as changing and bathing, and it can be applied to the learning of language and literacy.

Learning is always in a context. Human activity is dependent on context, and it does not exist independently of it. Scaffolding is provided by the situation; a crucial part of this is the support of the adult. We have mentors for new activities, knowledgeable people who guide us. The adult is part of the learning situation and is 'the supportive other' in an activity which takes two people. Parents, teachers, master craftsmen all act as supportive others in interactive learning situations. We could not imagine these forms of learning taking place without someone else being there. The idea of support is important (although in fact the concept of scaffolding may seem too fixed and mechanical a metaphor to capture the interactive nature of human learning) and the notions of apprenticeship in learning is useful here.[2]

The other crucial participant is of course the child. In the adult–child relationship, at birth the adult completely looks after and controls the child (ignoring for the moment all the other influences on the child). At the beginning the adult creates the structure of the interaction; the adult mediates the child's experience. Gradually the child takes over more and more; the adult relinquishes control. The scaffolding is removed. Later the child does more and comes to control its own learning. The child becomes adult. This approach also assumes that the child as a person is active, and is an active hypothesis maker. People think, people plan. Much human behaviour is self-regulated and is based on people's own thoughts, awareness, plans.

Related to this, each child in each generation recreates the world, reinvents it, to echo Andrew Lock's (1980) phrase about 'the guided reinvention of language'. Each generation's construction of the world is a new synthesis. Cultural history and individual development meet in the interaction of adult and child. The adult represents history. The social and the cognitive meet. The current generation of five year olds, for example, is incorporating computers into a world of technology and communications media. To a child, the computer is a fact of life, not necessarily more or less exciting than a football or a bicycle. It is important to emphasize here that computers are incorporated into a child's world as they are encountered. They are not added on to the end as they might be for an adult. The child is not repeating or recapitulating the adult's world, the child is creating a world anew. It may be a nice vision to think of the child as recapitulating history, but if one looks closely at the details of child development this does not make any sense. Any ordering or stages a child may pursue do not repeat historical development.

Gradually there is less mediation by adults and the child becomes more autonomous by internalizing the structures of social interaction. **Internalization** is a way of learning, a mechanism of acquisition. In Vygotsky's terms there are basic psychological processes and there are complex (or higher) ones. Complex social processes are first experienced by the child as social activities, for example between the child and its caregivers. They are then internalized inside the child's mind as psychological processes. The child, or adult (any person learning) gradually builds upon existing knowledge and abilities which become transformed by the new learning. The roots of reasoning, identity and awareness lie in early social interaction. The inner dialogue of reasoning is a reflection of the outer communicative interaction. The relation of the inner and the outer world is not solved by talking of internalization, but the term does provide a clear way of researching it, we have a metaphor for the relation of the two. There are still problems of what is internalized and what is not, and the relative contributions of internal structures and processes, but there are the beginnings of a way of uniting them.

Another useful concept which comes from Vygotsky is the **zone of proximal development**, or **Zoped**, as it is referred to. A common way of learning is that children learn things which are just beyond their abilities. The zone of proximal development, then, is the gap between what a child can do unaided and abilities exhibited when supported by social scaffolding. When supported, children can do much more. Socially supported activities are learned when they become internalized. What is important for teaching is the thing which can next be learned. In principle this provides an explanation of learning. Actually identifying these Zopeds is the puzzle for the researcher and for the teacher.

If we put together these various parts, the participants, the situation, the activity, a mechanism and ways of participation, we have the requirements for learning. This is a very powerful view of what is going on in situations of the transmission of culture, from the earliest interactions of infant and caregiver onwards.

Learning to speak

To repeat the beginning of this chapter, the roots of learning to read and write are in learning to speak, and more generally in children's early development. In a literate culture preparations for literacy are to be seen in early language development. It is important to emphasize this point because historically, learning to speak and learning to read have been seen as very different activities; this has been one aspect of the more general divide between written and spoken language. Standard books on one of these two subjects, either learning to read or learning to speak, have not mentioned the other and there has been little overlap in the theories they have drawn upon or the references they have cited. This can be explained in terms of the development of the field of language acquisition as an area of study with its roots in linguistics and psycholinguistics. It has also been part of a belief that learning to speak happens up to the age of five years, while learning to read happens after five years. Researchers and others now realize that learning to speak continues well beyond the age of five years and learning to read begins well before five years. What changes at age four or five, in Britain at least, is the onset of formal schooling.

The intertwining of written and spoken language noted earlier applies to children and their learning. Writing and speaking are very similar in many ways; similar processes underlie them and the mechanisms of learning described in the previous section apply equally to both learning to speak and learning to read. We want to go further than this and point out that they are inextricably entwined and cannot be separated: they are both part of learning to use language.[3]

There are standard ways of communicating with children which are almost built into the communicative system. Adults are bigger, stronger, more knowledgeable and more articulate than infants and if you pick up a small child in your arms it is most likely that you will be careful, gentle, you will take charge and you will communicate. You will hold the child so that it is comfortable and in western mainstream culture it is likely that in order to monitor its feelings and dispositions you will attempt to get and maintain eye contact. Communicating by speech and gesture is an important way of relating to a young infant. Inevitably, largely as a natural result of the communicative situation you are in, holding a small, defenceless and easily disturbed creature, you will adjust the way you communicate. Adults talking to young children adjust their language in consistent ways. In the English-speaking world you are likely to speak more quietly, more slowly, with exaggerated intonation, using short simple sentences, simpler sounds. What you talk about is likely to be constrained too. You talk about the here and now, what's going on around, personal feelings and needs. As we will see, these ways of adjusting are separate phenomena and some may be completely absent in other cultures, but in all cultures adults adjust themselves to children's behaviour.

People talk appropriately. What this means in practice changes over time. Adults adapt and are responsive to the growing and developing child. They are sensitive to the child's states and abilities. In learning to speak, and presumably in other areas, children seem to work on particular parts of their development and then move on to others. There is some evidence that adults are responsive to what the child is actually learning or working on. The ideas mentioned earlier of a zone of proximal development and of internalization fit in here and these interactions between adult and child are effectively mini language learning situations. There is an interplay between two things: adults to some extent fine-tune their language. At the same time, children choose what they attend to. This latter may be more important. In the interplay of the two can be found understanding and learning.

The different ways of adjusting our language may appear to be inextricably woven together in forming a coherent way of talking to children. However, the actual details vary from culture to culture. It is worth looking at some examples drawn from different cultures. Even within contemporary western culture, there are differences, for instance between different social groups in the United States. Shirley Brice Heath's study, mentioned earlier, contrasts how adults' concepts of childhood and parenthood affect how they interact with children in two communities in South Carolina. In Roadville, a small rural white working-class community, there is clearly a register for talking to children:

> Roadville parents talk to their babies, modifying their speech in ways they believe appropriate for speaking to children. Seen as conversational partners, children are expected to answer questions, read books cooperatively,

and learn to label and name the attributes of real-world and book objects . . . They are brought into tasks, asked to try activities, and supported and corrected in their efforts. (Heath, 1983, p. 146)

This is contrasted with Trackton, a black working-class community Heath studied. She documents very different ways of interacting with children and denies the existence of a specific register for addressing children. She implies that having a specific register for talking to children is part of the idea of children as communicative partners which in Trackton, according to her, they are not:

> As they come to talk, they repeat, vary the language about them, and eventually use their language to work their way into the streams of speech about them . . . Once old enough to be accepted in ongoing talk, children are expected to answer questions comparing items, events and persons in their world, to respond creatively to question challenges, and to report their own feelings, desires, and experiences. Without specific explication, they must learn to see one thing in terms of another, to make metaphors of the world about them. (1983, p. 147)

The temptation to turn these two contrasting communities into a dimension onto which all communities can be fitted must be resisted; these are two of many ways of being and they do not map simplistically onto oral versus literate, or black versus white. These two quotes exemplify many of the points being made in this chapter. They demonstrate how children's language is located in social interaction in particular settings and how this can be very different in different subcultures; we will return to this study for further examples when examining how learning to be literate is also embedded in the environment of a particular culture.

The details are not just questions of language but they are tied into other aspects of human communication. I related adjusting one's speech to a child to the physical situation of holding the child and maintaining eye gaze. There is evidence that in cultures where this is very different, for example where a child is carried on the mother's back and is in constant physical contact, then there may be very different ways of speaking to the child. There may be much less spoken language, and much less verbal adjustment to the child. Bambi Schieffelin, in her detailed study of the Kaluli of Papua New Guinea, documents some very different ways of addressing children.[4] These are striking examples of the social embeddedness of language development and make us question what can be claimed as generalizations or universals of language acquisition.

There are several routine and repeated situations in children's lives: feeding, bathing, changing are often carried out by the same adult in the same environment at the same time of day. The communication in these situations becomes regular and repeated. As we will see, there is a parallel in reading events. However, again we should be very cautious about making any generalizations and accept that we have described one limited culture. In particular it assumes one child and one caregiver. In many cultures the mother is not the only or the primary caregiver. There are many situations around the world where children are brought up in larger extended families and where the mother has less physical involvement in child rearing. Elinor Ochs gives an example from Samoa where older children take charge of the active care of babies and carry out changing, bathing and so on, the very tasks which are at the centre of western language routines. Typical interaction is three-way, not two-way. Put simply, the young child wanting attention appeals to the mother, the mother instructs an older child and the older child attends to the baby's needs (Ochs, 1983, 1988).

It is very difficult to compare what I have referred to as mainstream learning with that in other cultures and subcultures, partly because of the great imbalance in the amount of research and the degree of documentation. There has been far more research on middle-class white English-speaking children and their development. Nevertheless, where we do have research from other cultures on these topics, striking differences are immediately apparent. Here I have given just brief examples of individual ethnographies in separate cultures; at the very least, they suggest the richness of possible interactions around children and the limitations of attempting to generalize from one culture. They represent a strong critique of theories of learning which attempt to generalize out from western middle-class culture. They also demonstrate the value of detailed studies of specific situations. Their work is certainly a strong challenge to much standard work on social interaction and learning. For our purposes here, these studies are important in underlining the embeddedness of learning in the cultural context and the variety of ways in which this is achieved. With an idea of the basis of learning to speak, the next chapter now turns to the significance of this approach for the learning of literacy.

10 Emergent literacy

Reading to Children
Literacy events
Writing
Knowing about literacy

The ideas from the previous chapter on learning can be summarized. There are several ways of learning, and learning is part of all activities. It involves a situation, an activity and participants. There are common social practices associated with learning. It often takes place in the context of regular repeated activities with support from others and with active participation. Knowledge is internalized, building upon previous knowledge, and children follow individual coherent paths of development. In this chapter I now want to apply these ideas to the development of literacy. The point of this chapter in ecological terms is to demonstrate the strong social basis of children's early learning of literacy. The starting point will be a well-known and seemingly straightforward phenomenon of reading a bedtime story to children.

Reading to children

Reading to children is an activity which is easily identifiable and obviously related to literacy. By obviously I mean that adults read to children and that it is taken for granted that reading to children is 'a good thing' and that it contributes to their learning to read. I will deal in detail with the example of parents reading a story aloud to young children at home, usually at bedtime. It is an identifiable literacy event, recognized both by parents and by researchers, and is even named as **story time**. One reason for examining story time is that as an activity it is very similar to the routine situations of earlier language development mentioned in the last chapter. It is also similar in some ways to common school reading activities. The study of story time provides a link then with earlier spoken development and with later school learning.

A great deal can be learned from examining what is involved in reading by taking a detailed look at this one type of literacy event. It is an event which is shared, where the book is central, and where there is reading 'for its own sake'. A preliminary point to emphasize about bedtime stories is that there is not one thing called 'reading to children'. It takes many forms and can mean many things. There are many ways of reading to children and these will vary according to the age of the child, the situation, the participants. Reading will vary according to the type of text, according to the way it is used in the interaction, and according to such details as whether a child is hearing the story for the first time. The children's contribution can vary and this too changes over time.[1] Children change in the ways they participate in this event.

First, I should state the obvious. In Britain and North America there are books for children, books to read to children and books for children to learn to read. This has not always been true historically and it is not true now in all cultures. Cultures differ in the ways they simplify life for those being inducted into it. In contemporary mainstream culture there are many such books. They vary according to the age of child they are intended for and they are different from books aimed at children learning to read in school. Some have no words, just pictures. Some have thick cardboard pages, some are made of plastic and float in the bath. Book shops commonly have separate sections for these children's books, and they are often written by adults who specialize in writing such books. It is important to point out the obvious since it becomes so naturalized that we can fail to see its significance. It also needs to be located in children's developing use of other media, as in Marsh (2005).

I will use a variety of published examples along with instances from my own notes and experiences. I use my own examples partly because there is not a great deal of published documentation of children's early practices around literacy, but also because this is what I know best, with details covering several years. I start with an example from the life of my own child, using notes I have made on his language development and literacy development. He was growing up happily in north-west England in the late 1980s with his mother and father. Within the family's physical space of a house he had his own personal space, he had his own room with his own bed. There was also a bookshelf in the room with a growing number of books on it. First, some notes made when he was five years four months old:

> The bedtime story is an essential part of a regular routine of going to bed at night. It has also been used to persuade him to sleep during the day when necessary. The story fits into a regular routine. Immediately before it he cleans his teeth and goes to the toilet; he has the story, and, soon after it, he turns over in bed, gets a good night kiss and, often, goes to sleep within a few minutes.

As any parent will know this is only an idealized version of what happens and there are many variations. Usually one of his parents read the story although occasionally it would be a visitor or baby-sitter. At this point some form of story time had been part of his life for over four years and it had its earlier roots in his mother singing him to sleep. He had experienced some 1,500 bedtime story times by then, with many more to come. If we add this to stories at other times of the day we get a much greater number. This obviously constitutes a large amount of experience and it has been estimated that some children may have received 6,000 stories before starting school (see, for example Wells, 1986, p. 158).

Of course story time changes gradually and systematically over time. One of the changes is that there is more variety and less ritual as children get older. I will continue with notes from my child and then turn to studies of other younger children. Here is a particular example when he was aged five years four months:

> Last night he had finished cleaning his teeth in the bathroom. I said 'Right, you go and choose a story and get into bed and I'll come and read it in a minute.' He went next door to his room. A few minutes later I came into his room. He had chosen a book . . . and was sitting in bed with it waiting. I asked him to move over to make room for me, as I regularly do, and then I squeezed next to him on the bed. We both held the book and I began reading. When I had finished and said good night to him he sat looking at the book by himself for a few minutes and when I returned 10 minutes later he was fast asleep, the book closed on the floor by the bed.

A few years previously I would have carried him from the bathroom to the bedroom, I would have chosen the book, and I would have held it while reading. I would have structured the event as I did whenever I put him to bed by letting the blind down, making sure his bed was ready and turning on the light. (This description may make the event sound very scripted and organized, but, whether or not the participants are aware of it, such a routine is one of the regular and repeated events that constitute many young children's lives.) The books used in this earlier period had pictures but no words. I do not have detailed records from then but the interactions at story time have been studied in detail by several researchers and I will give three examples. Obtaining and examining the detailed transcriptions of the language is painstaking work but is revealing of what actually goes on and how it changes over time. The first is of a young child (Ninio and Bruner, 1978, p. 6):

Mother:	Look. [Attentional vocative]
Child:	(Touches picture)
Mother:	What are those? [Query]
Child:	(Vocalises and smile)
Mother:	Yes, they are rabbits. [Feedback and label]

The dialogue continues but we have enough here to discuss. Such interactions are very typical of early interaction and have been observed repeatedly. The adult is structuring the whole interaction and even turning the child's sounds into answers which act as turns in the conversation. The adult is creating the child's meanings. The child is learning to take part in a simple conversation. There are several alternative ways of analysing it, for example the conversation contains within it the seeds of the very common cycle found in classroom talk of getting attention, asking a question, providing an answer, and giving feedback. This little pattern is a common building block of spoken interaction.

Here is another example, from a child more than a year older than the first child, and it is clear that the child is participating in a different way. The mother is about to read a story. The mother's reading from the story book is in italics (Wells, 1985, p. 244):

Mother:	. . . *There's Eeyore. What's happened to him?*
Child:	I don't know.
Mother:	What do you think's happening to him?
Child:	He's getting cold.

> *Mother*:   He's getting cold. Why is he getting cold?
> *Child*:   I don't know.
> *Mother*:   I think it's the snow all over him – don't you think? [Short
>   pause] (*One day* . . .) [Starts to read]

All this conversation takes place before the mother actually starts reading the story. The mother is reading a story, but there is something else going on as well. They are talking about the story. The mother is involving the child in the story, even before they begin to read. Finally, here is a glimpse of a child aged two and a half years (Teale, 1984, p. 112):

> *Mother*:   (. . . *Come, look at what we grew. And we have so much, enough for us and all our friends too.*) What are you doing?
> *Child*:   I'm eating 'em.
> *Mother*:   Are you gobbling them all up?
> *Child*:   Uh-huh.
> *Mother*:   Can you tell me what some of those vegetables are? Can you show me where the tomatoes are? [Child points to tomatoes] And where's the lettuce . . .

The conversation continues. Once again they are talking about the story but they are doing more than this. The mother is expanding upon it, together they are bringing the child into the story and relating the story to everyday life. It is not necessarily the mother who initiates the interactions. Sometimes it is the child. We can see that this is not purely a story being told by one person to another, rather we have a story around a story, a narrative which is being **coconstructed** by the participants.

What can children get out of this regular repeated situation? They can learn many things about life, about adults, about the family, about knowledge and how to acquire it, about human interaction, about social practices. Here the discussion will keep to what they can learn about language and particularly about literacy.

The literacy event of story time provides a great opportunity for children to learn about language. As with the examples earlier of changing, washing and feeding, they get a chance to observe and participate in a regular and repeated situation where the language use has a great deal of contextual support. The most obvious area of language in story time is the language of the text; note that it is written language being spoken aloud. The child is hearing written language. In listening to stories children are exposed to the rhythms of written language being spoken. They are listening to extended discourse and they learn the structure of a story. They can attend to the function and structure of language. A broader range of grammatical structures and much wider vocabulary is available in stories than in ordinary everyday speech.

The language associated with story time is not just the text: equally important is the talk around the text, and this too is often richer in variety and complexity of linguistic structure than other everyday talk. One aspect of the language of story time is that children are exposed to a way of talking about language. There is talk to do with reading and writing – this is the metalanguage of literacy. Language is referred to in the discussions about the story. Adults might say 'Do you know what that means?', 'That's a new word', 'This is a long story'. In story time the written is embedded in the spoken and grows out of it. Again, here is an example of written and spoken language being intertwined.

Note that in these example it is spoken language around a written story. There is something special about this situation and it has grown up over time for the child. The event may be regular and repeated but it should be clear from the examples that there are many different forms of spoken interaction which can take place around an open book. To begin with when children are very young there is no story. Children's first books are often just pictures and first story times may consist mainly of the adult naming unconnected pictures. The labelling of objects in a picture – a symbolic representation of the world – is very similar to the naming activities with real objects. One can point to and name real cats and dogs, toy cats and dogs and two-dimensional drawn representations of cats and dogs. Pictures are not the first symbolic representations children will have encountered; dolls, plastic ducks and cars two inches long are all symbolic. However, there may be something crucial in the transition from toy to book: one cannot hold, feel or play with the object. The object moves from concrete to visual representation; what one can do with it moves from action to reflection. A child can do things with dolls as well as talk about them; with a picture the child can only talk about it. The next transition is from picture to written word.[2]

Whether oral or written, stories are important. Adults and children can do many things with the story: they can play and do pretend reading; they can memorize it word for word; they can do different voices for different characters; they can talk about the story and go beyond the present, go beyond the concerns of much early interaction with the here and now. Having a sense of story is a way of making sense of one's own life. It often starts with pictures and is related to using toys for play and fantasy. Children use stories to test out reality, to explore possibilities, and to go beyond the here and now, to the past and to the future. Stories can provide a way for children to understand other worlds, and to fantasize about what is not possible. The sense of story can come from the spoken stories in our culture as well as from the written ones, and solely from oral stories in a culture which emphasizes them.

Turning now to what is special about literacy, children are also learning about the nature of reading. First of all books are for reading. They are different from toys and other objects which are played with and manipulated. There is something special which marks out books as different from the other objects which children come across. Catherine Snow and Anat Ninio describe the distinctiveness of books as one of the 'contracts of literacy' which children learn to enter into, and they describe several instances of children learning that books are for reading, and not for biting, chewing or throwing. Of course it is more complex than this, there is not one thing books are for; as we have seen, even saying 'books are for reading' raises many complicated queries, as there are many ways of reading. Reading to children also provides a general familiarity with books of all kinds including instruction books, catalogues and magazines. Children learn about the mysteries of incidental parts of the book like the index and the small print of the title page. They learn about the functions of literacy, how print can be turned into words, and that one function is reading stories. Another of the contracts which children learn is how the picture, and later the story, constrains the topic; the story book comes to mediate children's experience. (For a list of the contracts of literacy see Snow and Ninio, 1986.)

During story time children can observe reading strategies and infer processes. There is, of course, a limit to what you can find out about reading processes by observing someone else doing it. Nevertheless, children are exposed to the rhythms of someone reading out loud and they may be able to notice when the reader stops and starts, how the story is broken into parts. In relation to the book the child may observe things like directionality, following the words of a story and turning the page.

The important things the child can learn are probably more subtle than this. There is not one way of reading. Reading is not extracting *the* meaning from a text; rather there are different ways of taking from the text, of taking different meanings from the text. Story time supports certain ways of interacting where meanings are created. These dialogues are the social bases of thinking which the child internalizes. In this way literacy becomes implicated in the creation of ways of thinking. As an example of this, one aspect of taking from the text is the way we learn to use our knowledge of the world to make sense of and do things with the text. We can see instances of this in the questioning used by the mother in the second short example of talk around a text above, where the mother asks *why*, 'Why is Eeyore getting cold?' To answer this the child has to draw on his or her general knowledge of the world to do with why living things get cold. Marilyn Cochran-Smith (1984) refers to this sort of dialogue as life-to-text interaction, bringing one's life experiences to bear on the text. Often the ways of questioning used by adults can provide particular examples of life-to-text interaction for the child. Similarly, the third example provides a different way of taking from the text, it shows text-to-life interaction, where the story is related to the child's life and the child is brought into the dialogue around the story.

More generally, children can learn attitudes and values associated with reading. Story time is typically a warm, friendly and safe experience. Time is set aside for it and it is an intimate event where children have an adult's complete attention and it may be the children's only time sharing an activity alone with an adult. It can have an important function within the family where the story is an integral part of the reward system used by the family in bringing up the child. A child can be told 'If you want a story, you will have to get to bed quickly'. Also if there have been arguments, story time can be a time for making peace, for being friendly and sympathetic. For the child who is learning, presumably these situations invoke other powerful mechanisms of learning mentioned at the beginning of the last chapter, such as the child identifying with the parent and the parent acting as a role model. Here and elsewhere the child sees what the adult gets out of reading. Part of the point of a story can be that it gives the child something pleasant to think about when going to sleep.

What is going on in terms of the theory of the previous chapter on learning? Initially scaffolding or support is provided by the situation and the adult's structuring of it. The adult mediates the child's behaviour. Children change the ways they participate, gradually taking over and developing their own practices. For example, there are many steps to becoming an avid book reader. First of all in story time, children choose their own book, initiate the interaction, and finally do it totally on their own. Children move to reading their own comic, to browsing through a book alone and finding information from the toy catalogue. Interactions become internalized. Reading is a shared experience which becomes a private experience as the child becomes older. This can go in several directions. The child can become lost in a book and enclosed in their own world, learning how reading is a way of being private in a public place, on a beach, in a bus. This is one development in the different sorts of reading children acquire. At the same time children can continue to develop much social reading with their peers around catalogues, magazines, and so on.

Obviously there is a lot more involved in reading to children than one might have first imagined. Much of it can be related to learning to read. As there are such different ways of reading to children the effects are not going to be straightforward. Chapter 12 includes a discussion of how reading to children might be significant for learning to read in school and how different aspects of reading to children might have different effects or be taken up differently by schools.

Literacy events

Story time is clearly to do with literacy, but there is no need to think of it as being the most frequent or the most important example of the literacy practices surrounding the developing child. There may be other activities within the home where literacy is the central concern, for example when people spend time reading, either separately or together. It is also true that literacy is embedded in much of children's play and many games can be construed as preparations for literacy. In addition there are magnetic alphabet letters on the refrigerator or radiator and early magazines and comics with letter and word games. These are all literacy-focused activities. However, in this section I want to concentrate on the significance of those activities where literacy is not the main concern, but where it has a more incidental role. Points made earlier can still be emphasized, such as that literacy is embedded in oral interaction, that there are different ways of learning and that learning is a component of all activities.

The family is an ecological niche in which literacy survives, is sustained, and flourishes. In contemporary society literacy is part of the web of family life. In addition to events like bedtime story reading where literate activities are central, many everyday activities invoke the use of literacy in some way. There is a great deal of print in the average house: it is on packaging, notice boards, instructions, junk mail, as well as magazines and books. Even in households without books there is still other environmental print. The activities of cooking, eating, shopping, keeping records, celebrating all make use of literacy in some way. Literacy is not the aim of these activities, their aim is something else – to survive, to consume, to act in the world – and literacy is an integral part of achieving these other aims. The aim of these activities is not to teach children literacy and with many of them the activities are not particularly for the child. They may be for the benefit of adults and have no obvious relevance to the child. Nevertheless, as with other family activities the children are brought into these activities.

Literacy is an essential part of these everyday activities and in many ways, in mainstream culture the household is structured around literacy, literacy mediates family activities. There are many ways of putting this. Heath locates literacy in the ways families use space and time and describes how literate traditions:

> . . . are interwoven in different ways with oral uses of language, ways of negotiating meaning, deciding on action, and achieving status. Patterns of using reading and writing in each community are interde-pendent with ways of using space (having bookshelves, decorating walls, displaying telephone numbers), and using time (bedtime, meal hours, and homework sessions). (Heath, 1983, p. 234)

I also like the vision of literacy flowing through the household, it pours in through the letterbox and goes out through the waste bin, hopefully to be recycled: in between, adults act on it, use it, change it (see Leichter, 1984, p. 40). I will concentrate for the moment on how this impinges on the child.

The print environment to which children in a range of Western cultures are exposed at home is extensive. There are studies of how children are surrounded by literacy.[3] Hope Jensen Leichter (1984, p. 41) lists the 'artefacts' relevant to literacy identified in an extensive observational study of literacy in the home. Her litany of some of the artefacts extends to 50 items, making a prose poem (and do not cover screen-based artefacts). They include 'Books; dictionaries; atlases and maps; encyclopaedias; school work books, reports and tests . . . postcards; political fliers; coupons;

laundry slips; cookbooks . . . diaries; Christmas cards; gift lists; record albums; sewing patterns; baseball cards; sweatshirts; photograph albums; identification cards; and tickets.' This is one of those lists which is never complete as each study finds more examples. In our own research we have made similar lists and are constantly adding to them.

The home is a particularly important domain in that it is the site for such a wide range of activities and several studies of children's emergent literacy have investigated this domain. In one of these studies of children's uses of literacy at home, William Teale wanted to identify the different forms of literacy around the children and he categorized the uses in terms of separate domains of activity, such as daily living routines, entertainment, school-related activity, religion. In each activity a different form of literacy was apparent. The full list was: daily living routines; entertainment, which was further subdivided; school-related activity; work, such as the Avon lady visiting the house; religion; interpersonal communication; participating in information networks; story-book time; and literacy for teaching. So within domains there can be subdomains, and often these can be broken down again.[4]

In some examples the child is primarily an observer. For example, the child can observe the different roles adults take in the home, such as who gets to read the newspaper first, who opens the mail; and sometimes the children may be excluded from activities: 'Leave me alone, I'm reading the paper', 'I'll be with you in a minute, I have some bills to pay'. Here the child can learn about literacy and know it is of value to adults, such as when the child wants attention and the adult's head is buried in a book. This is certainly important. Both observing a social interaction and participating in a social interaction contribute to literacy learning. However, I am assuming here, without proof, that participation is a more powerful form of learning. I am there-fore giving more attention to what often happens: that children are incorporated into family activities.

Outside the home, the child is in a world of signs, notices and advertisements. Shopping is another activity which in mainstream culture is often regular and repeated, where children take part with adults, and where literacy is involved but is not the main aim of the activity. Child care and shopping often go together and a local supermarket can be the scene of much induction into literacy. There are several strategies for juggling these two seemingly incompatible activities. One attempted strategy of sitting the child quietly in the trolley and getting on with the shopping only works with a few children at some ages and for short periods of time. What actually happens is that children are incorporated into the activities. They are asked what they want, they are asked to fetch goods which they have to recognize and they comment on what is being purchased. Just like the activities described earlier, this could be expressed in terms of adults structuring the situation by providing scaffolding for the child to learn by. This is an example of an everyday situation where the child can see what the adult achieves in practical terms with literacy.[5]

The active participation of the child in all this can be seen. Children want to know who the mail is for in the morning. At the supermarket they want to choose particular cereals and avoid other ones. They want to know on the calendar on the notice board when someone's birthday is approaching. They want to know from the newspaper when a particular television programme is going to be on. In all these activities children can see how reading mediates the activity, how they have to go via reading to get the results they want, how they have to go via someone who reads. Reading mediates even to the extent of getting in the way of the activities, it takes time. The adult stops to read the instructions before assembling a new toy, or starting a new card game, or to read the recipe before cooking a chocolate cake with the child. As with the story reading, above, there is a gradual shift as the child takes control of these activities and learns to get information from the calendar, to identify the desired breakfast cereal, and to find out from the listings what is on television.

The examples so far have been of households where literacy has a clear role. Even in seemingly less literate households, literacy has a significant role. Where researchers have taken very simple measures, such as the number of books in the home, it is very easy to find wide disparities – and to be shaken in one's literate world by the high number of homes containing almost no books. However, all homes in contemporary society are touched by literacy. There is still consumer packaging to get through, bills to pay, junk mail to sort and various official forms and notices to deal with. Junk mail cannot be avoided; you have to do something with it and people develop individual solutions to cope with the continuous tide (see Taylor, 1983, p. 27).

It is not a question of households being literate or not. It is not adequate to characterize this as a simple dimension of amount of literacy. What we have seen in several studies and most clearly in Heath's work is that households are part of whole communities which are oriented to literacy differently. This is not just to do with literacy but is part of the whole dynamics of the households. I will return to this in the chapter on schooling when investigating how these different orientations to literacy fare in school. It is important to emphasize that in places like Heath's Trackton, despite being unlike mainstream culture and being in many ways oral, literacy still impinges a great deal. Having said that, there may still be households and communities where children are getting little or no experience of handling books or holding pencils and are not being inducted into schools' 'ways with words'.[6]

To get more idea of how literacy is used in the home, I want to turn to studies which have listed the most common uses of reading and writing in the home. First, in her study of three communities in the United States, Shirley Heath provides such lists of the most common uses of reading and of writing. For Trackton, starting with the most common, she lists four main uses of reading (1983, p. 198):

Instrumental uses, 'to accomplish practical goals of daily life', such as reading price tags and street signs.

Social-interactional/recreational uses, 'to maintain social relationships, make plans, and introduce topics for discussion and story-telling'. This includes reading greeting cards, letters and newspaper features.

News-related uses, 'reading to learn about third parties or distant events', such as reading local news items or school circulars.

Confirmational uses, 'reading to gain support for attitudes or beliefs already held'. This would be reading the Bible or car sales brochures.

Similarly for writing, different uses in this community are listed (1983, p. 199):

Memory aids, 'writing to serve as a reminder for the writer, and, only occasionally, others'. Examples are writing telephone numbers and notes on calendars.

Substitutes for oral messages, 'when direct oral communication was not possible or would prove embarrassing', such as notes to school, greeting cards and letters.

Financial, 'to record numerals and to write out amounts and accompanying notes'. Writing cheques would be an example of this.

Public records, 'writing to announce the order of the church services'. This category includes other report-writing and record-keeping associated with the church.

This approach can provide an idea of the range of literacy practices in a community. The four uses of reading in Trackton, listed above, are also found in Roadville, the second community which Heath studied, although they differ in order of frequency. In addition social-interactional uses are separated from recreational, which become 'recreational/educational'. In the third community Heath studies, the 'townspeople', black and white middle-class people living in the suburbs, recreational is separate and there is an additional category of 'critical/educational'. Similarly with writing there are differences between the three communities. In Roadville there is no category of public records but there is one of social-interactional. With the townspeople there are Roadville's four categories with the additional category of 'expository'.

In their study of inner-city families in the north-eastern United States, Denny Taylor and Catherine Dorsey-Gaines (1988, pp. 124–90) compare their work with Heath's. For uses of reading in their inner-city neighbourhood, Shay Avenue, they list the four uses of reading found in Trackton, with the additional uses of 'socio-historical', 'financial' and 'environmental'. With writing they have the uses of writing found in Trackton, except for public records, and there are several additional uses of writing: instrumental, autobiographical, recreational, creative, educational, work-related, and environmental.

These lists are useful in giving an overview of the sort of activities which are most common in any one community, and when comparing communities, such as Heath's Trackton and Roadville, it is possible to identify uses of reading or writing which are absent from a community. However, there is a limit to the usefulness of listing functions since these lists overlap a great deal: reading a letter can be news-related and socio-interactional at the same time, for example, and much writing can be a memory aid at the same time as substituting for an oral message. Also, the various categories people have used seem to have different statuses, so that 'financial' seems to be a different sort of category from 'memory aid'. When looked at closely, seemingly obvious categories such as 'creative' and 'autobiographical' are surprisingly hard to pin down and define as particular sorts of writing. In our local literacies research we tried to avoid listing uses of writing. Concentrating on people's purposes in writing, we identified three broad areas of writing in the home: writing to maintain the household, writing to maintain communication, and personal writing, but even here there can be overlap and potential problems of definition.

Writing

The discussion so far has focused mainly on reading. Another direction for going beyond the example of story time is to consider children's early writing. There is much less writing than reading in the home: there is less writing by adults and, parallel to this, less pre-school writing by children has been reported.[7] The topic of early writing is usually treated as a separate subject with its own researchers and its own promoters. Several points can be made here which are parallel to those made about reading, showing how writing is embedded in everyday practices and that it draws upon similar forms of learning as speaking and reading.

Although there has been more work on reading, several researchers have observed children learning to write before they go to school. Some situate it back where children first learn to speak. For example, Carol Chomsky (1972) studied children who began the rudiments of writing as they learned to speak; she argues that in principle there is no difference between speaking and writing and that they can develop in harmony. Note that writing and speaking are parallel in that they are both ways of producing language. Other researchers concentrate on the tools of writing, pens and pencils, and they see the roots of writing, for some children at least, as being in drawing; and articles in Hall and Robinson (1996) concentrate on the development of punctuation.

Charles Read and others after him have analysed children's 'invented spellings', spellings which children spontaneously make up with little help from adults. These invented spellings demonstrate that young children teaching themselves to write do many coherent things and are actively making hypotheses about the nature of language; what are often taken to be errors of spelling are in fact coherent responses to a problem. For example, the child who writes YOT for 'yacht' is making an intelligent guess based on knowledge of the sound system of English, and is coming up with a more reasonable spelling than that which is actually utilized in the spelling system. Choosing to spell 'dragon' as JRAGIN, 'ship' as SEP, and 'fishing' as FEHEG also reflect sophisticated knowledge of the English sound system (see Read, 1971, 1986; Barton, 1992).

This active hypothesis making can be seen in other aspects of the writing system, not just spelling. Children make hypotheses about word boundaries, for example, how and where to split up the flow of writing into words. Some solutions are right for our writing system, such as leaving spaces between words. Others, like a dot between each word, sometimes chosen by children for a few months for instance, serve their purpose. They are not the solution chosen by our writing system. Nevertheless, these are intelligent guesses – and with this example it is certainly a plausible one: there have been writing systems where dots have been placed between words and today there are some computer word-processing packages which indicate the spaces between words with dots on the screen. Similarly some children when first writing English choose the syllable as the basic unit rather than the alphabetic segment, a reasonable choice, but not the one chosen in our writing system. The point is that the children are acting sensibly when they make guesses about how the writing system works.[8]

Learning to write involves two aspects associated with the two meanings of the word 'write', learning the mechanics of writing, or becoming a scribe, and deciding what to write, or becoming an author. I will explore these two distinct meanings of the English word 'write' more in the next chapter. For the moment, one problem with learning to write for young children and one which often constitutes a barrier for them as it stops them going any further concerns the practical, technical aspect of physically making the marks on the paper with a pen or pencil. Children and others experience the sheer difficulty of holding a pencil and forming letters, together with the unnecessary extra confusions of the orientation of letters. (The symmetry of *b p q d*, for instance, which many children find a problem, arises from haphazard historical development.) For all writers, but especially for the struggling beginning writer, there is the excruciating amount of time it takes, being so much slower than the thoughts to be expressed. This all gets in the way of expressing meaning.

The slowness of writing may seem to children to be intrinsic to the act of writing, but again it is tied in with the social practices around writing. The choice of writing implements is a social decision; the development of the pencil is a piece of technology as much as any modern computer technology. Now, with computers which have simple keyboards and printers, it is so easy and neat to form letters if one has access to the technology. These may have a great effect of lessening the physical difficulty of writing, along with further effects on the way children compose what they are writing. Such developments are changing the possibilities for children even more.

Turning now to children at home, what writing is there in the home? What are the literacy practices to do with writing which children observe and participate in? As I have already pointed out there may not be very much writing in the home. Nevertheless there is some. Typical writing activities involve notes, messages, calendars, paying bills, writing shopping lists. These are often public activities in the home and we can examine how children are incorporated into these activities. There has been little detailed study of this. Clark's (1976) study of children who could read and write when they arrived at school was retrospective. Much of the invented spelling research such as Read's work studied the products, the written messages containing invented spellings, and, in order to stress how these are invented by children, often researchers have provided little detail of how the activities are structured by adults. Nevertheless they are created within the family, and within particular social practices.

The first writing is often structured and supported by adults. In my notes of my own child's first writing, his own name, Tom, was important, and his first writing was the capital letter T when signing his own name on greetings cards and the bottom of letters. At first he wrote a T guided by an adult's hand, and later his own T and then the full name. Initially the letter T was a symbol for the word Tom. Other people have observed this gradual development, and pointed to the importance of the child's own name in early writing.

Children's early writing is often based upon the sort of things which adults use writing for in the home: signing names on greetings cards, making notices, sending messages. Children often ask adults to write words. Early on children do not necessarily want to write stories, but writing comes into games, making tickets for a show, or inventing an application form to join a club, adding words to pictures. Once again, early writing provides an example of children learning first through social interaction, and later internalizing their knowledge. In addition, the activity which the writing is part of is more important than the writing itself. The writing has a purpose. To take an example from my notes, for one child these purposes were putting his name on his door to demonstrate ownership; helping a less literate child fill in a toy club application form; and writing a note with a friend:

KNOW I WAD LAYC TOO GO HOME

This message, 'now I would like to go home', had a purpose in that this new friend was too shy to approach any adult. This new form of communication avoided face-to-face-interaction. This example is also a good illustration of children's early spellings: note the combination of conventional spellings, such as *home*, invented spellings, such as *layc* and half-learnt spellings such as *know*.

Children's writing develops gradually and some researchers, such as Ferreiro and Teberosky (1979), plot this development as a set of stages which children go through, starting out with drawing, and documenting children's gradually increasing co-ordination. I have some difficulty in fitting children I have observed and read about into a neat set of stages (see also Hall, 1987, p. 52 on these stages). Rather, the conclusions I would draw are parallel to what I have said about the development of reading and learning in general: that children actively undertake writing, that it serves other purposes for them and that they follow individual coherent paths of development. No less than reading, writing is a social practice similar to those described in earlier chapters. See Kress (1997) for more on the early development of writing.

Knowing about literacy

As a slightly different way of expressing the subject matter of this chapter we can examine children's developing awareness of spoken and written language. As part of learning to speak and learning the communication practices of their culture, children also learn some awareness of language. Children gradually use language to communicate on a broader range of topics in a wider variety of contexts. They use language, among other things, to demand, enquire and comment on themselves and their surroundings. Part of this context, part of the world to be commented on, is of course language itself, the child's own language and the language of others. So the child also acts upon, comments on and enquires about language. This happens in many different ways. For example a child at the age of two and a half years, when grammatical development is just taking off and vocabulary is expanding explosively, showed awareness in several ways; for example, he would ask for the names of objects he did not know and ask for clarification if he did not understand: 'What you say?' 'What she say?' He could also role-play, using appropriate voices for, among others, ticket inspectors and doctors (an example from Barton, 1986, p. 69). The early age at which this begins is often surprising to people.

It is clear from these and many other examples that at this age, and earlier, children demonstrate some knowledge or awareness of language beyond straightforward communication. Language use and language awareness go along together. As the child develops, awareness is closely bound up with acquiring literacy in contemporary culture. It is in learning to read and write, where language is explicitly taught, that adults talking to children reflect upon, comment on and draw attention to language. Once again we see the emphasis on the importance of spoken language in the development of written language. Some awareness is seen as a prerequisite for learning to read, while further awareness results from exposure to literacy: we learn about language by learning to read and write. Literacy instruction is, of course, only one source of awareness and insight into language. Exposure to another language, for example, seems a reasonable stimulus to awareness (as documented, for example, by Slobin, 1978). As we will see when we return to this when talking about schooling and the literacy practices associated with it, awareness is tied up with particular ways of teaching literacy.

For the child who has been immersed in the world of spoken and written language, learning to read and write and relying primarily on the written word involves a significant reorientation to language. Treated by itself, written language exists in a different modality, one which we can regard as being more tangible; unlike speech, writing does not disappear as soon as it is uttered, but it remains there open to inspection and available for all to see. Writing provides an explicit analysis of the language into (in English) letters, words and sentences. The child learning to read has to come to terms with language in this new modality. It is here that awareness has a role: the teaching of reading and writing normally assumes considerable awareness, and it is in acquiring literacy that the learner has to focus on language as an object independent of the medium of speech.[9] Having said this, it is important not to overdramatize the leap from spoken to written for the child. As we have shown in this chapter, the child is exposed to literacy from an early age. Meeting a reading book in the school classroom is not such a unique and strange event for many children, but there have been preparations for it for many years in literacy practices and in oral language use.

There has been a considerable amount of research on children's gradually developing knowledge of language and its relation to learning to read and write. There is also work on their knowledge of literacy practices, with studies showing young children not knowing if their parents can read, or not being clear about which part of books are read, nor being able to tell writing from drawing or scribble. All this awareness develops gradually.[10] The descriptions of home practices earlier in this chapter and the evidence of research on awareness suggests that, rather than asking whether children can read and write when they enter school, we want to ask what children know about literacy. This is particularly important for nonmainstream communities where teachers need to take account of the different knowledge children from different cultures bring. Gujarati-speaking children from a Moslem community in Britain, for example, will have been exposed to different language and literacy practices from children from mainstream culture.[11] Children's knowledge of these practices needs to be taken account of.

This early awareness of language and literacy is important as children try to sort out what sort of social practice literacy is. It also has a role in their developing thinking. Awareness is a crucial aspect of the approach to learning of the previous chapter. Children's awareness of self and of their thinking develops. The mind is socially constructed: this can be seen as children learn to talk about their thought processes. There is a remarkable time around four years of age, when having sorted out the sounds to get the words, and having sorted out some grammar to get some structures to convey meanings, the child creates awareness, a sense of identity, and begins to refer to him or herself and to comment on his or her mental faculties. When first uttered, these utterances recorded from a four year old are stunning statements: 'I said it in my brain but I did not say it to you.' 'When I say something, do I say it two times?'

The idea that mental activity is socially constructed is important when examining the relationship of literacy and thought, studying children's developing awareness provides further evidence that thinking cannot be seen as some 'given' activity which literacy is imposed upon. Early awareness is what is built upon as children come to learn to use different literacies and to develop critical awareness of literacy. Once again it is not writing which structures thought; it is social organization which does, and writing, or rather uses of writing, are part of that social organization.

11 Public definitions of literacy

The skill of reading
Writer as scribe and as author
The literary view of literacy
The professional writer

Having discussed home literacy practices and children's participation in them, there are two directions to pursue. First in this chapter I want to examine broader public definitions of literacy used in the media and in public debate, and then in the next chapter I will turn to schooling and literacy practices at school. I will identify two distinct discourses, the **skills discourse** of learning to read and write and the **literary discourse** associated with an elite view of literature and of culture. These are two common ways of talking about literacy in public discussion: they are powerful views, they are extremely prevalent and are part of media perceptions of reading and writing and what schools ought to do. They are sustained and nourished by various social institutions. There are clashes associated with these views of literacy in public debate and at all levels of education, from initial reading, through to advanced training. They support powerful public discourses about education.

The skill of reading

One of the most powerful metaphors for literacy in public discussions of reading and writing is that of literacy as a set of skills. It underpins the way politicians and the media discuss literacy issues. Behind discussions and headlines on falling standards, the need to improve the teaching of reading and the 'problem' of adult literacy, there is often the metaphor of skills. In this section I want to examine the roots of the skills metaphor in methods of teaching reading in schools, and discuss the extent to which it can be incorporated into an ecological view of literacy which emphasizes practices.

The idea of skills derives from psychology and its use was originally unrelated to language and reading. Today the skills metaphor is applied to reading and to many forms of learning, and it fits in well with general cultural moves towards measuring and monitoring human activities. Briefly, when applied to reading, it is an autonomous view of literacy: that reading is a set of skills which can be broken into parts and taught and tested. There is an emphasis on the mechanics of learning to read and the method of teaching is thought of as being of paramount importance. Learning to read is accomplished by breaking the skill into components starting from the simple and gradually building up. (In fact the historical origin of the meaning of the word 'skill' is 'to separate'.) This leads on to the notion of there being clear and discrete stages in learning, with the separate skills learned in a linear order. Underlying this, deep down, is the organizing idea of there being only one way of learning to read.[1]

As an extreme example of a stage approach to learning, it might be thought that there is a fixed order with learning mathematics. In fact, this is only true within a social conception of the subject. There is not one mathematics, rather any form of mathematics is socially constructed. New approaches to mathematics, such as teaching base systems to young children throw out the idea that there is some cognitive demand for a precise ordering. Another example of the social basis of these purported orderings is the way in which technological change affects what needs to be learned. In the past century log tables, slide rules and calculators have affected what children need to learn in mathematics and in what order. A more significant issue is whether the teaching of mathematics can keep pace, and also whether parents and public opinion understand the changes.

There are several ways in which the components of reading are isolated in the skills view of learning. Learning to read is seen as something individuals do and it is primarily an individual accomplishment. Secondly, it is taught as a separate subject which takes two or three years, and once it has been taught it is finished with. It is very hard for a child of nine years who has not learned to read to get support. Also, in the traditional

view, it is assumed reading and reading acquisition does not go on anywhere else except in the classroom and that it should not go on anywhere
else. Schools are seen as the natural place for learning to read. Until
recently it was a common view that parents should not be involved in
their child's education, and that helping a pre-school child with reading
and writing was harmful. While there is some shift in this view, schools
are still set up to teach children away from families and home life.

Another part of this is the idea that the age of five years is the right time
for beginning to learn to read. In Britain and North America, five years is
seen developmentally, that is psychologically or even physiologically, as
being the right time for learning to read, despite the fact that in several
other countries children are not taught to read until the age of seven or
eight years. This approach has been tied in with the idea of there being
precise physiologically based critical periods in children's development
which provide the precise window of opportunity for particular areas of
learning. The problems which arise in deviating from this idea of a precise
age for learning probably have their roots more in the management
of the classroom than in literacy. Such views are questioned by cross-
cultural comparisons, by pre-school literacy studies, and by ethnographic
studies of literacy, referred to in earlier chapters. The skills approach sets
up pre-reading as a stage just before reading, and it does not go back far
enough. It sets the prerequisites for successful learning to read as being
in a set of cognitive tasks with little room for the other factors which we
have been discussing here.

It is worth pointing out the seemingly obvious fact that there are
theories of how to teach reading, there are different methods, and there
is the belief, perhaps constructed by the media and publishers, that choice
of method is crucial. There are special books for learning to read, where
theories of what is simple are made explicit on the printed page. For
initial reading print is bigger; there is little on each page; some books
break lines with meaning, others do not; some favour illustrations, others
avoid them; some view simple words as being words which are frequent
in English, others see simple words as being those with regular spelling
patterns. However, they have in common the idea of starting from the
simple and moving gradually to the complex. In stating that there are
special books for learning to read I am apparently stating the obvious,
but it is not in fact obvious that there should be special books for learning to read. Historically, many people have started with the pages of the
Bible and have learned to read with an everyday book. It is salutary to

observe that children learn to read with all these methods and in fact there are not obvious large differences in the effectiveness of the particular methods which are currently being disputed. The choice of method is probably not that important in influencing whether or not most children learn to read.

The skills view of reading is closely tied in with the need to assess. Schools are required to be able to sort, grade, test and evaluate. Apart from the workplace, this is not something we do elsewhere in our everyday life in any precise way. It has its roots in intelligence testing, which was invented to sort children into different streams of schooling in order to prepare them for different jobs. Testing is always tied in with particular methods of instruction, and methods of testing strongly influence what is taught and how it is taught. In many parts of the world including North America, for example, there is a grade system for measuring reading, which is incomprehensible to the outsider – just as other systems presumably are incomprehensible to North Americans. Reading grades are defined in terms of the needs of testing. The only definition of grades when one gets beyond the earliest grades, in terms of external reference, is that grades refer to what a child in a particular class is expected to achieve. In the later grades, and probably the earlier ones too, the levels are not measuring the narrow view of reading they purport to but the practices of schooling, including vocabulary, general knowledge and ways of meaning.

I want to leave this here as I do not want to spend too much time criticizing. I will return to skills when discussing functional approaches in adult literacy. For the moment some comments on the relation of a skills approach to a practice account may be of value: I see a practice account as providing a broader way of conceptualizing literacy, one which can be applied to more and more areas as the theory is articulated more, even to areas which may seem challenging for a social account, such as testing, helping children with reading difficulties, or understanding form filling. Skills is one of those words which inevitably carries with it the burden of its past. It has its own intertextual links associated with functional approaches to literacy and ties in with a whole ideology about literacy and learning. Using skills often suggests you can abstract some neutral techniques which people possess, located somewhere inside the person, which are the same across all situations, and which can be added to piecemeal.

However, the notion of skills may be useful when examining a specific situation. One approach may be to see skills as situated within practices.

This goes back to Scribner and Cole's formulation that skills are located within practices and that the practices determine the skills. It is worth quoting what they say about the relation of practices and skills in detail:

> By a practice we mean a recurrent, goal-directed sequence of activities using a particular technology and particular systems of knowledge. We use the term 'skills' to refer to the co-ordinated sets of actions involved in applying this knowledge in particular settings. A practice, then, consists of three components: technology, knowledge and skills. We can apply this concept to spheres of activity that are predominantly conceptual (for example, the practice of law) as well as to those that are predominantly sensory-motor (for example, the practice of weaving). All practices involve interrelated tasks that share common tools, knowledge base, and skills. But we may construe them more or less broadly to refer to entire domains of activity around a common object (for example, law) or to more specific endeavors within such domains (cross-examination or legal research). (Scribner and Cole, 1981, p. 236)

Within this approach, skills always exist in a social context. Having accepted skills, it may still be that individual skills cannot be identified in a complex task, but that they are integrated in an indivisible way.[2] In Vygotsky's terms, reading is part of higher psychological processes; it is based upon lower order skills, but is not necessarily divisible into them.[3]

Writer as scribe and as author

In everyday life writing is often evaluated in terms of neatness of handwriting and correctness of spelling. A good writer is someone who is neat. This is a common view in society and I see the source of it as being in schools' view of literacy. To give one example of a woman recounting her childhood at the beginning of the twentieth century: 'Yes, I used to be a good writer at one time! In them days it was two fingers on your pen. The teacher would hit you if you only had one finger on your pen. The down stroke had to be thick. You had to do it properly!' This is one view of what is meant by writing where the emphasis is on the visual appearance of the writing. This view of handwriting of course depends on where along the social scale or education scale one is positioned, so that highly educated people such as academics and doctors can flout the conventions of handwriting at will, something which has been referred to as the arrogance of cultivated illegibility.

The word 'writing' has the problem mentioned already that it is ambiguous in English, carrying with it two distinct meanings, so that the question 'did you write this yourself?' is ambiguous. It can be asking about the handwriting or it can be asking about the content. The English word 'write' does not distinguish the *author* from the *scribe*. Referring to neatness, spelling and the mechanics of writing is to concentrate on the scribal aspects of writing. With both reading and writing we see a focus on quite rudimentary aspects of literacy being taken as the definition of it, aspects which we ourselves would not count as adequate in our own lives. Mace (2002) brings together different ways in which people act as scribes for others in contemporary life.

Turning to the idea of writing as authoring, of thinking about what is written, this too is seen in a simplistic manner. A common view of the process of writing is that it involves getting ready-made thoughts onto paper. In this view, writing is a form of *translation*. As we saw earlier, even at the technical level there is a great deal more to writing than this. With interest in composing and revising, there is a move to examining the process rather than the product: here writing is seen as a form of *thinking*. In our data we have a revealing quotation from a woman who left school aged 16 years not being able to read and write adequately returning to study several years later:

> I didn't realize the difference between being able to read, write and spell, and being able to use those other skills to put those three things to work – like the study skills thing of knowing two sides of the argument, of knowing the introduction, the middle bit, the conclusion – I just thought that anyone who could read and write could just do that automatically. I didn't realize that was like an additional skill as well. So that came as a shock, I thought 'Oh!', because I thought that anyone who could read and write must have no difficulty doing anything!

The clashes in terms of what is meant by writing are very evident when writing is assessed. As part of needing to evaluate, schools need to mark writing. The temptation to mark only those things which can be easily identified such as spelling and neatness is hard to resist. When trying to evaluate the content of writing the notion of good writing cannot be pinned down easily. There is little agreement in scoring, whether in school or university, partly because essays do not have a clear purpose outside of their narrow educational functions of acting as forms of assessment. However, there is no such thing as writing separate from a reader and a purpose. Writing can only be evaluated in terms of the purposes for which it is intended. There is no absolute evaluation of writing; the idea of what counts as a good school essay, for instance, is socially constructed and varies from culture to culture. Even within English-speaking countries with a great deal of contact, such as Australia, Canada, the United States and Britain, what constitutes a school essay differs in many ways.

In schools and colleges, of course, there have been moves to develop more sophisticated views of writing and to get beyond the initial stages of learning to write. Many teachers work with much more complex views of writing. One which has not been mentioned so far is the **process view** of writing, which focuses on the preparations for writing, such as planning, composing, revising, as much as upon the final products, that is, the essays which students produce. This is a shift to seeing writing as aprocess. From a teaching point of view and from a student's point of view, the understanding and reflection involved in a process approach can help students improve their writing. In terms of internalization, verbalizing is a reasonable step towards this. Introspecting on an activity is a step in becoming aware of something, and awareness is one way in which student writers and others can act to change what they do.[4]

A process approach is part way towards a practice account of writing. However, by focusing primarily on processes, such an approach may ignore contextual factors, and still assume that writing is a mental activity in which thoughts escape from the head onto the paper through the hand holding a pen. The social setting is ignored or denied (see Cooper and Holzman, 1989). The way to put writing into its social context is to construe it in terms of practices; the composing involved in student essays is one set of practices. The advance represented in the processing approach is in its acceptance that activities including composing, and ones like note taking, which in the past were often not even recognized as writing, and which have hardly been studied, are all writing. The advance is to realize that composing is part of writing, to realize that not all writing is neatly polished and printed final products. However, to think that all writing is like composing student essays is a mistake. Essays, with their ambiguity of purpose, are not the only things which get written. Writing also involves such activities as editing and revising one's own and others' writing, note taking, filling in forms, signing and copying. Looking back at the sample texts of chapter 5, it is clear that there would have been very different practices surrounding the production of each text.

The literary view of literacy

The original meaning of the words 'literary' and 'literature' was not tied up with meaning the approved fiction of a culture; this idea seems to have developed only in the past hundred years. In fact the words 'literate' and 'literary' have a common origin in the idea of being educated; in the twentieth century they moved far apart, so that literary now means something to do with novels, poetry or plays. Of course there is a more general meaning of the word literature, as in knowing the literature of a subject, whether it be arts or science, or browsing through some travel literature; this sense of literate as knowing the literature still exists. Nevertheless, the words literary and literature normally have a narrower sense and represent a particular theory of literacy. Literacy and literary have grown apart in an almost deliberate distancing of elite culture and mass culture,[5] an issue which is central in discussions of the significance of popular culture.

The view of school literacy outlined so far has been concerned with initial reading and writing. Within schools this exists alongside a quite different, and probably contradictory, view of literacy which children are exposed to later on in their school life. It is a view of literacy which comes from the study of literature and I will refer to it as the **literary view** of literacy. Like the other metaphors for literacy, it also pervades everyday views of reading and writing; it does not necessarily originate in schools but it is nourished and supported by the institution of schooling. The study of English and advanced reading and writing are located in the literature class. Taking meaning from texts, or **responding** to them, is often restricted to literary texts, particular genres. Book literacy is afforded higher status than other forms of print literacy. A certain sort of writing is taught and particular ways of evaluating it are offered. Again, this is a social practice.

Teachers of literacy can have many different backgrounds, each with their own ideology. A common background for many teachers of literacy is English literature, but there is no necessary reason for reading to be taught by experts in literature. This is elite literacy where writing is for 'writers'. At school and college students study a canon of great writers. In studying literature by developing criticism of literature, people are learning a literacy which is not available to them and which is intended as not being available. They are taught to be passive observers of others' greatness, to observe but not to participate in literate culture, with creative writing often a separate and distant subject from English, if creative writing exists at all in the curriculum. In this view of literacy a good writer is someone whose individuality you can recognize from any sentence which they write. Novelists are seen as inspired, where every word is chosen and cannot be changed. This is similar to the religious view of 'the Word', which is immutable and unchangeable as it is passed down through history, but it ignores the realities of writers' composing processes and the way they constantly revise their manuscripts.

The notion of a canon of books which any cultured person should know is a means of defining membership and including some people and excluding others. This is the idea of cultural literacy mentioned already, and attempts in Britain to define what every school child should know at particular ages. Overall this is an elite view of culture.[6] As an example of this view of writing, the novelist Mary Lavin, asked in an interview how she began writing, answered 'I never thought I would write . . . I just wrote. I took up the back of my Ph.D. thesis one day and began to write on it' (quoted in Chamberlain 1988, p. 140). As well as the image of turning her back on her thesis in order to write creatively, there is the very strong view of someone who has completed a PhD thesis – usually a few hundred pages of closely written text – not having written anything.

Related to this, I will now turn to a particular world of literacy, the daily practices of professional writers, looking at studies of successful professional writers and their everyday practices, examining how novelists for instance revolve their lives around literacy. It is important to demonstrate that literary practices are just one set of practices associated with literacy and that the literary theory of what constitutes reading and writing is just one theory of literacy.

The professional writer

One aspect of the literary view of literacy is its notion of who counts as a writer. The literary view of the writer is quite specific, with its own set of practices, values, and notions of identity. It is concerned with writing fiction – novels, poems and plays. This idea does not include those involved in nonliterary writing, such as textbook writers, technical writers, copywriters in advertising agencies, journalists, speech writers, although these people may all live by writing; nor does it include dictionary writers, academics writing science or social science books, articles, reports and proposals, nor student essay writing. It may exclude television and film script writers, and writers of popular fiction.

For the moment, by writer I mean someone who writes plays, novels or poetry and gets them published. These are the people whose practices I want to examine. Such writers often talk about the way they write, and there are several books which are collections of interviews with writers, carried out before the spread of computers for writing.[7] When first looking through them, the strong impression is of diversity and idiosyncrasy. Patterns are hard to see. For every writer who claims to have a regular work pattern, there is another who seems most erratic. For every writer who swears by drink, there is one who claims it is impossible to write and drink. To some extent a mythology surrounds writers which is colluded in by both writer and interviewer. It is important to get beyond the mythology. With drinking, for example, there has been the mythology of the male writer as a hard drinker, brilliant but driven, probably selfish, sexist, temperamental. William Faulkner, Norman Mailer, Tennessee Williams have at times promoted such an image. Examining what a range of writers actually say about drinking suggests the opposite. Their day-today lives are often austere. It is drinking which interferes with their writing.

Examining writers' everyday practices, seeing what they do, and how they plan and carry out their writing is one sense of practices. I am starting with the very practical ways in which people set about writing, the actual ways in which they organize their lives. However, I assume that in fact these activities reflect fundamental approaches to writing and what it means to people, both their own construction of themselves and how they are viewed by society – the second sense of social practices. We see in their literacy practices a mixture of the social and the psychological constraints and possibilities; we can see how writers organize their individual abilities strategically, structuring time differently and making appropriate use of memory and other abilities. In trying to make sense of people's day-to-day rhythms it is important not to be looking for just one pattern, one set of literacy practices. From the evidence of the writers talking about their lives, there actually seem to be two common patterns, although not everyone fits in with them.

Several writers have claimed to work regularly, starting in the morning and working for roughly four hours. Examples of such people are Edward Albee, Truman Capote, Annie Dillard, John Dos Passos, Arthur Koestler, William Maxwell, Edna O'Brien, Mary Sarton, Françoise Sagan, John Updike, H. G. Wells. Keith Waterhouse calls the morning 'primetime'. Anne Bernays speaks for several about the strain of this regimen but tinged with guilt, 'It sounds shameful, but on my best days I write only about three or four hours' (Winokur, 1986, p. 81). To get started they often have a set of rituals. They have a regular place to work with particular ways of writing. They like to be quiet and undisturbed.

The rest of the day is often seen as an incubation period, and may be spent on peripheral activities like correspondence or may be taken up with activities totally unconnected with the writing. The extremely productive popular writer Barbara Cartland was an example of this, although as she often pointed out, she is shunned by literary writers. Every morning she lay on a couch and dictated for several hours to a secretary. Eugène Ionesco also talked of regularly making himself comfortable and dictating, although he was forced into this as he got older and he could no longer write longhand. James Thurber said it took him 10 years to learn how to dictate his writing to a secretary. Sidney Sheldon, author of *The other side of midnight*, dictates for up to four hours a day and achieves up to 50 pages a day, but reports not knowing anyone else who worked like that.

A few writers worked longer hours. Philip Roth talks of writing eight hours a day every day of the year; Isaac Asimov talked of writing up to 18 hours a day. This gets us to the other group of writers, those who have a writing 'binge': they are more erratic and when they do write they will write for hours on end. Georges Simenon talked of writing a chapter a day until a novel was finished and then collapsing exhausted. This approach may be closer to the popular image of writers such as Faulkner, but from reading a wide range of interviews it strikes me as being less common.

The amount people claim to achieve varies greatly. Several pace themselves with a number of pages. William Styron writes two and a half to three pages a day, longhand on yellow sheets of paper, and it takes him five hours. Thomas Mann was reputed to write a page a day throughout the year, while Trollope trained himself to turn out 49 pages of manuscript a week, seven pages a day. Ernest Hemingway rigorously counted the number of words he wrote each day, and others poked fun at this.

He could regularly turn out five hundred words a day, but nevertheless felt good on a day with '320 words well done'. Days with 1,200 or 2,700 words 'made you happier than you could believe' (Phillips, 1985, p. 56).

When reflecting on writers' lives, the American author Annie Dillard is very cynical of the mystique surrounding writers and the way in which exceptional anecdotes are taken to represent the everyday reality. She likens Faulkner writing a novel in six weeks to rare feats such as lifting cars bare-handed or going over the Niagara Falls in a barrel. She guesses soberly that writers average 73 usable pages a year (see Dillard, 1989, pp. 12–16). While some writers claim to write every day of the year, as where Elizabeth Bowen talked of a need to write something each day, it seems more common for writers to have a time when they are writing a book and a time when they are not. Raymond Carver and Angus Wilson talked in these terms, while Ernest Hemingway claimed certain times of the year as being better for writing, a claim softly ridiculed by Annie Dillard.

Much has been written about how writers go about writing in the sense of planning, composing and revising. Again, many different approaches can be identified. A few writers (Georges Simenon was one) begin at the first page and write sequentially page by page, until they get to the end, making few additions or changes. Angus Wilson talked of doing only one draft and correcting as he went along. Others are happy to start anywhere and to move backwards and forwards repeatedly. Joyce Cary talked of writing the big scenes first and then fitting the rest around them. While some people (Anthony Burgess was an example) claim not to revise, others finish and then have a fixed number of revisions, going through the manuscript three or four times. Each cycle of revision was distinct for Truman Capote, with the third draft being on 'a very special certain kind of yellow paper'. Others make constant revisions: John Dos Passos revised six or seven times, Mary Lavin makes many drafts, Thurber talked of producing up to 15, while Raymond Carver referred to having 20 or 30 drafts.

Some researchers have looked for patterns, in terms of what different groups of people do, or the different strategies which people use. This has covered not just writers of fiction, but also academics and others writing.[8] A simple division can be made into people who start at the beginning and work straight through, and those who sketch out the whole piece and will work anywhere on it going back and forth between different parts. These have been referred to as 'serialists' and 'holists', respectively, and many writers would identify themselves as one or the other. Several further pairs of categories have been suggested, such as 'planners and discoverers', and 'thinkers and doers'. Reviewing the many categories researchers have used to classify the different strategies which writers use, Daniel Chandler (1995, pp. 229–36) suggests four strategies, which he gives memorable names:

The oil painting strategy, the 'typical Discoverer strategy of doing minimal pre-planning, jotting down ideas as they occur and reworking the text repeatedly'.
The architectural strategy, 'which involves conscious planning and organisation with only limited drafting and reviewing'.
The bricklaying strategy, 'polishing each sentence before proceeding to the next'.
The watercolour strategy, 'an attempt to produce a complete version relatively rapidly'.

For each of these strategies Chandler identifies writers who use them, with Kurt Vonnegut and Alberto Moravia using the oil painting strategy, John Barth using the architectural strategy, Tom Robbins and Anthony Burgess using the bricklaying strategy, and Katherine Anne Porter using a watercolour strategy. For each strategy there also appear to be writers hostile to it. Of course many writers utilize more than one of these strategies and they may use different strategies for different purposes. Some of the strategies may be better suited to word processing by computer than others. What is apparent is how distinct these approaches are, giving a variety which is not always taken account of in the teaching of writing. Not all people can be squeezed into any one model of how to write.

There is much more which can be said about practices from these interviews. The source of writers' inspiration varies. Some draw upon the world, some upon themselves, and some upon other books. While several keep notebooks, others treat them with disdain. E. M. Forster never kept a notebook and 'would have thought it improper to do so'. Neither did François Mauriac, Dorothy Parker, William Styron, James Thurber. William Maxwell gave up on a notebook and tried keeping file-cards instead, but found that he never looked at them. Others have copious notebooks which they draw upon when writing.

Literary writers do not collaborate. Agatha Christie and Evelyn Waugh derided collaboration. Many find it difficult to share what they are doing while they write. Hemingway's feeling that 'you lose it if you talk about it' is probably fairly common. On the other hand Truman Capote saw reading his unfinished works to his friends as an essential part of composition.

How writing fits into the rest of their lives is an important part of understanding these practices. In interviews many writers give the impression of having uncluttered days which they can dispose of as they please, unencumbered by child-care, doing the shopping or other household duties. As others have pointed out, men's and women's experience can differ radically in this. The people who are interviewed are generally successful writers and are interviewed at the point in their lives when they are well-known and well-off. Their practices reflect this. Usually they are able to write full-time; poets are the exception to this as it is virtually impossible for them to earn a living by writing full-time. Philip Larkin was a full-time librarian and said that when he was writing a poem he would work on it for two hours every evening, 'a routine like any other'. In many interviews people's social relations remain hidden; often there is the sense of the individual, with no notion of social responsibility or awareness of social positioning. This may in part reflect the questions being asked of writers. It is less marked in the collections of women writers.

All of the interviews have a certain pre-computer innocence about them, with discussions of pens versus typewriters and of writers demonstrating how impractical they are by buying a new typewriter rather than changing a ribbon. Part of the image of the writer has been to be mechanically incompetent and impractical, but this has all changed with the coming of computers and the internet.

I have focused mainly on 'literary' writers and their practices, partly to demystify the literary view of writing, but also because interviews with such writers are much more common than ones with other people who do considerable amounts of writing. As I have already said, there have been studies of academics and their writing. However there has been little study of other professional writers such as technical writers or journalists; nor of the theories of knowledge underlying professions where knowledge is to be found in books rather than in practices. In addition, the literacy practices of people who write extensively in their everyday lives have not been studied very much.[9]

12　School practices

Introduction

As has been pointed out already, in the earliest definitions of 'literate' the word meant educated. Today literate is sometimes used to mean educated, and sometimes a distinction is made between the two words so that literate is contrasted with educated or schooled. Therefore any discussion about the importance of literacy in education can become confusing. In contemporary society literacy, schooling and education are totally intertwined to the extent that successful schooling is largely measured in terms of abilities at literacy, and levels of literacy in different countries are often measured in terms of the number of years of schooling children have received. In many ways learning to read and write is seen as the point of education.

However, schooling was not the place where this investigation of literacy started. Schooling is not the main point of this book, since schooling is not the rationale for, or the end point of, literacy. Schooling is part of the picture, but literacy is not an end in itself: rather, in everyday life literacy serves other aims. The discussion of practices started out from people's everyday uses of literacy. If it had started from schooling, we would then have evaluated everything else in terms of school literacy. Schools are the places associated with the teaching and learning of literacy in our society; it is very hard to free ourselves from their perspective, and to take a look at literacy from a perspective other than the educational one. There is a danger in seeing home literacy just in terms of schools' demands. An example of this is that if school is the place where reading is taught then everything before starts being called 'pre-reading'. If reading gets taught in the classroom as a set of ordered skills, then home reading also gets defined as a set of skills with a set of stages. It is because this sort of defining goes on that it is important to examine what goes on in the home before turning to schooling.

In this chapter I want to examine literacy in the world of education; having started elsewhere, I now want to move on to schools. It should be possible to get some distance from schools and to see schools as strange, not as normal. In the ecological metaphor where literacy is viewed as something embedded in the everyday environment, schools can be seen as special places for encouraging certain forms of growth. There are some tempting metaphors: school is a glasshouse or greenhouse, where forcing in the hothouse takes place, a nursery in two senses. Both plants and people are trained. It is important to emphasize that this chapter is not intended to be exhaustive in its coverage of school literacy. Whole books can be and have been written about literacy and schooling and especially about the teaching of reading and writing; here the discussion will concentrate just on the topics which relate to the subject of this book, the ecology of literacy. The plan of the chapter is that first, I examine what actually goes on in schools, the everyday literacy there which children are part of; and then I look at the links between home literacy and school literacy practices. The discussion is continued in chapter 14, which examines some ways in which schools can take account of an ecological approach.[1]

Of course, there is not one school view of literacy, and certainly not a single view which I am setting up just to criticize. Schools are located in the wider society and reflect its multiplicity of values. As a separate point it is also hard to generalize as there is not one sort of school in the world or in a country. Within any country, schools are not homogenous. In Britain there are two systems of education side by side, a public state-supported system and a private system, and the former is studied and scrutinized much more than the latter. There are also hidden parts outside of the formal system such as out-of-school tutors and classes, which are hardly ever described. Views of literacy in schools are tied up with different methods of teaching, but even where a specific method of teaching is identified, what actually goes on in the classroom can vary a great deal. Currently in Britain and the United States education and literacy are in the public arena, with opposing theories of literacy clashing with each other. There are opposing definitions of literacy, often expressed as different methods of teaching. Nevertheless, schooling everywhere probably has something in common, and the comments above are all caveats to be borne in mind before slipping into generalizations about the ways schools work.

What goes on in schools

What goes on in schools? This is a different question from what and how literacy is taught. This is the ecological question, what actually goes on? Schools are powerful definition-generating institutions in our culture for many aspects of life, and especially in the area of literacy. School can be seen as an institution in that it is separated from other cultural activities. School-based forms of literacy are only one form of literacy. There is schooled literacy, and this has become the accepted literacy, to some extent marginalizing other literacies as it pushes into the home and other areas of life (see Street and Street, 1991 for discussion of this). As an institution school has distinct ways of doing things, and particularly a set of practices around language use and around literacy. School consumes a large part of children's lives and forms a significant reference point for their values and attitudes. This influence continues into adulthood and is reasserted as these adults become parents with children; for families with children at school, the school values enter the home. School attitudes and values influence society generally and it is probably true that the general public's view of reading and writing is influenced to some extent by schooling and images of what goes on in schools.

For schooling children are taken out of family life at a certain age and are taught in groups by adults. School is a particular domain, a place where only certain people go. They wear certain sorts of clothes and carry out certain sorts of activities, different from what might be done at home or at work, for instance. Physically, schools have distinct architecture and the boundaries are usually clearly demarcated. To enter them, often one passes a notice at the entrance announcing the name of the school, its status and ownership, the authority of the head teacher, with a list of degrees, and maybe other messages. Within school, space is divided up, so that children are often segregated by age and sometimes by ability and by sex. There are separate rooms called classrooms where up to 30 or 40 children may be gathered together with one adult. Time is also divided up fairly strictly. People go only on certain days at certain times and they carry out activities for precise lengths of time; these are often indicated by bells. Typically, everyone in schools follows the same demarcations of time. School life is marked by shared rhythms; there are common and repeated activities in the classroom that make up the routine of school life for teacher and child. Activities are broken up into subjects, which are pursued at separate times, often in different places, with different teachers and with different books. Socially, schools are arranged hierarchically with someone in charge and fairly clear statuses for different teachers. Teachers have more status and power than students and are paid to be there. Children have legal obligations to attend. Parents rarely enter schools, and usually only at the end of the day when official schooling is over. It is within this framework that children learn about literacy.

There are all sorts of practices which children are learning in schools: children are learning to conform, to be part of large groups, they are learning to sit still, to be regulated by time. Schools have their own ground rules of what you are allowed to do and what not, including rules about who may talk, when, to whom, and what about. These ground rules are different from those of home and community. There are many ways in which schools socialize children by the organization of day-to-day rhythms of schooling; language use is a central part of this.[2]

In examining reading and writing it is important to remember that schooled literacy is not the only form of literacy going on in schools. These are other literacies which are rendered invisible. We need to look at actual practices. There is a range of literacy activities, both official and unofficial. In the classroom there is graffiti and doodling, names are carved on desks, secret notes are passed. Children read comics and circulate illicit material, they have their own books and magazines brought in from the outside. In addition, the visual environment of notice boards, classroom displays and signs surround children. Children have their names on their clothes and lunch boxes. The young child takes written messages between home and school; here, the child acts as a carrier of messages, which, incidentally, may have to be explained orally. The child observes literacy events which are not part of the official teaching of reading and writing; for example, they may participate in the daily taking of the register and see other aspects of school record-keeping. As children get older they continue to do their own reading and writing both inside and outside of school.[3]

The official teaching within schools has its own set of practices. Just as there are special books for learning to read at home, so there are special books used throughout schooling. Often these belong in the school and are not removed from the classrooms. There are often many copies of the same book, which may not be available in book shops. They may be lent to children for a length of time; the children take responsibility for them and keep them in school – parents may never see them. Sometimes children get their own book, sometimes they share them. Textbooks are a distinct genre, a particular form of writing. Initially such books are used for learning to read and thereafter they are used to learn particular discourses which have been compartmentalized as distinct subjects, with specialist teachers. Often these books have been written by teachers, although many of them give the impression of not having an author. The way they are used is special in that often they are read in very short sections; there is a great deal of talk around these texts and their use is strongly mediated by the teachers.

When children write in school they produce writing in special books. In Britain these books are often supplied by the school; they are a certain size of paper different from the paper of personal letters or business life. Children are often restricted in the sort of writing instrument they may use and the colour of ink which is permitted. In other countries children buy their own books and different rules apply. In many countries low quality crayons are used by young children learning to write. Parents are sometimes invited to look at children's work; for example, piles of work may be laid out in classrooms for parents to peruse at the end of term, or they are sent home in a bundle with the child. What happens to the work is not clear, often it is taken home, and may be thrown away, or kept for many years.

Talk around texts

Children are learning schools' distinct ways of making meaning, in Olson's phrase, of 'learning to confine the interpretation to the meaning in the text' (Olson and Nickerson 1978), or as Wertsch puts it, learning to deal with **text-based realities** (Wertsch, 1991). Many of the classroom language practices where they do this are clearly identifiable. As part of the rhythms of school life there are common literacy events in classrooms, times when books are taken out, times when they are put away. There are times for reading, times for writing. In examining the uses of literacy in the classroom, the first point to make is that the literacy practices are totally bound up with oral language. In all sorts of literacy events, texts are talked about, whether they are books, worksheets, student writing, written tests. Much of schooling can be characterized as **talk around texts**. There are common uses of language associated with these events. The language and interactions of the classroom have been described in many places. It is the spoken language which has been analysed mainly but also the spoken and written together. Some of these uses of language have been identified as having important roles in the acquisition of literacy and, as has already been pointed out, are seen as crucial for success in mainstream schooling.[4]

Schooling is about text-based meanings, yet spoken language is of great importance. One way of emphasizing this is by describing what has been called the **two-thirds rule**, which captures the importance of speaking, and certain sorts of speaking.[5] There are three parts to the rule: that in classrooms someone is talking for about two-thirds of the time, two-thirds of this is the teacher, and two-thirds of this teacher talk is lecturing or asking questions. Particular forms of language are used in classrooms and there is less variety of language use than in other settings such as the home. The most common type of official talk in classrooms consists of routines where the teacher asks something, the child responds and the teacher then provides some sort of feedback or evaluation. In other words the teacher introduces the topic, and the child provides the comment. These routines, called IRE (initiation, response, evaluation) or IRF (initiation, response, feedback) sequences, have been widely studied, including their role in literacy lessons (see the review in Bloome and Green, 1992).

In these regularities of school interaction there are obvious similarities with the interactions described in the chapter on home literacy; activities have much in common with ones we have come across already. The labelling practices common in child rearing in middle-class literate culture of pointing to something and asking 'what's that?', when everyone knows the answer, is one such practice. This display of answering such questions is a very common and basic language routine in schools. Strangely, while it is used by adults with very young children, they gradually do less of it as the children learn to speak and take control of their own lives. Schools once again introduce this form of mediation into children's lives.

When thinking about home language, chapter 10 concentrated on two common language activities which are intertwined with literacy, **labelling** and **story telling**. These are two of many language activities in mainstream homes and they are also common activities in schools. Shirley Brice Heath draws attention to others which play important roles in mainstream homes and which feature in schools (Heath, 1985, 1986; see also Wells, 1989). Concentrating on the language in these activities, Heath (1985, 1986) identifies six 'genres of language use' which are common patterns of language use in schools. They are genres of oral language and ones which provide a way into written language. Labelling and story telling are two of the genres. Another genre is similar to labelling. This is what Heath refers to as **meaning quests**. This is when adults provide or request interpretations of what is said or meant. The other three genres are extensions of story telling in that they are further types of narrative. First there are **eventcasts**. These consist of providing a narrative on events currently happening or in the future. An example of an eventcast, taken from my own data, is a child saying:

> 'Let's build a den. We can use those sticks and build it under the tree. Will you help us?'

Second there are **accounts**. These involve providing information which is new to the listener. An example of an account would be when a child reports what has happened:

> 'Guess what we did in school? We're making a circus and these clowns came and we made up our faces. It was great.'

Third there are **recounts**. These differ from accounts in that they involve retelling experiences which are known both to the teller and to the listener. The distinction between accounts and recounts may not be immediately obvious; they differ crucially in the way in which the listener can contribute. An example of a recount is:

> 'D'you remember when we saw Haley's Comet. We went up to that tower and there were lots of people. And I was really cold coming back in the car.'

Having given these specific examples of language use it is still important not to evaluate literacy solely in terms of school's practices, with those of other domains such as homes and communities being evaluated only in terms of what they lack. We still need to know more about how meanings are made in different situations, both with and without the written word. Two issues I want to discuss about these different forms of language are first the ways in which they relate to forms of language in the home, and, second, the extent to which literacy events in the classroom can be disentangled from more general language events.

From home to school

This starting point of examining school-based definitions of literacy such as reading being an isolable skill leads us in very different directions from those opened up in chapter 10 where we started from young children's knowledge about language and literacy, even though at first sight the two investigations appear to be covering similar ground. From their experience in the home, children know about the particular language and literacy practices of their community. They have emergent theories about what language is, about what literacy is, and about how to learn. It is important to see how this knowledge is taken up by schools. Children from mainstream homes will know about mainstream ways of making meaning; children from minority communities will know about their community's ways of making meaning; particular literacy practices may be central to this, as with children who know about Koranic literacy, or they may not. Children who do not know mainstream ways of making meaning still know other ways, but, with or without print literacy, the ways different cultures make meaning rarely enter into the school when a minority child enters school. Several of the researchers mentioned already cover the mismatch between home and school practices (such as Heath, 1983, p. 235, and Bissex, 1984, p. 99). Even if mainstream or middle-class ways of meaning are more in tune with schools' ways, it is still important to be aware of the ways, mentioned already, in which home and school practices are still very different from each other.

There have been many studies attempting to identify what are the key elements of home literacy activities in relation to later school learning. New and richer links are being seen between home learning and school learning. The six genres of language use described above provide one bridge between home language use and school practices. Having reviewed the research on language use at home and at school, Heath argues that these six genres are the crucial ones for success in literacy and for success in school in general. She then examines different minority communities in the United States to see the extent to which these school-valued genres occur (Heath, 1986). She looks at Chinese-American families and Mexican-American families and argues that, whatever the language they are in, use of these genres by the communities is reflected in success in schooling. This example of specific uses of language, then, provides links between home and school, and also between different communities and school practices.

Other researchers (for example Weinberger, 1996; Compton-Lilly, 2003; Hull and Schultz, 2001) have also looked at this issue, stressing the range of home literacy events. Wells (1985) reports on a rare longitudinal study where certain home practices and later school achievement were compared. (It is rare in that the same children were studied at home and, several years later, in school.) He identifies having stories read to them as the most important variable linking the children's home and school achievement, more important than looking at books, drawing and colouring, or writing. Again, it is worth stressing the importance of oral language in this literacy event.

In all this discussion there are two quite distinct directions in which there can be links between home and school. First, there is whether school practices are reflected in home practices: whether children at home are being prepared for schools' ways of knowing. Second, there is the question of whether home practices are being acknowledged in schools; it is this latter question which is often ignored. As part of this second question it is also true that home literacy does not cease when children enter school, literacy does not shift from home to school. The home environment continues, with its own practices around reading and writing. (For some children, this presents a conflict of values which they have to resolve either by identifying with school or by maintaining home values and not accepting those of the school.)

To link up more with the earlier chapter on home literacy practices, what is of interest to schools should be what children know about literacy, much more than solely whether they can read or not. Of course some children enter school being able to read and write. Part of the interest by schools in what happens in the first five years of life has come from an interest in these early readers, children who learn to read before going to school. It has been found that a significant number of children turn up at school being able to read, the very job which schools devote so much energy to. How is it that children across a broad range of ability and social class can learn to read apparently effortlessly and with no formal teaching?

The idea of early reading has been well documented, discussed and promoted. For example in a classic study, Margaret Clark (1976) researched 32 children who could read when they entered school. She tried to find what these children had in common. She ruled out intelligence or social class and stated that the main thing the children had in common was a desire to read, and strong oral involvement of the parents. The parents were often keen readers and participated in a range of literacy practices which the children became involved in. Other researchers studied children who were learning to read as they learned to speak, including a child who learned to read some letters before beginning to speak.[6] There are now many books on helping children learn to read at home. This is part of a general shift in mainstream perception from seeing parents' involvement in children's literacy as a bad thing to seeing it as beneficial, making articles for parents such Bettelheim's in 1966 on 'The danger of teaching your baby to read' seem quaint today.

Literacy as language

So far I have tried to focus on print literacy and not extend it to include aspects of orality or visuals. However, several people within schooling have questioned whether it is possible to distinguish literacy events from other events. They have found the need to expand definitions of literacy to include other aspects of language, and have done so in several directions. Dealing with learning in the classroom it is very clear that events involving literacy are not neatly divided off from those which do not involve literacy, and in many events where the purpose is learning about literacy, there may be no text present. For example, in infant classrooms, children might go on a walk looking at buildings or spend the morning cooking partly in order to write about their experiences later. It is not clear where the literacy event begins and ends. Activities structured like this are precursors of common patterns throughout school, such as a discussion which comes before an essay, or carrying out an experiment which later has to be written up. However, there is probably no reason to regard the essay as more important for learning than the discussion, or the write-up as more important than the experiment. Throughout education there is no clear division between literacy and literacy-related events, and, once again, oral and literate are totally intertwined in western schooling. Crucially, texts are produced by talk and it is important to recognize that literacy practices are part of broader social practices.

Another point which makes the idea of literacy events difficult is that learning new forms of spoken language is going on in schools and mastering these may be equally part of becoming literate. For instance, concentrating on one aspect of literacy, Gordon Wells has defined literate to include 'all those uses of language in which its symbolic potential is deliberately exploited as a tool for thinking' (Wells, 1989, p. 252). The other area where the idea of literacy has been expanded is into other media, with notions mentioned already of film literacy or computer literacy. Certainly children's books are multimodal and it is hard to draw a line between the significance of print versus other forms of visual meaning making. Not focusing on education, Michael Cole and Helen Keyssar, for example, have a definition of literacy which is 'to be able to interpret any mode of communication' (Cole and Keyssar, 1985). This of course would include speech.

As a different way of solving the problem and to get away from just events involving print, David Bloome and his colleagues talk in terms of **language events**.[7] It is hard to exclude any activity involving language in contemporary society from being a literacy event. Outside schooling, the distinction is also blurred and again the idea of literacy events is not without problems. First, it is difficult to find a communicative activity where literacy does not have a role; its role varies and sometimes is central, such as reading a bedtime story to a child, but it can have a background role and may not even be present, for example in listening to the news being read on the radio or using a tool which is dependent on the written word for its manufacture or for understanding the instructions.

In conclusion, there are many reasons, especially in education, for grouping together written discourses and complex spoken discourses, to the extent that some would argue, as James Gee does, that it is pedantic to distinguish discourses which involve print from those which do not. He develops the idea of literacy as being one of several **secondary discourses**.[8] Nevertheless, as I hope this book has made clear, it is often useful to focus just on print media. The definition of literate implied in these discussions is similar to the one used in chapter 2: to do with confidence in the medium. To be literate is to be confident in the literacy practices one participates in. This emphasis on confidence has been a strong tradition in much adult literacy work. Also, it is similar to the definition used by Jennings and Purves (1991, p. 3) where they refer to literacy as 'the state of being comfortable inside a sign-sharing community'. This definition works with extended meanings of literate as well. Being literate in phrases like computer literacy, television literacy or political literacy means being confident in the area, and is similar to the meaning of literate when applied to reading and writing. One of the things schools can do is support children in their developing literacies.

13 Adults and world literacy

Introduction

In this chapter we turn to the area of adults and literacy, to issues around the topic of teaching adults to read and write. This is a concern both in developing countries, such as Nicaragua, Namibia and Nepal, where educational systems are still being created, and also in industrialized countries like Britain and Canada, where there has been over a century of compulsory schooling. The aim of the chapter is to give a brief overview of the world of adult literacy and to examine the dominant metaphors used here, especially those that create the discourse around the concept of **functional literacy**. I will discuss alternatives to this approach and I hope to show how an ecological view of literacy can contribute to discussions of adult literacy. This will include examining some of the strategies which adults with problems of reading and writing use in their everyday lives. In many countries one of the most important questions concerning literacy relates to the choice of language, and literacy in a language is connected in a complicated way with the health and survival of languages. This is discussed later in the chapter. I want to juxtapose these two sections which

may at first seem to be addressing different issues. However, there are connections: discussing issues about literacy and disappearing languages raises
fundamental questions about the purposes of adult literacy work.

This discussion of adults throughout the world and their learning of
reading and writing can draw on what has been said so far in the earlier
chapters. From the discussion of language, for instance, understanding
that there are different literacies and that there are systematic restrictions
on language use can be important for adult literacy. Similarly, there
are implications of realizing that texts can be read in different ways. To
make a set of connections with the discussions in earlier chapters, if we
are considering the state of literacy throughout the world today, many
of the conclusions on historical development are relevant. The study of
history demonstrates that different literacies are bound up with different
scripts and that they have spread by a combination of trade, migration
and colonization; that many developing countries have long histories of
literacy; and that there are other institutions associated with learning
besides schools, and many informal ways of learning to read and write.

Since two previous chapters have focused on children's learning and
on schooling, it is worth pointing out the connections and the differences. While it is important to see the links between adults and children,
at the same time it is fruitful to point out the ways in which adult
learning is a distinct topic. Although some countries, like the Scandinavian
countries, have long traditions of adult education, most countries do
not. When 'problems of adult literacy' are identified in a country, the
usual reaction is to turn to child education for inspiration. Both educators and learners conspire in this. Educators turn first to primary school
teachers and books. Meanwhile, learners come with expectations and
images from childhood education. The idea of 'learning to read' has such
strong associations with children, textbooks, classrooms, schools and
teachers that it is so easy to take this as the default, to see it as completely
natural. When thinking of adults each one of these associations can, and
should, be challenged (and in fact many of the assumptions can be challenged for children's learning as well). Just as schooling has the idea that
learning to read is complete after two or three years at school, it also has
the idea that education is complete and finished 10 years later. Schooling
often has no room for adult learning.

Fortunately, there are approaches to learning which start from adults
and which do not rely on children. A social approach to literacy underlines
some of the differences between adults and children: adults have a range

of ways of learning acquired in everyday life; they have their own experiences of culture and they have their own needs and purposes for learning. An exciting aspect of teaching adults is that because adult education is often outside of the traditional educational system it is possible to be innovative. Adult education can be marginalized, or it can be a vibrant area of education in its own right. It can have methods which take the embeddedness of literacy in everyday life for granted.

Thinking of all the different forms of adult literacy work going on in the world is very difficult. It may be useful to group contemporary adult literacy into three areas; there are three sorts of literacy campaigns which I will refer to as religious, political and developmental. As an example of the first sort, American Protestant missionary groups have often had literacy as a high priority in 'spreading the word' – teaching people to read has been an integral part of the missionary work. One such missionary, Frank Laubach, now has his name associated with a particular method of teaching literacy used worldwide and an associated slogan of 'each one teach one' – the idea being that each person who learns can then teach someone else. Another strand has been SIL International (formerly the Summer Institute of Linguistics), who are associated with the missionary organization Wycliffe Bible Translators, based in the United States. They operate by carrying out the linguistic work necessary in order to translate the Bible into previously unwritten languages and they are active in many parts of the world. In terms of a social view of literacy, they have been criticized for failing to respect other cultures. As pointed out earlier, throughout history maps of the spread of different literacies have reflected patterns of political and religious domination. This is no less true today.

I call the second group of campaigns political to draw attention to the fact that typically they have been initiated by the government of a country as part of a whole programme of social reform. These are mass literacy campaigns which have been held in places such as the Soviet Union, in Tanzania, in Cuba and in Nicaragua. They have reported spectacular results in terms of the numbers of people learning a basic level of reading and writing. In Nicaragua, for example, a literacy campaign was announced immediately after the revolution in 1980, the whole of the country's resources were devoted to it for a year, and the number of people in the country who could not read and write was reduced from 52 per cent to 12 per cent. These campaigns are important as they have had a high public profile and because they have been successful. Mass campaigns suggest many lessons, an important one in ecological terms being that literacy works when it is part of broader changes in society which have general public support. They have also drawn attention to problems which later campaigns have had to pay attention to, such as the possibility of forgetting how to read if it is not maintained and the need for 'post-literacy' support to sustain it.[1]

I refer to the third group of campaigns as developmental, in that they have had as their primary aim the economic development of countries, and that they have been initiated by international development agencies such as Unesco and the World Bank. Fundamental to their approach has been the idea that learning to read and write is influential, even causative, in the economic development of a country. They represent where most of the money on literacy is being spent and where most of the discussion about literacy takes place, but, as we shall see, they have not been particularly successful. It is the ideas about literacy which underlie this international effort which I want to examine further; this discussion will revolve around the concept of functional literacy.

Before getting on to this, it is worth emphasizing that this grouping of literacy campaigns into religious, political and developmental is fairly rough, as there is considerable overlap, and not all literacy work is encompassed by it. Certainly there are religious missionary organizations whose aims are similar to those of development agencies and there has usually been external aid money supporting the political literacy campaigns. In addition the developmental campaigns are intrinsically political in terms of international relations. Nevertheless, I feel the three groups differ in their prime motivation. Alongside these campaigns there has been considerable other work which does not fit into these categories. Often it is small-scale and outside the formal educational system and rooted in the community. This grassroots literacy work includes the original programme in Brazil associated with Paulo Freire and has been the source of some of the most innovative work in countries like Britain, Canada and the United States.

Functional literacy

Unesco, the United Nations Educational Scientific and Cultural Organization, was established after the Second World War along with a range of agencies concerned with world development. From the beginning Unesco gave high priority to literacy programmes. Early literacy programmes were based on the assumption of a strong, causative link between iteracy and social development. It was claimed that literacy, via the attitudes and cognitive skills that it fosters in individuals, promoted economic development and prosperity in society in general. Literacy therefore became an essential first step in the attempt to develop 'underdeveloped' countries. The aim was to eliminate poverty, disease and so-called 'traditional but unproductive' forms of social organization. As a result of this philosophy, literacy education has been one of the main planks of Unesco's modernization policies since the 1950s. The idea of a causal link between literacy and development has gone as far as quoting a figure, a 40 per cent literacy rate, as being the level of literacy needed in a society for economic take-off (see Anderson, 1966). Of course there has always been some criticism of this, but the idea of literacy being an essential catalyst for development has been underlying most literacy programmes throughout the period.

The literacy which development agencies have been promoting has been functional literacy. The idea of functional literacy is described in Gray's landmark book, *The teaching of reading and writing*, published by Unesco in 1956. It is interesting looking back at a book written more than 50 years ago. Examining it today, much of the book now seems very outdated: for instance, the research base the book draws on and the theories underlying its teaching proposals dwell at length on eye-movements and do not get far beyond word recognition in their view of what is involved in reading. However, alongside this, much of the rhetoric about the importance of literacy for everyday life does not seem outdated. The book is important in its acceptance of the social basis of literacy and in drawing attention to the need to make literacy appropriate to its cultural setting. Gray's definition of functional literacy is that someone is functionally literate if they are able to 'engage effectively in all those activities in which literacy is normally assumed in [their] culture or group' (1956, p. 24). This widely quoted definition obviously begs many questions, but it is important in making central the idea that literacy is a relative matter, relative to a particular society or group. Potentially, this definition is also a step forward from seeing literacy in terms of fixed minimum standards.

In practical terms, despite the above definition, functional literacy has often meant teaching literacy as a set of skills thought to be universal and applicable anywhere, with the idea of there being one literacy which everyone should learn in the same way. In principle the notion of functional literacy takes a useful first step forward in going beyond fixed set of skills. It does this by taking account of the fact that the demands of particular situations are different and that being literate is relative to the contexts in which literacy is used. In reality, looking back with hindsight at the basis of more than half a century's literacy work, we can see a continuing tension between the broad general statements on value and the narrow senses of functional.

In practice, the notion of functional literacy in international campaigns has usually been closely tied to employment and has been related to economic development.[2] Literacy has been treated as a variable, which is measurable and then related to other variables of development, such as economic development and modernity. The idea has been that resources are put into literacy and this then aids development. It has been seen as something external which is brought into a society. Unfortunately, in both developing countries and in industrialized countries functional literacy is associated with imposed literacy, imposing literacy on others, rather than starting from people's own perceptions of their needs.

Lastly, it is important to realize that early literacy programmes based on this approach were not in fact very successful, even in their own terms: Unesco evaluated its own programmes and found them lacking. The evaluation of the Experimental World Literacy Programme of the 1960s, for example, is an indictment of functional literacy programmes, and the criticisms are made more powerful by the fact that they were made by an organization critiquing its own activities (Unesco, 1976).

Since the Unesco programmes of the 1960s, there have been further programmes and further meetings and declarations. One significant international conference was held at Jomtien, Thailand, as part of activities for International Literacy Year in 1990. The participants of the Jomtien conference openly acknowledged the failure of the 1980s in terms of literacy work throughout the world and called for a decade of action up to the year 2000 to reverse this trend. A range of new initiatives and programmes on literacy in developing countries emerged. Many of these aimed to relate literacy and numeracy teaching closely to people's lives, livelihoods and local situations, resonating with a social view of literacy. More recently, Unesco is the lead agency in the United Nations literacy decade which runs until 2012. There has been renewed focus on literacy as key to the Education for All (EFA) goals and an emphasis on adults. At the time of writing, the fourth global monitoring report on Education for All (Unesco, 2005) attempts to bring together functional approaches with attention to people's literacy practices and the changing social context.

Some other initiatives are more politically oriented and seek to respond more to local people's concerns. The nongovernmental organization ActionAid developed a new, Freirean approach to teaching reading and writing to adults. REFLECT (Regenerated Freirean Literacy Through Empowering Community Techniques) aims to integrate literacy and numeracy teaching with broader efforts to stimulate development locally, and to address communities' social and political concerns. Rather than having a pre-defined curriculum, the starting point for learning is the analysis of learners' lives and concerns, and then developing materials with learners. It is now used in more than 50 countries. The US non-governmental organization World Education is supporting projects in Africa and Asia which promote an integrated approach to literacy and numeracy development.

This gulf between rhetoric and reality – to use a phrase common in adult education – is still there today. Books are still being published which talk about overcoming 'the scourge of illiteracy' and such phrases are still common. In my view, in such statements international bodies are trying to incorporate new approaches while still keeping hold of a rigid functional approach. This is one of several areas in the study of literacy where I see attempts to fit new ideas into the creaking framework of outworn theories which cannot take the strain. Unesco and other international agencies still need to reassess the ideas and theories underlying their aims and methods. It is apparent that there are still several philosophies alongside each other in the literacy and development field. There are different analyses of the literacy situation and different practical proposals for change. There is the gulf between the liberal aims of emancipation and the practical pro-grammes which are funded. The idea of conflicting definitions of literacy underlying the various approaches helps us see more clearly what is going on. From the grassroots there is often clear and articulate understanding of the issues; what gets carried out by governments and international agencies is still often centralized functional literacy programmes, imposed and often not particularly effective (Barton and Papen, 2005).

Industrialized countries

All the industrialized countries of the world have established systems of universal compulsory education over the past 120 years. They have done this gradually by increasing provision, extending legal requirements and enforcing these requirements. Although official statistics may hide the reality of attendance levels, all industrialized countries now claim that at least 95 per cent of their children enrol in school, and every country now provides at least nine years of compulsory schooling for children (see Unesco, 1990).

The ways in which provision has been made for adults to learn to read and write has varied from country to country. Adult literacy provision in most of Western Europe and North America has come about as people have realized that, despite well-established systems of schooling, all is not well. There has been a gradual recognition that the achievement of official universal schooling does not mean that literacy can be taken for granted: it has been observed that most people attain some competence in reading, and to a lesser extent writing, from attending school. However, there is a sense in which they are not fully literate. Many people leave school not feeling in control of the written communication they need in their day-to-day adult lives. Politicians, employers and educators express concern about people's reading and writing abilities. Responding to this realization, in the early 1970s some countries, including the United States and Britain, launched small-scale national campaigns, aimed to last a year or two.

Official recognition that the state school system of a country has not solved difficulties with literacy is often reluctant and it may come after pressure from campaigning community groups. Debate around the issue can be full of accusation, shock, disbelief and claims of falling standards. It is often centred around competing views of teaching methods and the way education should be organized. This attitude generates an atmosphere of 'crisis' and short-term measures are designed to solve it. In the 1980s and 1990s, despite the reluctance to accept problems with the school system, more and more countries came to accept the issue. The 'problem' in industrialized countries, then, has only recently been realized or constructed. The notion of the illiterate in a literate world is relatively recent. Even talking of a problem, as if it can be tackled and solved, is part of the metaphor. The metaphors for literacy as a disease, a crisis and a problem, discussed in the first two chapters, are widespread in the media and in public images of literacy.

As with developing countries, a wide variety of methods has been associated with literacy programmes in industrialized countries. Nevertheless, in several places there has been a coherent and consistent approach; the way it first developed in Britain in the 1970s, for example, can be seen as a distinct philosophy (see Hamilton and Hillier, 2006, for this history). The aim was to respond to people's expressed needs, to work individually or in small groups, to have flexible provision. At the same time there was, until recently, a conscious attempt to avoid external evaluation and assessment and to shun professionalism. There have been methods and materials which emphasize learner control and which make links with everyday life concerns. In developing a distinct approach, adult literacy kept a distance from the formal educational provision of schools.

An example of the distinctness of the approach has been the work on writing. Often there is an emphasis on the active process of writing, contrasted with reading, which is seen as more passive. Writing here means not just the physical act of writing, or even the process of it, but something much broader which can include the production and printing of books, magazines and newsletters. This relates to the different meanings of being a writer discussed in an earlier chapter. In adult literacy classes someone can be a writer in the sense of author even if they have difficulties with the physical act of writing; the technical problems of writing are overcome by one person being the scribe for another. The student writing movement in British adult literacy led to a great deal of innovative publishing giving a voice to writers who otherwise would have none. However, these approaches have come under attack more recently with changes in funding and moves towards more centrally controlled courses. A new wave of adult literacy provision, which is in many ways closer to the functional literacy of developing countries, has become more dominant since the 1990s. It is more often tied to narrow vocational ends, and through funding it is more controlled by national and international agencies.

There is a consensus among governments and policy makers in industrialized countries that we are moving into an 'information age', in which skills are becoming centrally important. This is said to be driven by a range of changes, particularly increased globalization of trade and business, and the emergence of a new so-called 'knowledge-based society' with an expansion in industries manufacturing or using high technology and a rapid increase in communications and computing infrastructures. The employment market is changing in industrialized countries, with an increase in the demand for highly skilled labour, a fall in the numbers of manufacturing jobs, and widening gaps between the earnings of the highly skilled and others. In this setting, it is argued that literacy (and numeracy) skills are increasingly important, both for individuals and for the economy as a whole. The European Union (EU) is one international organization which has encouraged an economically driven expansion of literacy programmes. The 'Lisbon agenda' of 2000 includes a commitment to invest in education and training throughout Europe. Improvement in the 'basic skills' of literacy and numeracy is one of the 13 key objectives of the education and training strategy.

The British Government's response to such moves was to put large amounts of funding into a massive programme in adult language, literacy and numeracy, called 'Skills for Life'. This began in 2000, with huge investment in developing centralized curricula and teacher training programmes, and demanding targets for the numbers of people participating in courses and passing literacy and numeracy tests. This investment has transformed the literacy, numeracy and language field in Britain. It has raised the profile of basic skills to an unprecedented extent. It is encouraging that governments and employers are becoming more interested in educational provision, but in terms of methods this centralized approach is very different from the tradition of community-based provision described above, and can pose a genuine threat to it. Ultimately, conflicting definitions of literacy underlie these different approaches.

It is very clear that these initiatives are promoting functional literacy in order to improve employability. The term 'functional literacy' has been deliberately chosen in an attempt to describe the distinct literacy problems of industrialized countries. The notion of **basic literacy** is used for the initial learning of reading and writing which adults who have never been to school need to go through. The term functional literacy is kept for the level of reading and writing which adults are thought to need in modern complex society. Use of the term underlines the idea that although people may have basic levels of literacy, they need a different level to operate in their day-to-day lives. However, there are still two different senses which are being confused: the term floats between meaning, on the one hand, some minimal competence thought necessary for everyday life and, on the other hand, quite specific and sophisticated abilities such as using computer-based technologies in the workplace. I am concerned that a concept has been borrowed from work in developing countries without taking notice of the problems associated with it. With industrialized countries throughout the world now taking an interest in questions of adult levels of literacy it is important for them to learn from what has happened in developing countries and not to ignore their wealth of experience. Crucially, it is important for them not to copy indiscriminately philosophies and methods which have failed.

It is important to stress, when talking about people in industrialized countries with problems of reading or writing, that they are ordinary people. Despite some media images, they are not strange, dysfunctional outsiders. The evidence from all sorts of studies is that, for the large part, they are ordinary people who lead ordinary lives and who function normally in society. They are also a very mixed group with different reasons for identifying problems with reading and writing in their everyday lives. The causes are many and varied. Literacy problems are clearly linked with poverty and social disadvantage of various sorts and, even in the richest of industrialized countries, there are still pockets of underdevelopment where people have only very fragmentary exposure to education. Some causes are rooted in cultural and social background. Others can be more directly related to schooling: such as large classes, lack of remedial help, children dropping out. For some people there are individual factors which have affected their learning, such as special learning needs due to disability, differences in the pace of learning, missing school for health reasons. I want to turn now to discussing the experience of having problems with reading and writing in modern life.

Not literate in a literate world

It is now accepted that many adults in all societies have some problems with reading and writing. Surveys in Canada, the United States, Australia and Britain using very different methodologies all point in the same direction, that very roughly one in 10 adults experience literacy problems in their everyday lives, with writing problems being the most common. How does someone with literacy problems fit into contemporary society? There is a common image of the loner, the outsider, having to cover up, hide and compensate for a secret disability. The person is a failure, someone who has to learn to cope with a problem. The image is of a seemingly ordinary person who constantly has to make excuses – carrying around an empty glasses case and claiming to have forgotten their spectacles, or the constantly bandaged writing hand. These images are powerful and they have been important in literacy campaigns in promoting general acceptance of the idea that it is ordinary people who have literacy problems and who might enrol in adult literacy programmes.

This last point needs reinforcing: those with literacy problems are usually ordinary people, who hold down jobs, have families, participate in society, pursue hobbies and, crucially, often do not see themselves as dependent or needing assistance. They have a variety of strategies for dealing with the written word. They do not necessarily see themselves as having problems, nor do they view themselves as outsiders or 'other'. They often do not identify with the media images they see around them where adults with literacy problems are portrayed. There is a definite tension between the views of people with low levels of literacy and the media images literate society transmits about them. The media image of 'The town that can't spell' (*Daily Mail*, February 1987), for example, is unlikely to be recognized by its inhabitants. Further, although some adults go to literacy classes, most adults would not think of doing so; those who do go to classes do not necessarily identify with the image of 'basic education student'.

A small study by Hannah Arlene Fingeret (1983) in a city in the northeastern United States emphasizes these points. She spent a year talking to and following around 43 adults. She refers to them as illiterate, but they are more accurately described as having low levels of literacy. She builds up a picture of their social life, describing it in terms of social networks. Most of the people she studied did not see themselves as dependent simply because they had some problems reading and writing; rather they were part of rich social networks where they were treated as equals and where there was considerable mutual exchange of skills. These networks were based on relations, neighbours, work colleagues and long-term friends. Skills and resources were exchanged and it was seen as unnecessary for everyone to develop every skill personally. These networks are no different from any social networks people may be part of, where people might look after each other's children, do shopping for someone else or provide gardening advice. Someone is known for fixing cars, someone else for good haircuts, a third person might 'help you figure out your problems'. Being able to fill in forms, show you how to use email, or understand the letter from the bank are also examples of these exchangeable skills which are the fabric of social life.

Fingeret shows the different ways people with literacy problems participated in these networks. Some people lived in a very literate cosmopolitan world while others lived more local lives where there were several people who could not read or write very well. People in the latter group were treated as equals in their networks and were accepted for what they could do, they were *interdependent* and swapped skills – to the extent that for some the ability 'to fix things' was a scarcer resource and was valued more than the ability to read and write. It is when these networks change or break down that people may identify problems in dealing with the written word.

In her study Fingeret describes only a very small number of the people she studied as *dependent*, rather than interdependent. These were people where there was a very basic asymmetry in their lives and where they needed to be supported without obviously giving anything back in return. She emphasizes that in these three cases it was not literacy itself which made them dependent, although it was a part of the dependence. Literacy contributed but was not the cause. We saw the same picture in our local literacies study, that there were a small number of people where literacy was one of several problems, such as extreme poverty or physical handicap, and that it was the combination of problems which made people dependent; other detailed studies and national surveys have come to similar conclusions. While not wanting to play down the problems and disadvantages associated with literacy difficulties in a highly literate society, such studies are obviously important when considering the images which literacy programmes can project. In pushing for a high public profile for literacy issues, there is a fine line between drawing attention to a neglected and underresourced area of education and creating a public image which stigmatizes people with difficulties.

An important aspect of the networks is that since these networks exist, problems with reading and writing do not arise; people have networks of support which help them avoid problems. This emphasizes the relative nature of difficulties. As I have said elsewhere:

> People do not need to identify literacy 'problems' in order to get a friend to help understand a tax form or to have the railway official write out some train times. We all do this and there are particular people used for support who we can regard as brokers for literacy activities. It may be a neighbour or friend who deals with figures or fills in the forms. It may be institutionalized, the railway officials who look up train times, the travel agents who fill in holiday forms for customers. (Barton, 1991, p. 9)

Looked at this way, literacy ceases to be an individual affair; rather, the resources available to a community become important. Of course not all social relations involve networks of support: being interviewed to claim unemployment benefit and filling in the associated forms, for example, involves people in quite different networks and can present people with new literacy challenges (see Hamilton and Davies, 1990). It is also true that social networks may be more apparent in a small town community. Nevertheless, they exist in quite different situations, and James Jennings, for instance, give an example of quite different networks of support in a community in Bangladesh (1990, p. 41).

In our local literacies study, as in Fingeret's study, there were various ways in which people with problems got by in their lives. They might be skilled at decoding particular formats, such as forms which were regularly encountered, or at finding the information they wanted from a complex document. Again, we all do this. Reading as getting a meaning from a text which we do not fully understand is a common situation for everyone and was described earlier when discussing what is meant by reading; it happens when reading instructions for using a video recorder, a train timetable, the small print of an insurance policy, or even James Joyce's *Ulysses* or Michael Halliday's *Language as a social semiotic*. In our study, adults with difficulties also placed greater reliance on other media such as television and on oral networks. When they needed help, people would choose appropriate readers for specific tasks: a next door neighbour might help with an official form, while someone might cross the city to ask a relative to read a personal letter. Writing difficulties hindered people but in our study they did not stop people from keeping diaries, writing accounts of their lives, and doing other personal writing.

A parallel to the difficulties people encounter with reading and writing is not knowing a language in a country, or, as is often the case, not knowing it very well. The strategies employed by people in the two situations may have much in common, whether they be a holiday maker or an immigrant. Monolingualism is the new illiteracy. In fact the two issues of knowing a language and knowing a literacy often merge in that it is frequently the written language which a person is trying to understand.[3]

Language issues in adult literacy

As we saw in the chapters on language and history: most countries use several languages; different languages have different statuses; only some languages have written forms; and the infrastructure of literacy is only available in some languages. Consequently, difficult choices have to be made when selecting the language of official life and of education. These are choices which have to be made everywhere, in Malaysia, in Namibia, in Wales, in Australia – all very different contexts with very different solutions. Implicitly or explicitly every country has a language policy and, as part of it, decisions have to be made about the language or languages for literacy teaching. With notable exceptions, often governments are not very sympathetic to nonofficial languages. In education a common disputed area is the choice of whether initial literacy teaching should be in some vernacular language, and if so for how many years. Moving up through the school system and on through higher education, there are decisions about the choice of language for different subjects, the language of instruction, the language of textbooks, and the language of examinations. It is not a simple choice and children can find the language used in the classroom changes as they move up the school, that it can be different in different subjects, and that the language they are taught in and examined in is a different language from the language of the textbooks.

First, focusing on the beginning of education and specifically learning to read, the received wisdom has always been the importance of starting to read in the vernacular language. This has been true both for children and for adults and it goes back to Unesco's handbook of 1953, *The role of vernacular languages in education*. In this book the authors argued the importance of using vernacular languages as a starting-point for making people literate and there is a definition of vernacular language, contrasting it with other terms including indigenous language, lingua franca, mother tongue, regional language. A vernacular language is defined as being 'a language which is the mother tongue of a group which is socially or politically dominated by another group speaking a different language. We do not consider the language of a minority in one country as a vernacular if it an official language in another country'.[4] Where the term **vernacular** has been used in other studies of literacy it has also been used in several senses. A group of linguists who reassessed the role of vernacular languages in education and investigated the state of the 'vernacularization of literacy' found problems with the term and were content to define it differently in different language situations in the world (Tabouret-Keller et al., 1997). The issues surrounding the word vernacular are crucial for decisions about what language is to be used for education.

Given these problems in defining what is meant by vernacular and with the benefit of the experience of worldwide literacy programmes since the 1950s, there is no single answer to the bare psychological question: 'is it easier to learn to read in one's vernacular?' There is something fundamentally wrong with the way the question is asked. It is posed primarily as a question of skills, as if one only needs to consider generalizable cognitive aspects of learning which are thought to transcend social practices. In the way in which the question is posed it ignores the embeddedness of language in culture – it ignores the ecological basis of literacy. The answer to the question can only be: 'it depends'. It depends on the social situation, on the value of the language to the speakers, on the motivations for learning to read and write, on the other languages in the area, and on many other things. Even if it made sense to answer the question from a psychological point of view, the question of language choice is like the question of script choice mentioned earlier: such decisions are taken within a social context. Decisions made for Britain might be very different from decisions made for South Africa or Spain; what one might want in one context may be different in another. The choice one might make on linguistic grounds may not be very practical; choosing a language for literacy is a complex political choice involving many issues. Teaching in the vernacular needs language to have a written form, but it also needs an infrastructure of literacy, including books and other reading materials, publishing, teachers and, in the long term, institutions to sustain literacy. Teaching in the vernacular can also be very expensive, especially if there are few reading books, and no higher level textbooks.

The question of what language to start literacy in has been tied up with the question of how best to preserve, maintain, support and sustain dying languages. However, they are not the same question and what is best for initial literacy is not necessarily the same question as how to sustain small languages. In terms of sustaining a small language, the vernacular is also a possibility for people who can already read and write; it is not just a medium for starting out from and then transferring away from. For a vernacular literacy to survive it has to be seen to be of value by those who are already literate. One support is if it is used by those who are already literate in a more major language, and where poets and other writers are involved in creating a literature. It is the literate who become biliterate! An example of this is Hubisi Nwenmely's experiences with literacy classes for St Lucian Creole speakers in London – often it is the people who are already literate in English who come along to classes in the Creole (Morris and Nwenmely, 1994). This is just one example, and in the remainder of this section I want to draw attention to more general ecological questions of how to support and sustain disappearing languages.

Languages are vanishing at a remarkable rate. Like species in the plant and animal worlds, once they are extinct they are lost forever. Linguistic species including literacies are disappearing. The figures are frightening. There are over six thousand languages in the world; the number cannot be precise, as more languages with small numbers of speakers are still being discovered and often there is not a clear distinction between a dialect and a separate language. When reviewing these languages, Michael Krauss (in a set of papers on endangered languages in the journal *Language* in 1992) distinguished **moribund languages**, **endangered languages** and **safe languages**. Moribund languages are likely to die out within a lifetime: they are languages which are no longer being spoken by children, so there is no new generation of speakers. In all parts of the world there are large numbers of languages in this condition: to give some examples, 18 out of the 20 native languages of Alaska are no longer being spoken by children; over one hundred of the four hundred languages of South America are moribund; and 90 per cent of Australian aboriginal languages are near extinction. Overall Krauss estimated that around 50 per cent of the world's languages are moribund and will disappear as the current speakers die. Endangered languages are ones which do not have official state support or a large number of speakers to make them viable; taking a figure of needing 100,000 speakers to be safe, Krauss estimates that a further 40 per cent of languages are endangered, and only 10 per cent of the languages of the world are safe. Of these safe languages, just four of them, English, French, Spanish and Arabic, are official languages in more than half of the countries of the world.

There are several reasons why languages are disappearing at such a rate; they range from 'outright genocide, social or economic or habitat destruction, displacement, demographic submersion, language suppression in forced assimilation or assimilatory education, to electronic media bombardment, especially television . . .' (Krauss 1992, p. 6). These are trends which have been growing in the past half century and which show every sign of continuing. Even Krauss's safe languages in fact do not seem that secure: the current spread of English, through economic and cultural dominance, is affecting major world languages, so that within Europe, for example, Danish, with over five million speakers, is surely under threat from the switch to English in many spheres of life, especially as English moves down through the education system. In just one generation there can be dramatic changes in language use.[5]

This is an environmental disaster on a global scale and it is not obvious what can be done. Governments often have little interest in protecting small languages, as they push for standardization in education and official life; speakers of lesser known languages are perceived as backward and not modern. There is little public awareness of languages and in many ways the situation seems hopeless. However, there is now more interest in the plight of endangered languages with a focused interest by linguists and others, as in Mühlhäusler (1992), Hinton and Hale (2001), and Ostler and Rudes (2001). Here I want to look briefly at the role of literacy in all this.

Most of the moribund languages are not written down, and where there is a writing system there is very little written in the language and only in a narrow range of domains. This is also true for many of the endangered languages. Literacy can have a role in slowing down language death, by giving a language status and widening its uses. Sustaining local literacies can be important. However, it is an equivocal role. Writing down and tape recording an unwritten language can help preserve it, but there are still many issues. The act of creating a written form changes a language; usually it is intimately connected with standardizing the language and this act can destroy much variety. Inevitably in writing a language down, some aspects get highlighted, and others are ignored or suppressed. So that missionary organizations, for instance, which have been at the forefront of writing down languages at the same time may be 'Christianizing' the vocabulary and ignoring other meanings in the culture. Their role in saving languages may not involve saving the cultures. Strangely, the supporters of indigenous languages may at the same time be the destroyers of the indigenous cultures. In addition, writing down a language is of little use if people stop using the language. Preserving a language for a museum-like archive is one step, but the language and the culture it embodies may still become extinct.

Literacy in a vernacular is also two-edged in that although it seems to give status and value to a language and widen the range of practices, all too often it is only a stepping-stone to literacy in a language of wider communication. Literacy can then become a way of escaping the vernacular and having access to a broader range of cultures. Initial literacy is

not in itself enough to protect a language. There are several other possibilities: a language probably needs speakers of dominant languages to
learn it and value it; it needs clear functions; it needs people to write in
it; and it needs a role in education. One of the problems is that minority
or marginal literacies are often not valued in a society, nor are nonstandard varieties, regional dialects, pidgins or creoles. It is this diversity which
is of value ecologically. It represents a source of cultural strength as well
as being important for much linguistic change and innovation. There is a
sense in which all the languages of the world represent an ecosystem,
all being interdependent upon each other. Different languages embody
different values, experiences and sources of ideas. It is important to widen
the range of discourses in a language, to value marginal nonstandard
discourses and give them a voice.

World languages such as English have a role in all this: they are the
source of much of the threat to dying languages. In addition, they are
not immune to these issues themselves, and much which has been said
earlier about variety in language and how languages change is relevant.
With the spread of English, people need to accept the range of Englishes
in the world, for instance. There is not one standard but several:
Nigerian English, Indian English, American English, British English, are
all standards. There are also dialects, creoles and a range of varieties associated with the language. One of the main ways in which languages
develop and adapt is by utilizing the variety within the language itself;
another is by borrowing from other languages. English represents a range
of cultures and has always drawn upon others for its development. All
attempts to claim that English embodies one particular culture are mis-
taken; moves to enforce one dominant culture need to be resisted. The
other issue, mentioned earlier, concerns the role of new technologies.
There are rapid changes in mass communication through technologies
such as the internet. Currently much of it is in English, which has been
spreading at the expense of other languages. However, technologies are
not inevitable; there are vernacular responses and they can be controlled,
but that takes political will. Like other literacies, these media are part of
social practices.

14 Some implications of an ecological view

Literacy in education
Global literacy

Literacy research is developing in many directions. Throughout this book references have been given to works which are taking the study of literacy forward, whether in understanding the changes the internet is bringing to people's writing, assessing the significance of literacy for minority languages, or clarifying the relation of home and school practices, or one of many other directions which are being pursued. Some areas are quite well developed, while for others work is only just beginning: there still need to be further studies, for instance, of how people actually use their literacies in particular situations, and tracking texts across different contexts.

Although this book is not primarily about educational practice, it began with questions about the public debate on reading and writing in schools and about issues in adult basic education; it is appropriate, then, to return to discussions about education and literacy. In this chapter I will provide some suggestions for ways in which education can take account of an ecological approach to literacy, first in the context of learning to read and write in schools, and second in the context of world literacy. Any implications apply as much to the public discussion of literacy issues as to educational practice itself.

Literacy in education

Schools and other educational institutions can take account of an ecological view of literacy. The implications are in the whole book, not
particularly in this chapter. For example, they are listed in terms of practices, in understanding what learning goes on in the home, in the recent
history of compulsory schooling, and elsewhere.

In Britain and elsewhere schools are at the centre of disputes with the
government and the media over reading and writing. I have concentrated
on the skills view of literacy and the literary view of literacy as two
powerful metaphors in schools because they are also public images, and
ones drawn upon by politicians, parents and the media. Of course much
education has gone beyond these approaches and other views of literacy
appear in the classroom, some of which have been referred to here. Contemporary classroom practices have developed beyond simplistic views
of reading and writing and in their different ways contain elements of a
social view of literacy. In primary schools, for instance, there are shifts in
how reading and writing are being taught. There are conflicts between
an emphasis on the child as an active learner and centrally imposed
curricula. These ideas are part of the current conflicts in the public
domain over reading and writing, which in many ways are clashes over
the definitions of literacy.

Several writers have discussed the ways in which schools can take
account of a social view of literacy. Roz Ivanič and Mary Hamilton have
provided a practical list of how schools can take account of new views
of literacy. I will start from their list (1989, pp. 15–17), putting it into my
own words and adding my own interpretations. It is of course accepted
that many of these ideas complement good practice which exists in
mainstream education and they fit in with approaches which aim to
'start from where the child is'.

The lists starts with some suggestions related to the curriculum:

1   School literacy is one of many forms of communication, and should
    be developed alongside other forms such as spoken language, physical
    communication, graphics. Maybe print literacy should not monopol-
    ize the education process.
2   Literacy practices beyond school are extremely varied, and often
    quite different from those in school. Teachers could work critically

on out-of-school literacies such as consumer literacy, examining the range of literacies in life.

3   It is important to see school as one context for learning amongst others. Children learn about literacy informally in their everyday lives, both before they go to school and when they are in school. 'This sort of learning does not follow any step-by-step pattern: people learn about uses, strategies and values simultaneously and haphazardly.'

4   There are social purposes for reading and writing. In everyday life people do not read and write without a purpose. This supports the idea of reading and writing for real purposes in schools. Exercises, materials and activities which only involve reading and writing for their own sakes should be avoided.

5   Everyday literacy involves collaboration and using networks of support. This should encourage those who are developing collaborative reading and writing in the classroom.

6   People who have gone through the school system without learning to read and write very well, such as adult literacy students, can provide insights into the process of education which teachers could take account of.

7   Children can reflect on their own and others' literacy practices and become ethnographers of literacy, 'documenting why, when, where and how their parents, grandparents, neighbours or role-models read and write'.

Some suggestions on diagnosis and assessment are:

8   Parents, politicians and educators should be more wary of standardized tests of reading and writing, and rely more on teachers' assessments and children's own self-assessments. With regard to adult literacy, 'Adults' assessments of their own literacy is defined by their current needs and aspirations in varying roles and contexts, not by independent measures and objective tests.'

9   Teachers should be wary of tests which isolate literacy from any context or simulate a context.

10   In all areas of reading and writing, when people make a mistake, they usually have a rationale for it. Adults and children are good sources of information about their own learning.

11   If teachers value marginalized literacies and literacy practices outside the educational domain, they will understand more about those children who reject school literacy.

And some points related to home–school liaison:

12   Home–school liaison is not just about initiating parents into school practices and expectations. It should be a two-way exchange and could include collecting information about community practices to inform what happens in schools. The educational system needs to make it possible for teachers to know what children are familiar with at home and to be willing to change school practices where necessary.
13   Children tend to feel excluded when their own literacy practices are not valued by the school. Schools should investigate which community practices should be legitimated by integrating them into the classrooms.

In most of the discussion of education, except when talking about literary views of literacy, I have focused on early reading. It is important to remember that initial schooling is concerned with learning to read, it then widens out to learning to deal with a range of texts, and relating to other media. It is in later schooling especially that the idea of practices is useful, as children address the demands of different subjects and learn to deal with a wider range of genres. This learning to read and write continues through life. In all jobs people encounter new literacies at work, whether as a firefighter, a social worker, or a factory worker. To be an academic, a lawyer or a physicist takes 10 or 20 years of learning about literacy. As well as work life, everyday life can make new demands; people are learning new literacies throughout their lives.

Global literacy

Looking at the global picture, in many ways it is very difficult to be hopeful about the future of education. There are overwhelming problems in developing countries: there is widespread poverty; there is great inequality within countries; there are poorly trained teachers, with large classes, and no facilities; there are mother tongues with little or no written tradition, a wide range of dialects, and no obvious uses of literacy. There are the difficult structural relationships which developing countries have with industrialized countries and with aid agencies. Nevertheless, there are what have been called 'small and beautiful' programmes, meaning that in many parts of the world there are examples of excellent literacy programmes in a field of not so effective ones; this is true in Britain as much as in any other country.[1]

The ecological view outlined earlier leads to several comments on the world literacy scene, both for developing and for industrialized countries. There are important differences between the two situations, such as industrialized countries with a literate infrastructure and developing countries without one, and differences associated with teaching adults who have been through an educational system as children, and teaching adults who have not. Nevertheless, it is still useful to look for similarities.

1.   *People need to re-examine metaphors for literacy.* The success or otherwise of international programmes starts in many ways from the language used to talk about reading and writing, the metaphors for literacy: the language affects the way the issue is defined, what counts as a 'problem' and what counts as an 'solution'. **Functional literacy**, the basis of much contemporary literacy work, is a vague term: sometimes it covers everything in that all literacy is functional, at other time it has a very narrow definition. It is not clear how useful this term is, especially when comparing across situations. **Universal literacy** is not meaningful, **universal schooling** may be. These terms are tied into a whole discourse which has the idea of there being a great divide between literate and illiterate as its foundation, and in the belief in literacy as a variable with cognitive consequences. Each piece of this metaphorical system has been criticized earlier, as the different aspects have been covered.

It is important to realize that the term functional literacy is just one way of talking about literacy in society today and that it is associated with a particular discourse about literacy, one which includes other not very useful terms such as functional illiteracy, universal literacy and the eradication of illiteracy. From these terms it is easy to drift into the media image of the need to eradicate some terrible disease from the face of the earth. People talk of the possibility of redefining the word, but with such a history of connotations it may be preferable to avoid the term. We are not just talking about one word but about a whole discourse, a whole way of talking: the words fit together and define each other.

The terms which need to be scrutinized include the very idea of a 'literacy problem'. As we saw in earlier chapters this is a relative concept. There is a sense in which everyone in contemporary society has literacy problems. Most of the people with problems of reading and writing in

Britain, most of the people attending literacy classes, can read and write to some extent. Everyone encounters literacy in their lives which they cannot fully comprehend. This relativity was in the original definitions of functional literacy, but it got lost somewhere along the line. Also, as we have seen, the idea of the person without literacy as being other, an outsider, is not generally true. Related to this, literacy has become defined as a problem in society. Other practices which some people are not part of are not considered as problems. Not being able to drive a car, or to add numbers, or to use a computer, or speak a foreign language, are less likely to be stigmatized as problems in today's world.

An ecological view of literacy, where it is embedded in its everyday context, can contribute two things to this discussion. First of all it makes clear that there are different metaphors for literacy, competing ways of talking about the issue. Secondly, a socially based view can provide a coherent alternative way of talking about literacy, with terms such as literacies, events, practices. A social view of literacy provides an alternative discourse, a different set of metaphors. To realize that there are different literacy practices in a culture, that there are different literacies and different domains, would be a good starting point. There is great need for international funders to realize that there are many literacies in any society, and that the workplace, for example, is but one domain of literacy use with its distinct practices. However, it is not just international decision makers who can examine how they talk about literacy. Trainee teachers can reflect on their own practices and observe those of others; similarly, critical readers of newspapers can examine the practices around them.

2.   *Literacy learning has a social basis.* Adult literacy is often assumed to be to do with the provision of classes and with methods of teaching. However, examining how people use literacy in their everyday lives makes it clear that the issue is much broader than this. Communities, not just individuals, become literate; there is more to a literacy campaign than inoculating individuals. It is important to think through the idea of helping a community become literate, rather than helping an individual. This could lead, for example, to supporting key people in a network, such as those who act as brokers or gatekeepers for literacy. Typically, when discussing levels of literacy in a country, the literacy rates of individuals are given. There is a lot more to it than this. There are also differences in writers, book shops, publishers, printers, libraries, amount of paper, availability of pens, computers, typewriters, postal systems, and other

communications technologies, as well as the existence of schools, colleges, the whole infrastructure of literacy.

Understanding literacy involves understanding how literacy use is embedded in the social structure and it involves examining, analysing and challenging the language in use in society today. This has several aspects. There are moves towards making written language more accessible, for instance, including simplifying forms and legal documents. Related to this it is important to understand and question the obscuring effects of the language of specific professions and academic disciplines. Literacy work raises questions about the control of language, power relations, and the accessibility of information. As has been mentioned already, helping people reflect on the importance of language, critical language awareness, is an important aspect of literacy teaching which grows out of a social view of language (see, for example, Ivanič and Moss, 1991).

There are many practical teaching implications of a social view of literacy, both for teaching adults and for teaching children. Many of the suggestions proposed earlier in this chapter when discussing children's learning are equally applicable to adults. Teaching adult literacy with a concern for its social context is different from teaching the acquisition of an autonomous skill, and there are many developments in this direction. In addition to the references given earlier, Lytle (1991), Papen (2005) and Tett et al. (2006) apply a social practices approach to adults learning to read and write. Reder (1987) suggests ways in which adult literacy can support communities rather than just teach individuals. Appleby and Barton (2006) have developed ideas for a social practices pedagogy when working with adults.

Part of the social basis of literacy is that new language practices are based on existing ones. Any community has established patterns of communication and any new practices have to bear some relation to the old. New literacy practices are based and grow out of established oral and literate practices. The starting point for literacy work should be the fact that every situation is different, with its own patterns of language use. Up until now literacy campaigns have been based on generalizations, on the idea that all world communities have much in common, that there is one invariable modern commodity of literacy which the whole world wants and can be given. This idea of the big generalization has been taken as far as it can be. Now it would be fruitful to take the opposite view, and to pursue it as far as possible: that every situation is different and each situation has to be examined in detail in order to understand literacy needs.

3.   *People change practices.* People have their own needs and purposes based on their own lives. This fact, like some of the others, may appear obvious. However, it is worth articulating this and making it explicit, as there is still resistance to the idea of taking account of people's own perceptions; this applies in every level of setting up literacy programmes, from initial discussion of funding and strategy, right on to the planning of individual lessons. It includes the right to have some influence over the language used.

People make sense of literacy; their awareness and perceptions of it are important, as are public perceptions of its role and its value. A thread which runs through from children's first awareness of language all the way to attempts at liberatory adult education is that learning is the active construction of knowledge; this should be the starting point for working out the role of teaching. It is people who decide to become literate, who actively learn and who decide to make changes in their lives. People's construction of literacy lies at the root of their attitudes and of their action. Literacy work needs to start from people's own definitions of literacy, from their own purposes and from their current communication practices. Literacy work for adults and for children needs to enable them to learn how to learn.

Adult literacy provision is required which responds to people's perceptions, not solely to the priorities of governments and international organizations. This point should not need stating. The ideas have been around for a long time and can be found in the various declarations of international organizations, but all too often they are lost by the time the ideas are translated into practical literacy programmes (see Barton and Hamilton, 1990; Rogers et al., 1999; Barton and Papen, 2005 for examples of this). There has always been a split between the language of literacy declarations and the reality of functional literacy programmes. The starting point for any literacy work has to be people's needs, with provision shaped to this. The assessment of need has to be ongoing as needs change. Inevitably, people's stated needs exist in relation to the possibilities; access to education gives different possibilities and people's demands will change accordingly. If taken seriously, this is different from needs analysis, which is common in some areas of teaching and which is something undertaken by teachers, but not usually in consultation with their students.

4. *There is an urgent lack of resources.* There are many problems facing adult literacy work in developing countries. In some of the poorest countries of the world the provision of education has got worse and in several the proportion of the country's wealth spent on education has been going down as part of a downturn in social funding. Adult education has to compete for resources with other areas of education such as child education with its aim of universal primary education. At the same time international organizations may be turning their attention more to other communications technologies and there is less concern for basic literacy.

In practical terms the issue is resources, with a need for such basic supplies as paper and pencils. Often what is needed are not ways of starting literacy, but ways of sustaining it, and it may be that questions about how to sustain literacy, post-literacy, should come before literacy programmes themselves. There is a need for sustainable literacy, that is, literacy which fits into sustainable development. Ideas of how this is possible have been developed in Street (2001), Robinson-Pant (2004) and Rogers (2005).

It is important to realize that in both developing countries and industrialized countries we are not talking about a short-term 'crisis' to be solved by some quick campaign, but rather this is to do with the provision of adult education. People need access to educational provision for a host of different reasons and at various times in their lives. Provision has to be long-term, it has to be flexible to respond to people's differing needs, it has to provide opportunities for people who have received the least educationally. It requires political commitment and it costs money. Ultimately literacy reflects inequalities in society: inequalities of power, inequalities in the distribution of wealth, and inequalities in access to education. These inequalities are both within countries and between countries. Literacy can only be fully understood in the context of these social relations. Literacy education will always be ineffective unless these other issues are addressed alongside questions of literacy. To the extent that it is meaningful, the eradication of illiteracy is possible, but only if it is preceded by the eradication of poverty.

Notes

1 An integrated approach to literacy

1   The term **literacy myth** was originally used by Graff (1979); the approach of explicitly listing a set of current myths has been used by Audrey Grant (1986), Frank Smith (1983, 1985), Carol Edelsky (1986) and Shirley Heath (1987), for example.

2 Talking about literacy

1   These ideas can be pursued in the work of Lakoff and colleagues, starting with Lakoff and Johnson's (1980) *Metaphors we live by*, especially the first few chapters.
2   In fact, in everyday writing the pejorative terms illiterate and illiteracy seem more common than the positive terms literate and literacy. From an examination of British newspapers discussing what goes on and what should be going on in education, it is apparent that the terms illiteracy and illiterate are the ones which are most used.
3   This may seem strange to the linguist or anthropologist who contrast literacy with orality but the adult basic education student has always taken exception to the term: people point out that International Literacy Year was really International Illiteracy Year and that literacy classes are really illiteracy classes.
4   We also got into knots when discussing the translation of the words teacher, trainer, student and learner into French.
5   Cole and Keyssar (1985).
6   Another powerful metaphor with literacy which will be useful later when discussing different literacies is that it creates a world. There are *Worlds of literacy* (Hamilton et al., 1994), 'children's worlds of literacy' (Dyson, 1991), and Frank Smith's (1985) use of the metaphor of literacy as being for creating worlds rather than for processing information. We read 'the word and the world' (Freire and Macedo, 1987) and there is *The world on paper* (Olson, 1993).
7   For example, Lave and Wenger (1991), Cole et al. (1997), Rogoff (2003), Holland et al. (2001), Holland and Lave (2001).
8   For more on Vygotsky, in addition to his two books (1962, 1978), see the work of others who have been developing these ideas (such as Kozulin, 1990; Moll, 1990; Wertsch, 1991, 1997) and the references on socio-cultural theory, above.

9 Other studies of language which talk in terms of ecology include work on multi-lingual classrooms (Creese and Martin, 2003) and, more generally, Creese and Martin (2006).

10 Lemke (1995) develops the notion of society as an 'ecosocial system', sharing all the complexity of an ecological system with the additional social complexities associated with meaning-making processes.

3 The social basis of literacy

1 For links with the broader sociological formulations of practice theory, see the discussion of the work of Bourdieu in Lave (1988). In another direction, Fairclough (1989, 1992) and Chouliaraki and Fairclough 1999 explore the notion of language as a set of social practices, in order to reveal how social institutions and power relations structure our uses of language, both spoken and written.

2 Colin Lankshear's work discusses this in more detail and demonstrates the inadequacy of this approach, showing that what test designers call basic and higher are quite different literacies serving different purposes. See Lankshear (1991).

3 See Holland and Quinn (1987), Cole (1998) and Wertsch's (1997) idea of seeing mind as action.

4 See, for example, Lave and Wenger (1991), Rogoff (2003).

4 Researching literacy practices

1 This approach to smaller-scale literacy research is described in more detail in Barton (2000), with examples of a range of different student projects. More examples with pictures of students' posters are available from www.literacy.lancs.ac.uk. See also Fowler and Mace (2005) on how teachers can research literacy with adult learners.

2 Guidelines for conducting ethical research in applied linguistics are available from the websites of professional associations such as the American Educational Research Association (AERA), the American Anthropological Association (AAA), or the British Association for Applied Linguistics (BAAL).

3 See for instance studies in Ferdman et al. (1994), Gonzalez et al. (2005), Guerra (1998) and Pérez (2004).

4 Alam (2000) and Hodge and Jones (2000) report on research with Panjabi speakers of Pakistani origin in Britain. In both of these studies, the speakers speak Panjabi, a language primarily used in its written form, but write Urdu, a language which is seen as carrying greater prestige.

5 Given this seeming stability it is equally important to know how and why the other invented scripts of Liberia, Glebo and Kru, did not survive, as reported by Elizabeth Tonkin in Le Page (1990).

6 And, giving a historical dimension, there are examples of women being associated with personal letters from the beginnings of literacy four thousand years ago (Barton and Hall, 2000).

7 See Jennifer Horsman's and Kate Rockhill's studies of women's lives and adult literacy (Horsman, 1994; Rockhill, 1993); studies of girls' and boys' school literacies

such as G. Moss (1989) and Millard (1997); studies of teenagers (Finders, 1996; Smith and Wilhelm, 2002); Jane Mace's (1998) study of the meaning of literacy to mothers; and various articles in Hamilton et al. (1994).

8   These points are made by Hull (1997) in her introduction to *Changing Work, Changing Workers*, a collection which includes several workplace ethnographies referred to in this section.

9   We have identified five distinct types of restriction by examining historical studies of writing; see Barton and Hamilton (1996).

10   Historical examples can be found as in Hindu India. See Goody (1968, p. 12) and Gaur (1984, p. 84).

5 Literacy embedded in language

1   A simple introduction to the genre approach and to the dispute between it and process approaches to teaching writing is to be found in Cairney (1992).

2   Rather than seeing language use as holding groups together, an alternative perspective is one which emphasizes common activities. This is work which emphasizes **communities of practice**, as in Wenger (1998), Barton and Tusting (2005), and for a comparison with discourse communities see Swales (1998, 1990).

3   For general ideas on how to analyse such texts, see the approaches to linguistic analysis represented in Fairclough (1989, 2003), and for examples applied to education, see Fairclough (1992), Rogers (2004), Bazerman and Prior (2004). To locate the analysis of texts in broader multimodal analysis, see LeVine and Scollon (2004).

4   More discussion of a previous version of this form and the problems it presents claimants can be found in Davies (1994).

5   See Fairclough (1992) for a more detailed analysis of different sorts of intertextuality.

6   For ideas of the ways in which texts act in place of people, see work on actor-network theory, for example, Clarke (2002), Hamilton (2001), Barton and Hamilton (2005), Brandt and Clinton (2002).

7   To give three disparate examples, Fawns and Ivanič (2001) provide a detailed study of what people actually do when they fill in forms. Examining a very different literacy practice, Radway (1987) carried out an ethnographic study of how people read one sort of novel, popular romances. Nell (1988) has investigated what it means for people reading to be lost in a book.

6 Configurations of language

1   This list continues; a thorough review of the work from this period on differences can be found in Akinasso (1982), where much of this list is taken from. On idea units and other possible units of spoken language see Chafe (1985).

2   On the language of oral cultures, see Feldman (1991) and the contributors to Bloch (1975). For the variety of spoken genres, Akinnaso's (1982) analysis of Yoruba ritual communication demonstrates this point, as do studies of oral poetry and oral literature (Finnegan, 1977). For more discussion and examples, see also Street (1984, 1993), and contributors to Duranti (2001).

7 Writing systems and other notations

1   Halle (1969, p. 18) and Ong (1982, p. 87) are two examples where the writing system has been misunderstood. For details of the Chinese writing system, see DeFrancis (1984).

2   There is, however, some research on adults learning second language writing systems; see, for example, Cook and Bassetti (2005).

3   A standard reference for this claim is Makita (1968), but also see Paradis et al. (1985) where the claim is disputed, and the establishment in the late 1990s of the Japan Dyslexia Society NPO Edge (www.npo-edge.jp/eng/index.html).

4   Significantly, one study of English-speaking children experiencing reading problems (Rozin et al., 1971) claimed that such children had no difficulties when beginning to read with a method that involved teaching them to read English using Chinese characters.

5   But see the work of Tzeng and colleagues on other scripts, such as Tzeng et al. (1978).

6   See Martin (1972), for example, on Japanese texts being shorter than comparable English ones and in some ways quicker to read.

7   See, for example, the work of Rogoff and Lave mentioned already, and Crump (1990); on gender, the collection of articles in Burton (1986); on numeracy as social practice, Baker (1998); on home and school numeracy practices, Street et al. (2005); on transfer between adult mathematics and everyday life, Evans (2000).

8 Points in history

1   The two most widely quoted authorities on the development of writing are two works which were first published more than half a century ago: they are Diringer (1968, first published 1948) and Gelb (1963, first published 1952). Both are rich in sources of data and anecdote which are presented within a framework of gradual development toward our modern western alphabet. They are important in discussing what writing is and in setting a framework, but it is necessary to go beyond their work. Other overviews are presented by Goody (1981), Gaur (1984) and Harris (1986). The ideas in this chapter originated in an article written by Mary Hamilton and myself (Barton and Hamilton, 1996); further evidence and sources for the claims made here can be found in this article.

2   Certainly as Albertine Gaur points out (1984, p. 35), when looking at later examples 'writing on imperishable material is nearly always preceded and accompanied by writing on perishable material'. So only some of the evidence remains: this is most probably also true of the first writing.

3   Baines (1983) provides a clear description of the development of literacy in ancient Egypt.

4   Havelock (1963, 1976). It has been developed and spread by David Olson (1977) and others, and it is in danger of becoming accepted fact, for example with Michael Cole and Peg Griffin (1983) surmising that perhaps 'the ability to send astronauts into space owes a lot to the analytic power of the alphabet'. Ivan Illich and Barry Sanders claim to believe that there are 'certain constructs which cannot exist without reference to the alphabet – thought and language, lie and memory, translation, and particularly the self' (1989, p. x).

5   Literacy studies owes McLuhan a great debt, in both a positive way and a negative way. His are both the most refreshing and the strangest ideas on literacy (1962, 1964).

6   For more information on this, Harris (1986) describes in detail how an evolutionary account of writing obscures our understanding of the origin of writing, and other books on writing such as Sampson (1985) have also criticized aspects of the evolutionary approach. For more details of my criticisms, see Barton (1993).

7   Unesco's important study of vernacular languages also concluded that the only solution to Japan's 'problem' was to adopt a phonetic system of writing (Unesco, 1953, p. 35). See also Havelock's attribution of Japan's failure to 'catch up' with the West to its syllabic writing system (1982, pp. 346–7). Havelock seems not to realize (pp. 66–9) that many spoken languages have more regular syllabic systems than English.

8   Burnaby (1997) describes how ethnocentrism and a faith in the power of English went largely unquestioned in Britain and North America during the twentieth century, leading to the idealization of phonemic orthographies over other types of writing systems.

9   See Walker (1981) for an example of an invented Native American system.

10 Aitchison (2000) provides a simple introduction to the subject of language change.

11 I draw primarily on the ideas of Elizabeth Eisenstein (1979, 1981) and on the 1996 paper by Mary Hamilton and myself mentioned earlier.

12 These developments in Europe were apparently independent of those in Asia, although Chinese block printing techniques were known in Europe, as discussed by Febvre and Martin (1984).

13 Vincent's (2000) analysis of the rise of mass literacy in modern Europe describes such contradictory tendencies and results of the growth of printing, demonstrating clearly the dangers of ascribing any deterministic causal attributes to literacy in itself without taking into account social, cultural, economic and historical contexts.

14 Similar claims about life in thirteenth-century Denmark are made in Schousboe (1989, pp. 154–7).

15 See Marshall (1983), Staikos (2000) on libraries; Brooks and Pugh (1984) on the teaching of reading; Petroski (1989) on the pencil; and Carvalho (1971) for a history of ink.

16 See the summary and discussion of this in Swales (1990), also Bazerman and Prior (2004). For other examples of the development of particular sorts of texts, see studies by Olson (1991) and Halliday (1988).

9 The roots of literacy

1   An additional point is that the question of innateness is often not an empirical question, in the sense that it cannot be solved by practical research.

2   Harste (1984, p. 61), for example, is critical of the idea of scaffolding. The other ideas of learning such as apprenticeship or using people as supportive others are probably more revealing. See Brown et al. (1986) for appropriate references and for expansion on the term 'supportive other'. They demonstrate how such an approach can be applied to poor readers. See Wells (1986) for more on apprenticeship in literacy learning, and Padmore (1994) for an example from adults, and Brandt's notion of 'sponsors of literacy' (2001). Jane Mace examines the significance of scribes in many areas of life (2002) and Baynham (1993) examines mediators of literacy.

3 Of course some people have long realized the connections. The similarities were noted by Ragnhild Soderbergh (1977, p. 8), for example, when arguing that children could learn both reading and speaking 'at the same age and in the same way'. In a key article in the field of language acquisition Catherine Snow (1983) explores the parallels between learning to read and learning to speak; from a different direction Shirley Brice Heath's book (1983), which I have already referred to, traces the web between learning to speak and literacy in contrasting communities.

4 Schieffelin (1979) and articles in Duranti (2001). Another study is the work of Clifton Pye (1981) on Mayan communities in Guatemala.

10 Emergent literacy

1 For more on some of the different ways of reading to children, see Teale (1984, pp. 111–14).

2 Of course there are many books with moving parts, windows to look through, and finger puppets; these all make the distinction between books and toys less clear-cut.

3 Such as Taylor (1983, 1986), Leichter (1984), Heath (1983) and our own work.

4 See Teale (1986, pp. 185–7); also Anderson and Stokes (1984, pp. 28–34).

5 As another example, religious activities often incorporate children and may have special regular roles for them involving language.

6 Ironically it is the poorest households which often have the greatest demands put on them in terms of the official literacy of benefits and social security (see Taylor, 1996).

7 Nevertheless, writing can have a central role in some homes. This is demonstrated in the work of David Bloome, Dorothy Sheridan and Brian Street studying the writing of participants, and the British Mass-Observation Archive. See Sheridan et al. (2000).

8 Glenda Bissex (1984, p. 100) has more examples of the intelligent choices children are constantly making as they teach themselves to write. See also Kress (1998).

9 This is a separate point from whether or not the teaching should focus explicitly on language.

10 For examples of a range of this research see Sinclair et al. (1978), Downing and Valtin (1984), and the journal *Language Awareness*.

11 As in Hartley (1994) and Saxena (1994), referred to in chapter 4.

11 Public definitions of literacy

1 One of the attractions of approaches such as phonics is that something complicated is broken down into components and there is an apparently rigid ordering in which it can be taught. While teachers may want to break an activity into parts for teaching purposes, it is a mistake to think that the phenomenon of reading is made up of components which can be taken to bits and put together again at will.

2 I still find it instructive to see what happens if one avoids the word skills and replaces it with a practices framework. As an example of this, it may be very fruitful to avoid the notion of **study skills** in schools and colleges and replace it with ideas of **academic literacies**. This changes the nature of the problem, and the nature of the possible solutions (see, for example, Lea and Stierer, 2000).

3   Incidentally, in a sense I am puzzled over why a belief in the importance of breaking literacy into skills is so often tied in with an overemphasis on phonics in teaching, in correct spelling and in learning mathematical tables, and why they are associated with right-wing movements and general beliefs in the need for more discipline. It is conservative in a very basic way of being resistant to change. However, being able to spell becomes irrelevant with a spell checker. Slips of grammar or spelling rarely impede communication. Why do newspapers and politicians support these things so passionately? Why are they all so desperate for it to be true and to impose these approaches on education? Why do mature adults still write heated letters to the editors of the most prestigious national newspapers complaining about misplaced apostrophes or the misspelling of words like 'occurrence' or 'separate'?

4   The consciousness-raising ideas of writing which develop from the process view of writing are being brought into British schools (for example, Czerniewska, 1992), and links between consciousness raising and critical literacy are explored by Clark and Ivanič (1991).

5   In fact the disdain felt by 'literary' writers, such as Virginia Woolf, for ordinary people is argued coherently, if contentiously, by John Carey in a book entitled *The intellectuals and the masses* (1992).

6   There are parallels in art, the theatre and academia. Universities are for creating PhDs and everyone else is a failure. In Britain at the level of bachelors degrees there are 'good degrees' and 'bad degrees'. We have the absurd outcome of many people leaving universities with the idea of not having done very well. It is something which has its root in an elite view of education, and is exacerbated by a culture of testing, targets and league tables.

7   The ones I have read through include: several of the classic *Writers at Work* series edited by George Plimpton which are collections of interviews with well-known writers (e.g. Plimpton 1988); collections of interviews with women writers including Chamberlain (1988); also a book of Hemingway's quotations edited by Phillips (1985); and Dillard (1989). Nearly all write in English and most are American. It is now much more common for writers to reflect on how they write (e.g. Hoggart, 2005).

8   See for example Hartley and Branthwaite (1989) for work on successful academic writers.

9   For examples of everyday writing see Barton and Padmore (1991), Sheridan et al. (2000).

12 School practices

1   Two books which explore in detail this view of literacy and its relation to school education are Larson and Marsh (2005) and Pahl and Rowsell (2005). Pahl and Rowsell (2006) and Street (2005) bring together many different areas of education. Papen (2005) provides a social view of literacy in relation to the education of adults.

2   Willett and Bloome (1992) summarize the ways in which schools socialize children. They also provide extensive references to the research on this.

3   In a study of the unofficial literacies in schools, Janet Maybin (2006) reports on the unofficial writing of 12 year olds in and out of school; see also the studies of older children by Camitta (1993) and Shuman (1993) and papers in Scheiffelin and Gilmore (1986).

4   For a focus on analysing the language of the classroom see Cazden (2001).

5   The two-thirds rule is summarized by Edwards and Mercer (1987, p. 25).

6 Steinberg and Steinberg (1975). A classic popularization of explicitly teaching young children to read is Glen Doman's best selling paperback originally published in 1963. There are now many books on this.

7 See Bloome and Bailey (1992). A similar conclusion is reached by Jo Longman and Neil Mercer in a study of a quite different event – counselling interviews with unemployed adults. They conclude that such interviews 'are not aptly described as literacy events or as oral events: they are language events with oral and literate dimensions' (1992, p. 16). Similarly, in examining children's talk Janet Maybin and Gemma Moss (1993) conclude that children's talk around texts involves making sense of the written word, and is reading.

8 As in Gee (1996), and he talks of being literate as 'mastery or fluent control over a secondary discourse' (pp. 142–3). However I am not convinced of the distinction between primary and secondary discourses. It seems to me that all adult talk is part of secondary discourses in his sense.

13 Adults and world literacy

1 'Post-literacy' concerns the literacy support which is provided after a literacy campaign. Often it involves trying to provide more long-term support after the initial burst of enthusiasm in a literacy campaign. It may well be that all literacy work should be post-literacy and that it provides a more ecological view of reading and writing than is provided in standard literacy campaigns. See Rogers et al. (1999), Barton and Papen (2005).

2 For more on this see Kenneth Levine's (1985) early criticism of functional literacy.

3 Cecil Klassen (1991), has examples of the strategies bilingual learners use in their daily lives. See also Martin-Jones and Jones (2000a), Gonzalez et al. (2005).

4 Unesco (1953, p. 46). It is worth pointing out that even within the Unesco report, the authors do not keep to this definition of vernacular: their review of vernacular languages in education includes Chinese, Japanese and other world languages.

5 There are also examples of the opposite happening: where languages such as Irish and Cornish are being 'resurrected'. Here there is great dependence on written records. Such examples bring up complex issues about language, identity and nationhood.

14 Some implications of an ecological view

1 Educators from almost any country of the world can point to examples of small but effective literacy programmes in their country, even where the overall practice is not encouraging. For examples from Africa, India and elsewhere, see Barton (1994).

References

Aijmer, K. and Stenström, A.-B. 2004. *Discourse patterns in spoken and written corpora.* Amsterdam: John Benjamins.

Aitchison, J. 2000. *Language change: progress or decay?*, 3rd edn. Cambridge, UK and New York: Cambridge University Press.

Akinnaso, F. N. 1982. On the differences between written and spoken language. *Language and Speech*, 25, 97–125.

Alam, Y. 2000. Gender, literacy and community publishing in a multilingual context. In M. Martin-Jones and K. Jones (eds). *Multilingual literacies: reading and writing different worlds.* Amsterdam: John Benjamins, pp. 247–72.

Anderson, C. A. 1966. Literacy and schooling on the development threshold: some historical cases. In C. A. Anderson and M. Bowman (eds) *Education and economic development.* London: Frank Cass, pp. 347–62.

Anderson, A. B. and S. J. Stokes. 1984. Social and institutional influences on the development and practice of literacy. In H. A. Goelman, A. Oberg and F. Smith (eds) *Awakening to literacy.* London: Heinemann, pp. 28–34.

Anderson, A. B., W. H. Teale and E. Estrada. 1980. Low-income children's preschool literacy experiences: some naturalistic observations. *Q. Newsletter of the Laboratory of Comparative Human Cognition*, 2, 59–65.

Appleby, Y. and D. Barton. 2006. *Social practices pedagogy.* London: National Research and Development Centre for Adult Literacy and Numeracy.

Archer, D. and S. Cottingham. 1996. *The REFLECT mother manual: regenerated Freirean literacy through empowering community techniques.* London: ActionAid.

Auerbach, E. and N. Wallerstein. 2004. *Problem posing at work.* Alberta: GrassRoots Press.

Baines, J. 1983. Literacy and ancient Egyptian society. *Man*, 18, 572–99.

Baker, D. 1998. Numeracy as social practice, *Literacy and Numeracy Studies*, 8(1), 37–51.

Barton, D. 1986. Metalinguistic awareness and children's acquisition of literacy. In C. Antaki and A. Lewis (eds). *Mental mirrors.* London: Sage, pp. 68–78.

Barton, D. 1988. Exploring the historical basis of contemporary literacy. *Q. Newsletter of the Laboratory of Comparative Human Cognition*, 3, 70–6.

Barton, D. 1991. The social nature of writing. In D. Barton and R. Ivanič (eds). *Writing in the community.* London: Sage, pp. 1–13.

Barton, D. 1992. The emergence of sounds: parallels between learning to read and learning to speak. In C. Ferguson, L. Menn and C. Stoel-Gammon (eds). *Phonological development*. Timonium, MD; York Press, pp. 539–52.

Barton, D. 1993. Some problems with an evolutionary view of written language. In S. Puppel (ed.). *Biology of language*. Amsterdam: John Benjamins, pp. 19–32.

Barton, D. (ed.). 1994. *Sustaining local literacies*. Clevedon, UK: Multilingual Matters.

Barton, D. 2000. Researching literacy practices: Learning from activities with teachers and students. In Barton, D. Hamilton, M. and Ivanič R. (eds). *Situated literacies: reading and writing in context*, London and New York: Routledge, pp. 167–79.

Barton, D. 2001. Directions for literacy research: analysing language and social practices in a textually-mediated world. *Language & Education*, 15, 92–104.

Barton, D. and N. Hall. 2000. *Letter writing as a social practice*. Amsterdam: John Benjamins.

Barton, D. and M. Hamilton. 1990. *Literacy research in industrialised countries: Trends and prospects*. Hamburg: UIE Reports 2.

Barton, D. and M. Hamilton. 1996. Social and cognitive factors in the historical elaboration of writing. In A. Lock and C. Peters. *Handbook of human symbolic evolution*. Oxford: Oxford University Press, pp. 793–858.

Barton, D. and M. Hamilton. 1998. *Local literacies: reading and writing in one community*. London and New York: Routledge.

Barton, D. and M. Hamilton. 2005. Literacy, reification and the dynamics of social interaction. In D. Barton and K. Tusting (eds). *Beyond communities of practice: language, power and social context*. Cambridge, UK and New York: Cambridge University Press, pp. 14–35.

Barton, D., M. Hamilton and R. Ivanič (eds). 2000. *Situated literacies: reading and writing in context*. London and New York: Routledge.

Barton, D. and S. Padmore. 1991. Roles, networks and values in everyday writing. In D. Barton and R. Ivanič (eds). *Writing in the community*. London: Sage, pp. 58–77.

Barton, D. and U. Papen (eds). 2005. *Linking literacy programmes in developing countries and the UK*. London: National Research and Development Centre for Adult Literacy and Numeracy (NRDC).

Barton, D. and K. Tusting (eds). 2005. *Beyond communities of practice: language, power and social context*. Cambridge, UK and New York: Cambridge University Press.

Bateson, G. 1972. *Steps to an ecology of mind*. New York: Ballantine Books.

Baynham, M. 1993. Code switching and mode switching: community interpreters and mediators of literacy. In B. Street (ed.). *Cross-cultural approaches to literacy*. Cambridge, UK: Cambridge University Press, pp. 294–314.

Bazerman, C. and P. Prior. 2004. *What writing does and how it does it: an introduction to analyzing texts and textual practices*. Mahwah, NJ: Lawrence Erlbaum Associates.

Becker, J. D. 1984. Multilingual word processing. *Scientific American*, 251(1), 82–93.

Belfiore, M. E., T. A. Defoe, S. Folinsbee, J. Hunter and N. Jackson. 2004. *Reading work: literacies in the new workplace*. Mahwah, NJ: Lawrence Erlbaum Associates.

Berry, J. 1958. The making of alphabets. In E. Siversten (ed.). *Pro. VIII International Congress of Linguistics*. Oslo: Oslo University Press, pp. 752–64.

Berry, J. 1977. The making of alphabets revisited. In J. A. Fishman (ed.). *Advances in the creation and revision of writing systems*. Hague: Mouton, pp. 3–16.

Besnier, N. 1988. The linguistic relationships of spoken and written Nukulaelae registers. *Language*, 64, 707–36.

Besnier, N. 1989. Literacy and feelings: The encoding of affect in Nukulaelae letters. *Text*, 9, 69–91.

Besnier, N. 1993. Literacy and feelings: the encoding of affect in Nukulaelae letters. In B. Street (ed.). *Cross-cultural approaches to literacy*. Cambridge, UK: Cambridge University Press, pp. 62–86.

Bettelheim, B. 1966. The danger of teaching your baby to read. *Ladies Home Journal*, 83, 38–40.

Bhatt, A., D. Barton, M. Martin-Jones and M. Saxena. 1996. *Multilingual literacy practices: home, community and school*. Lancaster University: Centre for Language in Social Life Working Papers no. 80.

Biber, D. 1991. *Variation across speech and writing*. Cambridge, UK and New York: Cambridge University Press.

Bissex, G. L. 1984. The child as teacher. In H. A. Goelman, A. Oberg and F. Smith (eds). *Awakening to literacy*. London: Heinemann, pp. 87–101.

Blackledge, A. 2000. Power relations and the social construction of 'literacy' and 'illiteracy': the experience of Bangladeshi women in Birmingham. In M. Martin-Jones and K. Jones (eds). *Multilingual literacies: reading and writing different worlds*. Amsterdam: John Benjamins, pp. 55–70.

Bloch, M. 1975. *Political language and oratory in traditional society*. Academic Press.

Bloome, D. and F. M. Bailey. 1992. Studying language and literacy through events, particularity, and intertextuality. In R. Beach, J. Green and T. Shanahan (eds). *Multiple perspective research on language and literacy*. Urbana, IL: National Conference on Research on English, pp. 181–210.

Bloome D. and J. L. Green. 1992. Educational contexts of literacy. *Annual Review of Applied Linguistics*, 12, 49–70.

Bowler, P. J. 1986. *Theories of human evolution*. Oxford: Blackwell.

Brandt, D. 2001. *Literacy in American lives*. Cambridge, UK and New York: Cambridge University Press.

Brandt, D. and K. Clinton. 2002. Limits of the local: expanding perspectives on literacy as a social practice. *Journal of Literacy Research*, 34(3), 337–56.

Breen, M., W. Louden, C. Barratt-Pugh et al. 1994. *Literacy in its place: literacy practices in urban and rural communities*. Western Australia: Edith Cowan University.

Brien D. (ed.). 1992. *Dictionary of British sign language/English*. London: Faber & Faber.

Bronfenbrenner, U. 1979. *The ecology of human development*. Cambridge, MA: Harvard University Press.

Brooks, G. and A. K. Pugh. 1984. *Studies in the history of reading*. Reading, UK: University of Reading Centre for the Teaching of Reading.

Brown, A. L., A. S. Palincsar and L. Purcell. 1986. Poor readers: teach, don't label. In U. Neisser (ed.). *The school achievement of minority children: new perspectives*. Hillsdale, NJ: Lawrence Erlbaum, pp. 105–44.

Burnaby, B. 1997. Writing systems and orthographies. In V. Edwards and D. Corson, (eds). *Encyclopedia of language and education, volume 2: Literacy*. Dordrecht: Kluwer, pp. 59–68.

Burton, L. (ed.). 1986. *Girls into maths can go*. London: Holt Rinehart and Winston.

Cairney, T. 1992. Mountain or mole hill: The genre debate viewed from 'Down Under'. *Reading*, 26, 23–9.

Camitta, M. 1993. Vernacular writing: varieties of writing among Philadelphia high school students. In B. Street (ed.). *Cross-cultural approaches to literacy*. Cambridge, UK: Cambridge University Press, pp. 228–46.

Carey, J. 1992. *The intellectual and the masses*. London: Faber.

Carvalho, D. N. 1971. *Forty centuries of ink*. New York: Burt Franklin.

Cazden, C. B. 2001. *Classroom discourse: the language of teaching and learning*, 2nd edn. Portsmouth, NH: Heinemann.

Chafe, W. L. 1982. Integration and involvement in speaking, writing, and oral literature. In D. Tannen (ed.). *Spoken and written language: Exploring orality and literacy*. Norwood, NJ: Ablex, pp. 35–53.

Chafe, W. L. 1985. Linguistic differences produced by differences between written and spoken language. In D. Olson, N. Torrance and A. Hildyard (eds). *Literacy, language, and learning*. Cambridge: Cambridge University Press, pp. 35–55.

Chamberlain, M. (ed.). 1988. *Writing lives: conversations between women writers*. London: Virago.

Chandler, D. 1995. *The act of writing: a media theory approach*. Aberystwyth: University of Wales.

Chatwin, B. 1988. *Utz*. London: Picador.

Chomsky, C. 1972. Write first, read later. *Childhood Education*, 47, 296–99.

Chouliaraki, L. and N. Fairclough. 1999. *Discourse in late modernity: rethinking critical discourse analysis*. Edinburgh: Edinburgh University Press.

Clammer, J. R. 1976. *Literacy and social change*. Leiden: E. J. Brill.

Clanchy, M. T. 1993. *From memory to written record*. Oxford: Blackwell.

Clark, M. M. 1976. *Young fluent readers*. Oxford: Heinemann Educational Books.

Clark, R., N. Fairclough, R. Ivanič and M. Martin-Jones. 1990. Critical language awareness 1: a critical review of three current approaches to language awareness. *Language and education*, 4(4), 249–60.

Clark, R., N. Fairclough, R. Ivanič and M. Martin-Jones. 1991. Critical language awareness 2: towards critical alternatives. *Language and education*, 5(1), 41–54.

Clark, R. and R. Ivanič. 1991. Consciousness raising about the writing process. In P. Garrett and C. Jones (eds). *Language awareness in the classroom*. London: Longman, pp. 168–85.

Clarke, J. 2002. A new kind of symmetry: Actor-network theories and the new literacy studies. *Studies in the Education of Adults*, 34(2), 107–22.

Clyne, M. 1982. *Multilingual Australia: resources, needs, policies*. Melbourne: River Seine Publications.

Cochran-Smith, M. 1984. *The making of a reader*. Norwood, NJ: Ablex.

Cole, M. 1998. *Cultural psychology: a once and future discipline*. Cambridge, MA: Harvard University Press.

Cole, M., L. Hood, and R. P. McDermott. 1978. Concepts of ecological validity: their differing implications for comparative cognitive research. *Q. Newsletter of the Laboratory for Comparative Human Development*, 2, 34–7.

Cole, M. and H. Keyssar. 1985. The concept of literacy in print and film. In D. Olson, N. Torrance and A. Hildyard (eds). *Literacy, language and learning*. Cambridge, UK: Cambridge University Press, pp. 50–72.

Cole, M. and P. Griffin. 1983. A socio-cultural approach to remediation. *Quarterly Newsletter of the Laboratory for Human Comparative Cognition*, 5, 69–71.

Cole, M., Y. Engeström and O. Vasquez. (eds). 1997. *Mind, culture and activity: seminal papers from the laboratory of comparative human cognition*. Cambridge, UK: Cambridge University Press.

Collins, J. and R. Blot. 2003. *Literacy and literacies: texts, power and identity*. Cambridge, UK: Cambridge University Press.

Compton-Lilly, C. 2003. *Reading families: the literate lives of urban children*. New York: Teachers' College Press.

Cook, V. J. and B. Bassetti (eds). 2005. *Second language writing systems*. Clevedon, UK: Multilingual Matters.

Cook-Gumperz, J. 1986. *The social construction of literacy*. Cambridge, UK: Cambridge University Press.

Cooper, M. M. and M. Holzman. 1989. *Writing as social action*. Portsmouth, NH: Heinemann.

Coulmas, F. 1991. The future of Chinese characters. In R. L. Cooper and B. Spolsky (eds). *The influence of language on culture and thought*. Berlin: Mouton de Gruyter, pp. 247–43.

Coulmas, F. 1996. *The Blackwell encyclopaedia of writing systems*. Oxford: Blackwell.

Creese, A. and P. Martin (eds). 2003. *Multilingual classroom ecologies: inter-relationships, interactions and ideologies*, Clevedon, UK: Multilingual Matters.

Creese, A. and P. Martin (eds). 2006. *Ecology of language. Encyclopedia of language and education*, vol. 9. Heidelberg: Springer.

Cressy, D. 1980. *Literacy and the social order: reading and writing in Tudor and Stuart England*. Cambridge, UK: Cambridge University Press.

Crump, T. 1990. *The anthropology of numbers*. Cambridge, UK: Cambridge University Press.

Czerniewska, P. 1992. *Learning about writing*. Oxford: Blackwell.

Daniels, P. T. and W. Bright. 1996. *The world's writing systems*. Oxford: Oxford University Press.

Darrah, C. 1997. Complicating the concept of skill requirements: scenes from a workplace. In G. Hull (ed.). *Changing work, changing workers: critical perspectives on language, literacy, and skills*. Albany, NY: State University of New York Press, pp. 249–72.

Davies, P. 1994. Long-term unemployment and literacy: A case study of the restart interview. In M. Hamilton, D. Barton and R. Ivanič (eds). *Worlds of literacy*, Clevedon, Avon: Multilingual Matters, pp. 41–51.

De Castell, S., A. Luke and K. Egan (eds). 1986. *Literacy, society and schooling*. Cambridge, UK: Cambridge University Press.

DeFrancis, J. 1984. *The Chinese language: fact and fantasy*. Honolulu: University of Hawaii Press.

Dillard, A. 1989. *The writing life*. New York: Harper & Row.

Diringer, D. (1948) 1968. *The alphabet: a key to the history of mankind*, vols I & II, 3rd edn. London: Hutchinson.

Doman, G. 1965. *Teach your baby to read*. London: Jonathan Cape.

Downing, J. and R. Valtin. 1984. *Language awareness and learning to read*. New York: Springer-Verlag.

Duranti, A. (ed.). 2001. *Linguistic anthropology: a reader*. Oxford: Blackwell.

Dyson, A. 1991. Towards a reconceptualization of written language development. *Linguistics and Education*, 3, 139–61.

Edelsky, C. 1986. *Writing in a bilingual program*. Norwood, NJ: Ablex.

Edwards, D. and J. Potter. 1992. *Discursive psychology*. London: Sage.

Edwards, D. and N. Mercer. 1987. *Common knowledge*. London and New York: Methuen.

Eisenstein, E. 1979. *The printing press as an agent of change*, 2 vols. Cambridge, UK: Cambridge University Press.

Eisenstein, E. 1981. Some conjectures about the impact of printing on western society and thought: a preliminary report. In H. Graff (ed.). *Literacy and social development in the West: a reader*. Cambridge, UK: Cambridge University Press, pp. 53–68.

Evans, J. 2000. Adult mathematics and everyday life: Building bridges and facilitating learning 'transfer'. In D. Coben, J. O'Donoghue and G. FitzSimons (eds), *Perspectives on adults learning mathematics: research and practice*. Dordrecht: Kluwer Academic Publishers, pp. 289–305.

Fairclough, N. 1989. *Language and power*. London: Longman.

Fairclough, N. 1992. *Discourse and social change*. Cambridge, UK: Polity Press.

Fairclough, N. 2003. *Analysing discourse: textual analysis for social research*. London and New York: Routledge.

Fawns, M. and R. Ivanič. 2001. Form-filling as a social practice: taking power into our own hands. In J. Crowther, M. Hamilton and L. Tett. *Powerful literacies*. Leicester, UK: National Institute of Adult and Continuing Education (NIACE), pp. 80–93.

Febvre, L. and H. Martin. 1984. *The coming of the book*. London: Verso.

Feldman, C. F. 1991. Oral metalanguage. In D. R. Olson and N. Torrance (eds). *Literacy and orality*. Cambridge, UK: Cambridge University Press, pp. 66–89.

Ferdman, B. M., R.-M. Weber and A. G. Ramirez (eds). 1994. *Literacy across languages and cultures*. Albany, NY: State University of New York Press.

Ferreiro, E. and A. Teberosky. 1979. *Literacy before schooling*. New York: Heinemann.

Finders, M. J. 1996. *Just girls: hidden literacies and life in junior high*. New York: Teachers' College Press.

Fingeret, A. 1983. Social network: A new perspective on independence and illiterate adults. *Adult Education Quarterly*, 33, 133–46.

Fingeret, H. A. and C. Drennon. 1997. *Literacy for life: adult learners, new practices*. New York: Teachers' College Press.

Finnegan, R. 1977. *Oral poetry: its nature, significance and social context*. Cambridge, UK: Cambridge University Press.

Fishman, A. 1988. *Amish literacy: what and how it means*. Portsmouth, NH: Heinemann.

Fishman, A. 1991. Because this is who we are: writing in the Amish community. In D. Barton and R. Ivanič (eds). *Writing in the community*. London: Sage, pp. 14–37.

Fowler, E. and J. Mace (eds). 2005. *Outside the classroom: researching literacy with adult learners*. Leicester, UK: National Institute of Adult and Continuing Education (NIACE).

Freire, P. and D. Macedo. 1987. *Literacy: reading the word and the world*. London: Routledge.

Gaur, A. 1984. *A history of writing*. London: The British Library.

Gee, J. 1996. *Social linguistics and literacies: ideology in discourses*, 2nd edn. London: Taylor and Francis.

Gee, J., G. Hull and C. Lankshear. 1996. *The new work order: behind the language of the new capitalism*. London: Allen and Unwin.

Gelb, I. J. (1952) 1963. *A study of writing*, 2nd edn. Chicago: University of Chicago Press.

Gibson, J. J. 1979. *The ecological approach to visual perception*. Dallas: Houghton Mifflin.

Ginzburg, C. (1972) 1982. *The cheese and the worms: the cosmos of a sixteenth-century miller*. Harmondsworth, UK: Penguin.

Giroux, H. A. 1983. *Theory and resistance in education*. London: Heinemann.

Gonzalez, N. E., L. Moll and C. Amanti (eds). 2005 *Funds of knowledge: theorizing knowledge in households, communities and classrooms*. Mahwah, NJ: Lawrence Erlbaum Associates.

Goodman, Y. 1984. The development of initial literacy. In H. Goelman, A. Oberg and F. Smith (eds). *Awakening to literacy*. London: Heinemann, pp. 102–9.

Goody, J. (ed.). 1968. *Literacy in traditional societies*. Cambridge, UK: Cambridge University Press.

Goody, J. 1977. *The domestication of the savage mind*. Cambridge, UK: Cambridge University Press.

Goody, J. 1981. Alphabets and writing. In R. Williams (ed.). *Contact: human communication*. London: Thames and Hudson.

Goody, J. 1983. Literacy and achievement in the ancient world. In F. Coulmas and E. Ehlich (eds). *Writing in focus*. Hague: Mouton, pp. 83–97.

Goody, J. and I. P. Watt. 1963. The consequences of literacy. In *Comparative Studies in Society and History* 5(3), 304–45. Reprinted in J. Goody (ed.) *Literacy in traditional societies*. Cambridge, UK: Cambridge University Press, pp. 27–68.

Gough, K. 1968. Implications of literacy in traditional China and India. In J. Goody (ed.) *Literacy in traditional societies*. Cambridge, UK: Cambridge University Press, pp. 69–84.

Gowen, S. G. 1992. *The politics of workplace literacy: a case study*. New York: Teachers College Press.

Graff, H. J. 1979. *The literacy myth: Literacy and social structure in the 19th century city*. New York and London: Academic Press.

Grant, A. N. 1986. Defining literacy: common myths and alternative readings. *Australian Review of Applied Linguistics*, 9, 1–22.

Gray, W. S. 1956. *The teaching of reading and writing*. Paris: Unesco.

Gregory, E. 1996. *Making sense of a new world: learning to read in a second language*. London: Paul Chapman.

Gregory, E. and A. Williams. 2000. Work or play? 'Unofficial' literacies in the lives of two East London communities. In M. Martin-Jones and K. Jones (eds). *Multilingual literacies: reading and writing different worlds*. Amsterdam: John Benjamins, pp. 37–54.

Guerra, J. C. 1998. *Close to home: oral and literate practices in a transnational Mexicano community*. New York: Teachers College Press.

Hall, N. 1987. *The emergence of literacy*. London: Edward Arnold.

Hall, N. and A. Robinson (eds). 1996. *Learning about punctuation*. Clevedon, UK: Multilingual Matters.

Halle, M. 1969. Some thoughts on spelling. In K. S. Goodman and J. T. Fleming (eds). *Psycholinguistics and the teaching of reading*. Newark, DE: International Reading Association, pp. 17–24.

Halliday, M. A. K. 1985. *Spoken and written language*. Geelong, Victoria: Deakin University Press.

Halliday, M. A. K. 1988. On the language of physical science. In M. Ghadessy (ed.), *Registers of written English*. London: Pinter, pp. 162–77.

Hamilton, M. 2001. Privileged literacies: policy, institutional process and the life of the IALS. *Language and Education*, 15, 178–96.

Hamilton, M., D. Barton and R. Ivanič. (eds). 1994. *Worlds of literacy*. Clevedon, UK: Multilingual Matters.

Hamilton, M. and P. Davies. 1990. *Written communication and long-term unemployment*. Centre for the Study of Education and Training, Working Paper 19, Lancaster University.

Hamilton, M. and Y. Hillier. 2006. *Changing faces of adult literacy, language and numeracy: a critical history*. Stoke on Trent, UK: Trentham Books.

Hammond, N. 1986. The emergence of Maya civilization. *Scientific American*, 255(2), 98–107.

Harris, R. 1986. *The origin of writing*. London: Duckworth.

Harste, J. C. 1984. *Language stories and literacy lessons*. London: Heinemann.

Hartley, J. and A. Branthwaite. 1989. The psychologist as wordsmith: a questionnaire study of the writing strategies of productive British psychologists. *Higher Education*, 18, 423–52.

Hartley, T. 1994. Generations of literacy among women in a bilingual community. In M. Hamilton, D. Barton and R. Ivanič. (eds). *Worlds of literacy*. Clevedon, UK: Multilingual Matters, pp. 29–40.

Haugen, E. 1972. *The ecology of language*. Stanford, CA: Stanford University Press.

Hautecoeur, J. P. 1990. Illiteracy: from the myth to the reconstruction of the facts. Paper presented in 'Functional Literacy in Eastern and Western Europe', UIEUNESCO/ EC/OECD-CERI, Hamburg.

Havelock, E. 1963. *Preface to Plato*. Cambridge, MA: Harvard University Press.

Havelock, E. 1976. *Origins of western literacy*. Toronto: Ontario Institute for Studies in Education.

Havelock, E. A. 1982. *The literate revolution in Greece and its cultural consequences*. Princeton, NJ: Princeton University Press.

Heath, S. B. 1980. The functions and uses of literacy. *The Journal of Communication*, Winter, 123–33.

Heath, S. B. 1983. *Ways with words*. Cambridge, UK: Cambridge University Press.

Heath, S. B. 1985. The cross-cultural study of language acquisition. *Papers and Reports on Child Language Development*, 24, 1–24.

Heath, S. B. 1986. Sociocultural contexts of language development. In Bilingual Education Office. *Beyond language: social and cultural factors in schooling language minority students*. Los Angeles: California State University, pp. 143–86.

Heath, S. B. 1987. The literate essay: using ethnography to explode myths. In J. A. Langer (ed.). *Language, literacy and culture*. Norwood, NJ: Ablex, pp. 89–107.

Henriques, J., W. Holloway, C. Urwin, C. Venn and V. Walkerdine. 1984. *Changing the subject: psychology, social regulation and subjectivity*. London: Routledge.

Henderson, L. 1982. *Orthography and word recognition in reading*. London: Academic Press.

Hill, C. and K. Parry. 1994. *From testing to assessment: English as an international language*. London and New York: Longman.

Hinton, L. and K. Hale. 2001. *The green book of language revitalization in practice: towards a sustainable world*. San Diego: Academic Press.

Hodge, R. and K. Jones. 2000. Photography in collaborative research on multilingual literacy practices: images and understandings of researcher and researched. In M. Martin-Jones and K. Jones (eds). *Multilingual literacies: reading and writing different worlds*. Amsterdam: John Benjamins, pp. 299–318.

Hoggart, R. 2005. *Promises to keep*. London and New York: Continuum International Publishing Group.

Holland, D. and N. Quinn. 1987. *Cultural models in language and thought*. Cambridge, UK: Cambridge University Press.

Holland, D. and J. Lave. 2001. *History in person: enduring struggles, contentious practice, intimate identities*. Oxford: James Currey.

Holland, D., W. S. Lachicotte, D. Skinner and C. Cain. 2001. *Identity and agency in cultural worlds*. Cambridge, MA: Harvard University Press.

Hornberger, N. 1989. Continua of biliteracy. *Review of Educational Research*, 59(3), 271–96.

Hornberger, N. (ed.). 2003. *Continua of biliteracy: an ecological framework for educational policy, research, and practice in multilingual settings*. Clevedon, UK: Multilingual Matters.

Horsman, J. 1994. The problem of illiteracy and the promise of literacy. In M. Hamilton, D. Barton and R. Ivanič. (eds). *Worlds of literacy*. Clevedon, UK: Multilingual Matters, pp. 169–81.

Hull, G. (ed.). 1997. *Changing work, changing workers: critical perspectives on language, literacy and skills*. Albany, NY: SUNY Press.

Hull, G. and K. Schultz (eds). 2001. *School's out! Bridging out-of-school literacies with classroom practice*. New York: Teachers' College Press.

Hurford, J. 1987. *Language and number: The emergence of a cognitive system*. Oxford: Blackwell.

Hymes, D. 1962. The ethnography of speaking. In T. Gladwin and W. Sturtevant (eds). *Anthropology and human behaviour*. Washington, DC: Anthropological Society of Washington, pp. 13–53.

Illich, I. 1981. *Shadow work*. London: Marion Boyers.

Illich, I. and B. Sanders. 1989. *The alphabetization of the popular mind*. Harmondsworth, UK: Penguin.

Irvine, P. and N. Elsasser. 1988. The ecology of literacy: negotiating writing standards in a Caribbean setting. In B. A. Rafoth and D. L. Rubin (eds). *The social construction of written communication*. Norwood, NJ: Ablex, pp. 304–20.

Ivanič, R. and M. Hamilton. 1989. Literacy beyond schooling. In. D. Wray, *Emerging partnerships in language and literacy*. Clevedon, UK: Multilingual Matters.

Ivanič, R. and W. Moss. 1991. Bringing community writing practices into education. In D. Barton and R. Ivanič (eds). *Writing in the community*. Newbury Park, CA: Sage, pp. 193–223.

Jennings, J. 1990. *Adult literacy: master or servant?* Dhaka: University Press Ltd.

Jennings, E. M. and A. C. Purves. 1991. *Literate systems and individual lives: perspectives on literacy and schooling*. New York: State University of New York Press.

Johnson, S. 2001. *Emergence: the connected lives of ants, brains, cities and software*. London: Penguin.

Jones, K. 2000. Becoming just another alphanumeric code: farmers' encounters with the literacy and discourse practices of agricultural bureaucracy at the livestock auction. In Barton, D. Hamilton, M. and Ivanič, R. (eds). *Situated literacies: reading and writing in context*. London and New York: Routledge, pp. 70–90.

Kapitzke, C. 1995. *Literacy and religion: the textual politics and practice of Seventh-day Adventism*. Amsterdam: John Benjamins.

Kelly, T. 1970. *A history of adult education in Great Britain*. Liverpool: Liverpool University Press.

Kintgen, E. R., B. M. Kroll and M. Rose. 1988. *Perspectives on literacy*. Carbondale: Southern Illinois University Press.

Kirkwood, G. and C. Kirkwood. 1989. *Living adult education*. Milton Keynes, UK: Open University Press.

Klassen, C. 1991. Bilingual written language use by low-education Latin American newcomers. In D. Barton and R. Ivanic (eds). *Writing in the community*. Newbury Park, CA: Sage, pp. 38–57.

Kozulin, A. 1990. *Vygotsky's psychology*. New York: Harvester Wheatsheaf.

Krauss, M. 1992. The world's languages in crisis. *Language*, 68, 4–10.

Kress, G. 1997. *Before writing: rethinking paths to literacy*. London: Routledge.

Kress, G. 1998. *Children's early spellings: creativity and convention*. London and New York: Routledge.

Kress, G. 2003. *Literacy in the new media age*. London and New York: Routledge.

Kress, G. and T. van Leeuwen. 1996. *Reading images: the grammar of visual design*. London and New York: Routledge.

Kress, G. and T. van Leeuwen. 2001. *Multimodal discourse: the modes and media of contemporary communication*. London: Arnold; New York: Oxford University Press.

Kress, G., C. Jewitt, J. Ogborn and C. Tsatsarelis. 2001. *Multimodal teaching and learning: the rhetorics of the science classroom*. London and New York: Continuum.

Lakoff, G. and M. Johnson. 1980. *Metaphors we live by*. Chicago: University of Chicago Press.

Lankshear, C. 1991. Getting it right is hard: redressing the politics of literacy in the 1990's. In P. Cormack (ed.). *Selected papers from the 16th ARA National Conference*. Adelaide: Australian Reading Association, pp. 209–28.

Lankshear, C. and M. Knobel. 2003. *New literacies: changing knowledge and classroom learning*. Maidenhead, UK: Open University Press.

Larson, J. and J. Marsh. 2005. *Making literacy real: theories and practices for learning and teaching*. London: Sage.

Lave, J. 1988. *Cognition in practice*. Cambridge, UK: Cambridge University Press.

Lave, J. and E. Wenger. 1991. *Situated learning: legitimate peripheral participation*. Cambridge, UK: Cambridge University Press.

Lea, M. R. and B. Stierer (eds). 2000. *Student writing in higher education: new contexts*. Milton Keynes, UK: Open University Press.

Leichter, H. J. 1984. Families as environments for literacy. In H. A. Goelman, A. Oberg and F. Smith (eds). *Awakening to literacy*. London: Heinemann, pp. 38–50.

Lemke, J. 1995. *Textual politics: discourse and social dynamics*. London: Taylor & Francis.

Le Page, R. B. 1990. *Proceedings of the workshop of the University of York, International group for the study of language standardization and the vernacularization of literacy*. York: York University.

Levine, K. 1985. *The social context of literacy*. London: Routledge & Kegan Paul.

LeVine, P. and R. Scollon. 2004. *Discourse and technology: Multimodal discourse analysis*. Washington, DC: Georgetown University Press.

Lewin, R. 1984. *Human evolution: an illustrated introduction*. Oxford: Blackwell.

Livingstone, D. W. (ed.). 1987. *Critical pedagogy and cultural power*. Toronto: Garamond Press.

Lock, A. J. 1980. *The guided reinvention of language*. London: Academic Press.

Longman, J. and N. Mercer. 1992. Forms for talk and talk for forms: oral and literate dimensions of language use in Employment Training interviews. Open University, Centre for Language and Communications, Occasional Paper, 29.

Luke, A. 2005. Evidence-based state literacy policy: a critical alternative. In N. Bascia, A. Cumming, A. Datnow, K. Leithwood and D. Livingstone (eds). *International handbook of educational policy*. Dordrecht: Springer, pp. 661–75.

Luke, A. and C. Walton. 1994. Teaching and assessing critical reading. In T. Husen and T. Postelthwaite (eds), *International encyclopedia of education*, 2nd edn. Oxford: Pergamon Press, pp. 1194–8.

Lytle, S. 1991. Living literacy: rethinking development in adulthood. *Linguistics and Education*, 3, 109–38.

Mace, J. 1998. *Playing with time: mothers and the meaning of literacy*. London: UCL Press.

Mace, J. 2002. *The give and take of writing: scribes, literacy and everyday life*. Leicester: National Institute of Adult and Continuing Education (NIACE).

Mahiri, J. 2004. *What they don't learn in school: literacy in the lives of urban youth*. Oxford and New York: Peter Lang.

Makita, K. 1968. The rarity of reading disability in Japanese children. *American Journal of Orthopsychiatry*, 38, 599–614.

Marsh, J. (ed.). 2005. *Popular culture, new media and digital literacy in early childhood*. London and New York: RoutledgeFalmer.

Marshall, D. N. 1983. *History of libraries*. New Delhi: Oxford & IBH Publishing Co.

Martin, S. E. 1972. Nonalphabetic writing systems: some observations. In J. F. Kavanagh and I. G. Mattingly (eds). *Language by ear and by eye*. Boston: MIT Press, pp. 81–102.

Martin-Jones, M. and K. Jones (eds). 2000a. *Multilingual literacies: reading and writing different worlds*. Amsterdam: John Benjamins.

Martin-Jones, M. and K. Jones. 2000b. Introduction: Multilingual literacies. In *Multilingual literacies: reading and writing different worlds*. Amsterdam: John Benjamins, pp. 1–16.

Maybin, J. 2006. *Children's voices: talk, language and identity*. Basingstoke, UK: Palgrave Macmillan.

Maybin, J. and G. Moss. 1993. Talk about texts: reading as a social event. *Journal of research in reading*, 16, 138–47.

McKitterick, R. 1989. *The Carolingians and the written word*. Cambridge, UK: Cambridge University Press.

McLuhan, M. 1962. *The Gutenberg galaxy*. London: Routledge & Kegan Paul.

McLuhan, M. 1964. *Understanding media*. New York: McGraw-Hill.

Meadows, S. 1986. *Understanding child development*. London: Hutchinson.

Merrifield, J., B. Bingham, D. Hemphill and K. P. Bennett de Marais. 1996. *Life at the margins: language and technology in everyday life*. New York: Teachers College Press.

Millard, E. 1997. *Differently literate: boys, girls and the schooling of literacy*. London and New York: RoutledgeFalmer.

Moje, E. B. and D. G. O'Brien (eds). 2000. *Constructions of literacy: studies of teaching and learning in and out of secondary schools*. Mahwah, NJ: Lawrence Erlbaum.

Moll, L. C. (ed.). 1990. *Vygotsky and education*. Cambridge, UK and New York: Cambridge University Press.

Moll, L. 1994. Mediating knowledge between homes and classrooms. In D. Keller-Cohen (ed.). *Literacy: interdisciplinary conversations*. Creshill, NJ: Hampton Press, pp. 385–410.

Morris, C. and Nwenmely, H. 1994. *The Kweyol language and literacy project*. In M. Hamilton, D. Barton and R. Ivanič. (eds). *Worlds of literacy*. Clevedon, UK: Multilingual Matters, pp. 81–94.

Moss, B. J. 1994. *Literacy across communities*. Creshill, NJ: Hampton Press.

Moss, G. 1989. *Un/popular fictions*. London: Virago Press.

Mühlhäusler, P. 1992. Preserving languages or language ecologies. *Oceanic Linguistics*, 31, 163–80.

Neisser, U. 1982. *Memory observed*. San Francisco: W. H. Freeman.

Nell, V. 1988. *Lost in a book: The psychology of reading for pleasure*. New Haven, CT: Yale University Press.

Ninio, A. and J. Bruner. 1978. The achievement and antecedents of labelling. *Journal of Child Language*, 5, 1–15.

Ochs, E. 1983. Cultural dimensions of language acquisition. In E. Ochs and B. B. Schieffelin (eds). *Acquiring conversational competence*. London: Routledge, pp. 185–92.

Ochs, E. 1988. *Culture and language development*. Cambridge, UK: Cambridge University Press.

Olson, D. R. 1977. From utterance to text: the bias of language in speech and writing. *Harvard Educational Review*, 47, 257–81.

Olson, D. R. 1991. Literacy and objectivity: the rise of modern science. In D. Olson and N. Torrance (eds). *Literacy and orality*. Cambridge, UK: Cambridge University Press, pp. 149–64.

Olson, D. R. 1993. *The world on paper*. Cambridge, UK: Cambridge University Press.

Olson, D. R. and K. Nickerson. 1973. Language development through the school years: learning to confine interpretation to the information in the text. In K. E. Nelson, *Children's language*, vol. 1. New York: Gardner Press, pp. 117–69.

Olson, D. R., N. Torrance and A. Hildyard (eds). 1985. *Literacy, language, and learning*. Cambridge, UK: Cambridge University Press.

Ong, W. J. 1982. *Orality and literacy: the technologizing of the word*. London: Methuen.

Ostler, N. and Rudes, B. (eds). 2001. *Endangered languages and literacy: proceedings of the fourth FEL conference*. Bath: Foundation for Endangered Languages.

Padmore, S. 1994. Guiding lights. In M. Hamilton, D. Barton and R. Ivanič (eds). *Worlds of literacy*, Clevedon, UK: Multilingual Matters, pp. 143–56.

Pahl, K. and J. Rowsell. 2005. *Literacy and education: understanding the new literacy studies in the classroom*. London: Paul Chapman.

Pahl, K. and J. Rowsell (eds). 2006. *Travel notes from the new literacy studies: instances of practice*. Clevedon, UK: Multilingual Matters.

Papen, U. 2005. *Adult literacy as social practice: more than skills*. London: Routledge.

Paradis, M., H. Hagiwara and N. Hilderbrandt. 1985. *Neurolinguistic aspects of the Japanese writing system*. New York: Academic Press.

Pérez, B. (ed.). 2004. *Sociocultural contexts of language and literacy*, 2nd edn. Mahwah, NJ: Lawrence Erlbaum Associates.

Petroski, H. 1989. *The pencil*. London: Faber & Faber.

Phillips, L. W. (ed.). 1985. *Ernest Hemingway on writing*. London: Granada.

Plimpton, G. (ed.). 1988. *Writers at work: the Paris Review interviews*, 7th series. Harmondsworth, UK: Penguin.

Postgate, J. N. 1984. Cuneiform catalysis: the first information revolution. *Archaeological Review from Cambridge*, 3(2), 4–18.

Prinsloo, M. and M. Breier. 1996. *The social uses of literacy: theory and practice in contemporary South Africa*. Amsterdam: John Benjamins.

Pye, C. 1986. Quiche Mayan speech to children. *Journal of Child Language*, 13, 85–100.

Radway, J. 1987. *Reading the romance*. London: Verso.

Read, C. 1971. *Children's categorization of speech sounds in English*. National Council of Teachers of English, Research Reports 17.

Read, C. 1986. *Children's creative spellings*. London: Routledge.

Reder, S. 1987. Comparative aspects of functional literacy development: three ethnic American communities. In D. Wagner (ed.). *The future of literacy in a changing world*. Oxford: Pergamon Press, pp. 250–70.

Reder, S. 1994. Practice-engagement theory: a sociocultural approach to literacy across languages and cultures. In B. Ferdman, R.-M. Weber and A. G. Ramirez (eds). *Literacy across languages and cultures*. Albany, NY: State University of New York Press, pp. 37–74.

Richards, G. 1987. *Human evolution*. London: Routledge & Kegan Paul.

Robinson-Pant, A. (ed.). 2004. *Women, literacy and development*, London and New York: Routledge.

Rockhill, K. 1993. Gender, language and the politics of literacy. In B. Street (ed.). *Cross-cultural approaches to literacy*. Cambridge, UK: Cambridge University Press, pp. 156–75.

Rogers, A. (ed.). 2005. *Urban literacy: communication, identity and learning in development contexts*. Hamburg: Unesco Institute for Education.

Rogers, A., B. Maddox, J. Millican, K. Newell Jones, U. Papen and A. Robinson-Pant. 1999. Redefining post-literacy in a changing world. *Occasional Paper on Education 29*. London: Department for International Development.

Rogers, R. 2004. *An introduction to critical discourse analysis in education*. Mahwah, NJ: Lawrence Erlbaum Associates.

Rogoff, B. 2003. *The cultural nature of human development*. Oxford and New York: Oxford University Press.

Rozin, P., S. Poritsky and R. Sotsky. 1971. American children with reading problems can easily learn to read English represented by Chinese characters. *Science*, 171, 1264–7.

Sampson, G. R. 1985. *Writing systems*. Oxford: Blackwell.

Saxena, M. 1994. Literacies among Panjabis in Southall. In M. Hamilton, D. Barton and R. Ivanič (eds). *Worlds of literacy*, Clevedon, Avon: Multilingual Matters, pp. 195–214.

Saxena, M. 2000. Taking account of history and culture in community-based research on multilingual literacy. In M. Martin-Jones and K. Jones (eds). *Multilingual literacies: reading and writing different worlds*. Amsterdam: John Benjamins, pp. 275–98.

Schieffelin, B. B. 1979. Getting it together: an ethnographic approach to the study of the development of communicative competence. In E. Ochs and B. B. Schieffelin (eds). *Acquiring conversational competence*. London: Routledge, pp. 73–108.

Schieffelin, B. and P. Gilmore (eds). 1986. *The acquisition of literacy: ethnographic perspectives*. Norwood, NJ: Ablex.

Schmandt-Besserat, D. 1992. *Before writing*. Austin: University of Texas Press.

Schousboe, K. 1989. Literacy and society in medieval Denmark. In K. Schousboe and M. Trolle Larsen (eds). *Literacy and society*. Copenhagen: Akademisk Forlag, pp. 149–70.

Scollon, R. and S. W. Scollon. 2003. *Discourses in place: language in the material world*. London and New York: Routledge.

Scribner, S. and M. Cole. 1981. *The psychology of literacy*. Cambridge, MA: Harvard University Press.

Sealey, A. and B. Carter. 2004. *Applied linguistics as social science*. London and New York: Continuum.

Searle, J. 1999. Online literacies at work. *Literacy and Numeracy Studies*, 9(2), 1–18.

Searle, J. 2002. Situated literacies at work. *International Journal of Educational Research*, 37, 17–28.

Serpell, R., Baker, L. and S. Sonnenschein. 2004. *Becoming literate in the city: the Baltimore early childhood project*. Cambridge, UK and New York: Cambridge University Press.

Sheridan, D., B. Street and D. Bloome. 2000. *Writing ourselves: mass observation and literacy practices*. Cresskill, NJ: Hampton Press.

Shor, I. (ed.). 1987. *Freire for the classroom*. London: Boynton/Cook Heinemann.

Shuman, A. 1993. Collaborative writing: appropriating power or reproducing authority. In B. Street (ed.). *Cross-cultural approaches to literacy*. Cambridge, UK and New York: Cambridge University Press, pp. 247–71.

Sinclair, A., R. J. Jarvella and W. J. M. Levelt (eds). 1978. *The child's conception of language*. New York: Springer-Verlag.

Slobin, D. I. 1978. A case study of early language awareness. In A. Sinclair, R. J. Jarvella and W. J. M. Levelt (eds). *The child's conception of language*. New York: Springer-Verlag, pp. 45–54.

Smith, D. 1990. Textually mediated social organization. In *Texts, facts and femininity: exploring the relations of ruling*. London and New York: Routledge, pp. 209–24.

Smith, F. 1983. *Essays into literacy*. London: Heinemann.

Smith, F. 1984. The creative achievement of literacy. In H. Goelman A. Oberg and F. Smith (eds). *Awakening to literacy*. London: Heinemann, pp. 143–53.

Smith, F. 1985. A metaphor for literacy: creating worlds or shunting information. In D. Olson, N. Torrance and A. Hildyard (eds). *Literacy, language, and learning*. Cambridge: Cambridge University Press, pp. 195–213.

Smith, M. W. and J. D. Wilhelm. 2002. *'Reading don't fix no Chevy's': literacy in the lives of young men*. Portsmouth, NH: Heinemann.

Snow, C. 1983. Literacy and language: relationships during the preschool years. *Harvard Educational Review*, 55, 165–89.

Snow, C. and A. Ninio. 1986. The contracts of literacy: what children learn from learning to read books. In W. H. Teale and E. Sulzby (eds). *Emergent literacy: writing and reading*. Norwood, NJ: Ablex, pp. 116–38.

Snyder, I. (ed.). 2002. *Silicon literacies: communication, innovation and education in the electronic age*. London and New York: Routledge.

Soderbergh, R. 1977. *Reading in early childhood*. Washington, DC: Georgetown University Press.

Spivey, N. N. 1990. Transforming texts: constructive processes in reading and writing. *Written Communication*, 7, 256–87.

Staikos, K. 2000. *Great libraries: from antiquity to the Renaissance*. London: British Library.

Stallings, W. 1975. The morphology of Chinese characters: a survey of models and application. *Computers and the Humanities*, 9, 13–24.

Steinberg, D. D. and M. T. Steinberg. 1975. Reading before speaking. *Visible Language*, 9, 197–224.

Street, B. 1984. *Literacy in theory and practice*. Cambridge, UK and New York: Cambridge University Press.

Street, B. (ed.). 1993. *Cross-cultural approaches to literacy*. Cambridge, UK and New York: Cambridge University Press.

Street, B. (ed.). 2001. *Literacy and development: ethnographic perspectives*. London and New York: Routledge.

Street, B. (ed.). 2005. *Literacies across educational contexts: mediating learning and teaching*. Philadelphia: Caslon.

Street, B., D. Baker and A. Tomlin. 2005. *Navigating numeracies: home/school numeracy practices*. Dordrecht: Kluwer.

Street, J. and B. Street. 1991. The schooling of literacy. In D. Barton and R. Ivanič (eds). *Writing in the Community*. London: Sage, pp. 143–66.

Stubbs, M. 1980. *Language and literacy: the sociolinguistics of reading and writing*. London: Routledge & Kegan Paul.

Swales, J. M. 1990. *Genre analysis*. Cambridge, UK: Cambridge University Press.

Swales, J. M. 1998. *Other floors, other voices: a textography of a small university building*, Mahwah, NJ: Lawrence Erlbaum Associates.

Swann, C. 1991. *Language and typography*. London: Lund Humphries.

Szwed, J. F. 1981. The ethnography of literacy. In M. F. Whiteman (ed.). *Writing: the nature, development, and teaching of written communication*, Hillsdale, NJ: Erlbaum, pp. 13–23.

Tabouret-Keller, A., R. B. Le Page, P. Gardner-Chloros and G. Varro. 1997. *Vernacular literacy: a re-evaluation*. Oxford and New York: Oxford University Press.

Talbot, M. 1992. The construction of gender in a teenage magazine. In N. L. Fairclough, *Critical language awareness*. London: Longman, pp. 174–99.

Tannen, D. 1985. Relative focus on involvement in oral and written discourse. In D. Olson, N. Torrance and A. Hildyard (eds). *Literacy, language and learning*. Cambridge, UK: Cambridge University Press, pp. 124–47.

Taylor, D. 1983. *Family literacy*. London: Heinemann Educational.

Taylor, D. 1986. Creating family story. In W. H. Teale and E. Sulzby (eds). *Emergent literacy: writing and reading*. Norwood, NJ: Ablex, pp. 139–55.

Taylor, D. 1996. *Toxic literacies: Exploring the injustices of bureaucratic texts*. Portsmouth, NH: Heinemann.

Taylor, D. (ed.). 1997. *Many families, many literacies: an international declaration of principles*. Portsmouth, NH: Heinemann.

Taylor, D. and C. Dorsey-Gaines. 1988. *Growing up literate*. Portsmouth, NH: Heinemann.

Taylor, I. 1981. Writing systems and reading. In T. G. Walker and G. E. MacKinnon (eds). *Reading research: advances in theory and practice*, vol II. New York: Academic Press, pp. 1–51.

Teale, W. H. 1984. Reading to young children: Its significance for literacy development. In H. Goelman, A. Oberg, and F. Smith (eds). *Awakening to literacy*. London: Heinemann, pp. 110–21.

Teale, W. H. 1986. Home background and young children's literacy development. In W. H. Teale and E. Sulzby (eds). *Emergent literacy: writing and reading*. Norwood, NJ: Ablex, pp. 173–205.

Teale, W. H. and E. Sulzby (eds). 1986. *Emergent literacy: writing and reading*. Norwood, NJ: Ablex.

Tett, L., M. Hamilton and Y. Hillier (eds). 2006. *Adult literacy, numeracy and language: policy, practice and research*. Buckingham, UK: Open University Press.

Trolle-Larsen, M. 1989. What they wrote on clay. In K. Schoesbou and M. Trolle-Larson (eds). *Literacy and society*. Copenhagen: Akademisk Forlag, pp. 121–48.

Tusting, K. 2000. The new literacy studies and time: an exploration. In D. Barton, M. Hamilton and R. Ivanič (eds). *Situated literacies: reading and writing in context*, London and New York: Routledge, pp. 35–53.

Tzeng, O. J. L., Hung, D. L. and L. Garro. 1978. Reading the Chinese characters: an information processing view. *Journal of Chinese Linguistics*, 6, 287–305.

Unesco. 1953. *The use of vernacular languages in education: monographs on fundamental education VIII*. Paris: Unesco.

Unesco. 1976. *The experimental world literacy programme: a critical assessment*. Paris: Unesco.

Unesco. 1990. *Basic education and literacy*. Paris: Unesco.

Unesco. 2005. *Education for all: literacy for Life: EFA Global Monitoring Report 2006*. Paris: Unesco.

van Dijk, F. 1994. Gender specific images in reading and writing. *PaPal Bulletin*, 23, 1–8.

Venezky, R. L. 1977. Principles for the design of practical writing systems. In J. A. Fishman (ed.). *Advances in the creation and revision of writing systems*. Hague: Mouton. pp. 256–70.

Venezky, R. L., D. A. Wagner and B. S. Ciliberti. 1990. *Toward defining literacy*. Newark, DE: International Reading Association.

Vincent, D. 1989. *Literacy and popular culture: England 1750–1914*. Cambridge, UK: Cambridge University Press.

Vincent, D. 2000. *The rise of mass literacy: reading and writing in modern Europe*. Cambridge, UK: Polity.

Vygotsky, L. S. 1962. *Thought and language*. Boston: MIT. Press.

Vygotsky, L. S. 1978. *Mind in society*. Cambridge, MA: Harvard University Press.

Wagner, D. A. 1993. *Literacy, culture and development: becoming literate in Morocco*. Cambridge, UK: Cambridge University Press.

Walker, W. 1981. Native American writing systems. In C. A. Ferguson and S. B. Heath (eds). *Language in the USA*. Cambridge, UK and New York: Cambridge University Press, pp. 145–74.

Weinberger, J. 1996. *Literacy goes to school: the parents' role in young children's literacy learning*. London: Paul Chapman.

Wellisch, H. H. 1978. *The conversion of scripts: its nature, history and utilization*. New York: Wiley.

Wells, G. 1985. Preschool literacy-related activities and success in school. In D. Olson, N. Torrance and A. Hildyard (eds). *Literacy, language and learning*. Cambridge, UK: Cambridge University Press, pp. 229–55.

Wells, G. 1986. *The meaning makers*. London: Hodder and Stoughton.

Wells, G. 1989. Language in the classroom: Literacy and collaborative talk. *Language and Education*, 3, 251–73.

Wenger, E. 1998. *Communities of practice: learning, meaning, and identity*. Cambridge, UK and New York: Cambridge University Press.

Wertsch, J. V. 1991. *Voices of the mind*. Harvester Wheatsheaf.

Wertsch, J. V. 1997. *Mind as action*. Oxford and New York: Oxford University Press.

Willett, J. and D. Bloome. 1992. Literacy, language, school and community: a community-centred view. in C. Hedley (ed.). *Whole language and the bilingual learner*. Norwood, NJ: Ablex, pp. 35–57.

Williams, R. 1981. *Contact: human communication*. London: Thames and Hudson.

Willinsky, J. 1990. *The new literacy*. London: Routledge.

Wilson, A. 2000. There is no escape from third-space theory: borderland discourse and the 'in-between' literacies of prisons. In Barton, D. Hamilton, M. and Ivanič, R. (eds). *Situated literacies: reading and writing in context*, London and New York: Routledge, pp. 54–69.

Winokur, J. 1986. *Writers on writing*. Philadelphia: Running Press.

Index

Page numbers in bold type refer to main treatment of topics and chapter headings or sub-headings